Women of Vail

Those Who Walked This Bridge
1962-1970

Elaine Kelton and Carolyn Pope

Foreword by Warren Miller

conquestgraphics
Affiliated Companies: Lewis Creative Technologies
Lorraine Press

Library of Congress Cataloging-in-Publication Data

Kelton, Elaine White
Pope, Carolyn Woodward

Women of Vail
Those Who Walked This Bridge 1962-70

Most of the narratives were written and submitted by the women included in this book. Several were written based on taped interviews.

The photographs used in this book were loaned to the publishers by the women. Many of the old newspaper photos are courtesy of the *Vail Daily*, owner of *The Vail Trail*.

ISBN 978-0-615-61018-4

1. Vail, CO - early life
2. Narratives about the West
3. Women's history in Vail, CO
4. Colorado history
5. Ski Resorts - Skiing - Sports and Recreation

Edited by Rosalie Jeffrey Isom
Design by Joanne Morgan

Printed by Conquest Graphics, Salt Lake City, Utah

iii

FOREWORD

When I got to Vail the first year with my camera, there were no quad chairlifts, but there was a gondola, two chairlifts, one Poma lift, and accommodations for as many as 42 people.

Just as for frontier women of a generation or two earlier, it was not an easy life for the women. Money was hard to come by as they found their places in this new town - perhaps this would be the gold mine they had dreamed of owning a piece of. But quite unlike those earlier frontier women, some arrived with only a suitcase or two, a pair of skis, and with the future shining brightly in their eyes. They found places to live and jobs to live by. Not many homes were built those first two years, but those that were built had a room to rent when the owner was in a city somewhere else making enough money to afford the luxury of a ski house in Vail.

The women were mostly college graduates and strong-willed enough to get out of the city and seek a better life in the mountains. All they needed was a place to park their belongings and a bed to sleep on. In the sixties, there were still boy jobs and girl jobs - so the women sometimes fell into the stereotypical jobs as waitresses with college degrees or kept the paperwork flowing for whoever the management was at the time. Shelter and privacy were hard to come by. Vail was definitely a frontier town, and occasionally on payday someone would ride their horse into The Copper Bar where almost everyone went after work.

As was everyone, the women were also looking for freedom and adventure, and the first years of the Women of Vail set a standard that still identifies someone who moved to the valley to find an opportunity in the white gold on the side of a hill.

The histories of most frontier towns in the West have been written by men and, therefore, are mostly about men. This one is written by the Women of Vail, about the women.

— WARREN MILLER

iv

THE
WOMEN

ANNE STAUFER

I went to school in England before my family moved to Eleuthera in the Bahamas. After that, we went up to Canada where I lived for five years and attended school, worked at IBM, and then found my way to Bermuda. I met my husband, Joe, while working at the Elbow Beach Surf Club in Bermuda. Eventually, we left Bermuda to work in Santa Barbara, but stopped first in Vail, and never made it to Santa Barbara. At first, I worked in reservations at The Lodge at Vail, then at the Christiania. I subsequently created and ran Annie's specialty store on East Meadow Drive.

We stayed because my husband said we couldn't afford to leave. As far as a social life, I have been too busy to have one. But I have enjoyed hiking in the woods every summer morning, mushroom hunting and gardening. I used to cross-country ski but now head for the Caribbean to swim and sail every winter. Our nightlife consisted of going to the old Casino, Sheika's nightclub at Gramshammers, and the Outback at the old Vail Village Inn.

I didn't have any expectations because there was nothing there, and nobody had heard of Vail - including Hertz Rent-A-Car at the Denver Airport – they told us there was no Vail, only Vail Pass and that the nearest town was Minturn. We drove up anyway in the middle of a snowstorm, met a Swiss man who was living in a log cabin at the bottom of Vail Pass and was there to help install the Bell Gondola in Vail. We found a few small buildings in the middle of nowhere and spent the night at the We Ask You Inn, which is at the entrance to what is now Beaver Creek. Next day, my husband went up the mountain with Pete Seibert on a snowcat; he came back down and said we were not going on to California. "If this place doesn't make it, nothing will," he said, and that's been our motto ever since.

Joe and I have been married now for 53 years and have the joy of a loving son, plus the closeness with my husband's brothers, and a few wonderful old friends we call family.

The special people we met in the early days of Vail made us love the place and stay to do what we could to make it a success – that's all any of us cared about. We knew we had one of the best skiing mountains in the world and, with a lot of hard work, sleepless nights (when it did not snow), anxiety over staying afloat, it gradually became a little village and a close community.

ANNELIESE FREEMAN

I was born in Garmisch-Partenkirchen, Germany. I started skiing at age four and was a member of the German Ski Team from 1958 to 1962. I came to the US to race in the 1960 Olympics in Squaw Valley. I liked what I saw and wanted to see more, so I returned in 1963 on a storm-tossed coal freighter and cross-country Greyhound bus rides (with several pairs of skis). I arrived in Colorado and spent the winter working both

for Max and Edna Dercum at Ski Tip Ranch and Willy Schaeffler and Erich Windisch (both from Garmisch) at Arapahoe Basin. There, I met Clay Freeman who later made me part of the Howard Head ski family, and his own Freeman family.

We moved to Vail in 1965 and lived in the Clock Tower Building with neighbors - the likes of John Donovan and his St Bernard, Bandit. Exciting and colorful evenings at Bill Whiteford's Casino across the street added more excitement. I reconnected with David and Renie Gorsuch, whom I had met on the European race circuit and again in Squaw Valley. I went to work for them in their new Vail ski shop, and the rest is history. I'm still working there.

Sons Michael and Stefan both enjoyed the wonderful and carefree Vail childhood possible in those early years --- skiing, mountain kid fun hockey, tennis, and freedom.

I have made many enduring friendships in Vail. The beautiful mountain environment and those special bluebird days of skiing on Vail Mountain will keep me here forever.

ANNETTA DIXON RAPPA

Skiing brought me to Vail. I came from Michigan in 1964 where I'd gone to high school in Jackson and attended Michigan State University in Lansing. I learned to ski at Boyne Mountain and worked at a hotel in Lansing while I went to school. I moved to Vail to ski bum in November 1964 and never left.

My list of jobs includes Pepi's, Red Lion, A Place on Earth, and the First Bank of Vail. I got married and had two kids: Eric and Troy Dixon. They loved skiing, hiking, biking, and the lore of the mountains. As for social life, I have to say I like it all. When I wasn't working I went hiking, biking, downhill skiing, cross-country skiing, snowshoeing, exercising, and swimming.

I came to Vail to ski, but I don't remember having expectations - only that I fell in love with the mountains. I am happy I stayed through all the growth of the valley. If I had left and returned 10 years later, it would not have been the same. As it is, I grew with the changes, and I plan to stay.

ATHENA BUXMAN

Prior to moving to Vail in 1966, Athena and John Buxman lived in Denver Colorado, where John was an executive with the Red Owl Corp. and Athena was a busy mother of three focused on raising her family.

Their family passion for skiing and love of outdoor life in the Rockies took them to the slopes at every opportunity. Most summers they hiked and played in Glenwood or shared a friend's cabin in Red Cliff. The children began skiing as soon as they could walk, and the two youngest, Christine and Johnny, were soon racing on the junior ski team at Arapahoe Valley.

The road to Vail really began when Johnny won the honor of forerunning a World Cup race at Arapahoe. Among the competitors was his hero, the French skier Jean Claude Killy. Johnny must have been skiing on cloud nine that day because he turned in a remarkable time. When he reached the finish line Jean Claude was waiting for him. Making a little boy's dreams all come true, Jean Claude invited him to take a few runs and later asked to meet Johnny's parents. Killy saw Johnny's promise and felt he had the potential to be a world-class competitor. He wanted Athena and John to understand that Johnny's competition, especially in Europe, would be living on the mountain, going to special schools in summer and training every day in winter. Equivalent programs currently did not exist for American skiers, and if Johnny were to meet his full potential, it would be up to them to provide similar conditions. Life plans gave way to finding a way to give their child every opportunity to go as far as he could doing what he loved.

That opportunity soon arrived when the Super Foods Grocery Store in Minturn came up for sale. Recognizing the potential of the Vail Valley, they partnered with Kaiser Morcus and purchased Super Foods in 1966. Athena and the family lived in the Catholic Rectory in Minturn for a time before moving to an apartment above Wild Bill's on Wall Street in downtown Vail.

Athena's next few years were occupied with running the bakery in the new store, The Village Market, which opened when Crossroads was built in 1968. They built a home in East Vail and met the challenges of raising a teenager and two grade-school children in a town focused on developing a primarily adult resort. There was no infrastructure, no schools, no church and only a handful of other mothers trying to overcome those same challenges. Like other pioneers, Athena did the best with what she had and when Nancy Kindel hired a teacher, the early families found

a space in the Gondola building, and a one-room schoolhouse K-12 became Vail Country Day school. Daily time on the slopes became a priority at the school, and Johnny was able to live and breathe his sport.

Athena helped Father Stone establish Sunday services in Casino Vail. Although Sunday Mass smelled more like stale beer than incense, the beginnings of a place for families to worship was born. She also worked at Wild Bill's Emporium.

Soon, two of the kids were in the Junior Olympic Program, and Athena always had a house full of children from all over the world. Hosting winter exchange students from Argentina provided Chris and Johnny with summer training in South America. American skiers living with her in Vail then hosted her children at races all across the USA.

Among Athena's favorite Vail pastimes was skiing with a group of Vail women who called themselves "The Superchickens." Athena also led women in three-day cross-country ski trips over Shrine Pass.

Elaine speaking: Athena Buxman shared her Greek heritage with us all when she patiently taught us the joy of making Baklava. She lives in Glenwood Springs near family and in the mountains she loves.

5

Barbara Larese

My husband Ernst Larese and I were running a ski lodge in Thredbo, Australia, when we heard about Vail from Roger Staub, who was then Vail's director of skiing. We came to the US and decided to investigate what opportunities there might be at Vail. At first, I worked the front desk at the newly opened Holiday Inn. Soon, I became the Head Start nurse at the middle school in Minturn and later worked at the Clinic with Dr. Tom Steinberg. We saw a need for a restaurant with entertainment and opened The Blue Cow. We also started and ran the Baskin Robbins ice cream store and the Swiss Hot Dog restaurant.

It was a lot of fun living in the new resort because everyone knew everyone else in town. Most parties were held in friends' homes. We went sometimes to the Nu Gnu, saw movies in Minturn, and had steak dinners at the Diamond J in Eagle. Of course, we enjoyed dinner and dancing at the Blue Cow, too.

I raised three kids here, and I think they had healthy young lives. All of them were ski racers and enjoyed the outdoors. Two still live here, and my daughter is taking over and expanding The Swiss Hot Dog.

I remember that even with the businesses, we skied as much as possible. I had not really expected much except to ski and have a new adventure. Vail became a place for us to stay and make a living, as well as to enjoy the mountain life, surroundings, and weather. We made life-long friends from all over the globe and loved having visits from our many Australian friends.

BARBARA PARKER

I was working on my Master's in social work when I met Bob Parker and decided that skiing was more fun, and being married to him would be more fun than being a social worker. I had never had a job. When I moved to Vail, Bob and I had returned from France and Austria where we had lived for six years.

Bob was the editor of Skiing Magazine, and Merrill Hastings was the publisher. At a World Cup race in Chamonix, Merrill told Bob not to talk to anyone of the "opposing" magazine, which was Ski Magazine. This got Bob's ire up, and he promptly spoke to the people from Ski Magazine and was fired. That left him with no way to get home and not a cent in his pocket. So, he called Pete Seibert. He and Pete had already talked about the possibility of Bob's coming to work for Vail Associates, and Bob started when it was still just a dream of Pete's. Exactly what Bob did, I don't have any idea. He went to work every day, so he and Pete must have figured out something for him to do. We were very much part of Vail Associates before it became a reality.

On Labor Day in 1960, before moving to Vail, we camped on what would later be Forest Road, then just a track on the side of the mountain above where The Lodge is. We put out our sleeping bags and spent the night. We had a little primus stove and cooked our dinner and breakfast on it. When we woke up the next morning, it had snowed a couple of inches. We never did figure out where they were going to put this new resort nor where we were going to ski, because it didn't look like much when you simply looked up the hill from our campsite.

At the end of 1961, Bob had already gone ahead to Vail. I put my grapefruit tree, my dog, and two children in the VW and went over Loveland Pass in a terrible storm, ending up in Vail on Christmas Eve. We spent the night in The Lodge where Sigi Fowler was the manager and Daphne Slevin was his secretary. We had just gotten to bed when there was a loud knock on the door and somebody said, "The pipes are frozen; there's a big flood. We need all hands to help." So everybody got out of bed to help. It was in Daphne's room. The children slept through the whole thing. The next day, we moved into our house. There was no electricity, and I got water from the stream that flowed into the beaver pond. We had construction power to one outlet and a light bulb on a long, long cord, and whichever room we needed to be in we'd carry the light bulb on the long cord from one room to the next. We cooked most of our meals in the fireplace. It was all kind of jolly and fun and one big adventure.

Our house was complete because Bob timed it well. The only other house that was visible was the Bishop house; quite possibly, Dick Pownall had started his cabin. There were Kuehn children and three Seibert boys and two Parker children and at least two Shepards. We had decided to homeschool our children, Katherine and Guy. We found very quickly that homeschooling was more complicated and bothersome than we thought it would be because you can't do anything else if you're homeschooling your kids. We hired Allen Brown and his wife to come and teach for us, and that worked beautifully. He taught what homeschool directed, and the kids had a good time. They had school up at Betty Seibert's house. She had a pet goat, and they battled up and down the stairs with the goat, and he was in their classroom. It was all pretty loose, and every year they were in a different place. When the Plaza Building was complete, they went there; when the firehouse was complete, they went up above the firehouse. Eventually, it evolved as the Vail Country Day School.

The next thing was the procuring of food. Our nearest grocery store was in Minturn, and I ended up going fairly frequently to Denver. On my birthday in '63 I went alone to Denver to pick up groceries and heard that Kennedy had been assassinated. When I went home I needed news, and we had no television and just a very crackly radio because we didn't have a good antenna. I remember Don Almond shinnying up the closest pine tree and putting up a great big antenna so we could at least listen to the news of Kennedy's burial.

June Simonton

The winter of '62 they asked me to sell ski school lessons, but VA didn't ask me back the second year. I could never, ever reckon my books at the end of the day and I swear I didn't take a cent, but I could not figure out the number of tickets that were sold. The amount of money in the cash drawer at the end of the day never reconciled. They decided I wasn't a very good bet, "Let's forget her and send her off to do something else." So, they sent me off to do something else. Daphne and I ran the Vail Resort Association office one year, after the Plaza Building was complete. Every now and then another building would go up, and it was fun to walk down Bridge Street and see what they were doing. There was always in the background the noise of cranes and saws that construction makes. For years, we never had quiet with only the sound of birds and skiing.

The first year, they needed someone to get

the mail. I took my own VW bus to the post office in Minturn, picked up a heavy sack, then drove to The Lodge and hauled that thing into the lobby and upended it on the floor. Nobody sorted it – so everybody came and just helped himself. That's why they called me Vail's first postmistress, which was pretty ridiculous because I really wasn't a postmistress. I was the mail procurer.

Bob was very involved in the sale of Vail. The annoying part was that every morning about 2 o'clock somebody from New York would call. Apparently their news people worked through the night, and they called in the middle of the night, because they knew they could get you. It was always to see what news Bob had to impart to some newsperson asking for information.

At one point, Joanne Miller and I started a business renting houses in the winter. We never made any money, but we had a lot of fun. I was a relatively avid skier and really loved it, although I was never very good. Bob would stand at the bottom of the slope and yell, "Let 'em run" (laughter!), and it just made me angry as anything, so I'd try another curve or two.

People think living in a resort is an idyllic sort of life, but it's not. It's really quite difficult, because everybody else is on vacation, and you're not. But there were fine friends, and most of the friendships we made are still alive if the people are, and some of those are the dearest friends I have. The first year we were there, John Donovan lived in the little apartment in our house with his dog, Bandit. Diana Donovan (Mounsey) met him in Vail,

and they married. She and I have remained good friends.

We were never worried about locking our doors or having a burglar come in. Once, we went away and couldn't find the key to our front door because we never locked it, and we just left for our Mexico vacation.

A very important part of our life was summer in Vail. We could go into the mountains and hunt mushrooms, paint, hike, pick berries, and do those wonderful fun things that I thoroughly enjoyed. Many friends came along on picnics, and it was great for the kids. Perhaps we enjoyed the mountains more thoroughly than we had the skiing of the winter before.

9

BETTAN WHITEFORD LAUGHLIN

I completed my baccalaureate in Sweden and came to the USA to study at the Institute of Finance in New York City. After work that included modeling, being a registered stockbroker, and working in investment banking at Bear, Stearns & Co., I found Vail.

Bill Whiteford was building Casino Vail and asked me to come out for a weekend. He offered me a job as a "disceuse" for his new venture, and I accepted. During 1964-65 I ran the disco at Casino Vail. I also did accounting and anything else that was needed. I married him in 1966.

I loved the small town atmosphere, the beautiful surroundings, the "pioneer" spirit, the friendships, the skiing and other sports, and all the cultural offerings.

Most of the social life took place at Casino Vail from 1964-1969 (we could seat 500 people), where we had European-style tea dances most afternoons, many times with a live band. During dinner, we showed movies (mostly Warren Miller and Roger Brown ski films), and then at night a full-out disco or live acts. To name a few, we featured acts like The Hustlers, The Wilshire Boulevard Buffalo Hunters, Odetta, the Irish Rovers, Dizzy Gillespie, Ethel Ennis, James Cullum Dixieland

Band, the Queen City Jazz Band, and Dick Gibson's Jazz parties. We also gave dance lessons to the ski school and ski patrol so they would know the latest dances when the tourists were here. The Casino also served as Vail's church, and Father Stone said mass there every Sunday. We had weddings and conventions (Colorado Sheepherders, Miss Tall America, and Airline Week, among others). We had shows like Bill McHale's "Highlights of Broadway" starring lovely Pam Zarit. One summer "The Sounds of Ireland" performed with the Irish Rovers, the Pattersons, Irish dancers, and harps. We were the movie theater in town and showed older 16 mm. films and ski movies. Other favorites were turtle races, upside-down Christmas tree contests, and other funny, crazy inventions that Bill came up with. The Casino was the place to be.

I loved skiing and tennis (I believe the first courts became reality in 1968), hiking, hunting, and partying. Bill and I married and had two children. We divorced, and I married Tom Laughlin. We were together until his death in a plane crash. I really didn't have any expectations about Vail since I hadn't planned to come here. I just thought it would be a great way to spend the winter, working, skiing, and having fun.

Vail has changed dramatically from the small Bavarian-style village of the '60s where everyone knew each other but didn't know if the resort would survive. It is very special to have been part of its development and growth into a world-famous, successful mecca. I loved the place in the beginning, and I still do.

BETTY SEIBERT

As one of Vail's earliest residents, I arrived in 1962 with my husband Pete, a founding member of Vail Associates. In those early years, most of my time was devoted to raising our three sons. The good times were skiing together, winter birthday picnics, and summer wild mushroom picnics above Camp Hale.

Most meaningful to me during those early years were the people in my life who helped me with the children. We welcomed several young women ski instructors to live with us during the winter season to help with the boys. Elizabeth, Hanne, Heidi, and Ruth were all part of our "bigger" family. Another good friend was my housekeeper of 17 years, Rosabelle Cordova who raised her brood along with mine.

Photo by John Bonath

Vail gave the boys early job opportunities. Calvin worked as a photographer for Allen Knox and did ticketing for Vail Village Travel. Jim Reinecke gave Peter and Brent hammers and jobs in construction. Of course I took advantage of living amongst the mountains. Thanks to Lyle, Joan, and Pia, I perfected my skiing skills by learning how to anticipate and carve my turns.

One of my happiest memories was returning to school at the University of Denver to finish my education—a BFA and then a Master's in Art History.

As a little girl growing up back East, I always loved the snow, Lake Placid, and winter sports. Little did I know that someday my wish to live in the mountains would come true.

BETTY STILES STONER

My parents were close friends of Bunny and Joe Langmaid in our hometown of Swampscott, Massachusetts. The Langmaids went on to become original investors in Vail. I have been a best friend of their daughter, Jane, for my entire life. It is these friendships that resulted in my coming to Vail with Jane and another close friend, Robin Apple, in the fall of 1964.

I had learned to ski as a young child in the White Mountains of New Hampshire. Vail founder Dick Hauserman was a good friend of the Langmaids, and he introduced me to Joan Carnie of the children's nursery in the Plaza Building on Bridge Street. I worked for Joan for two seasons developing a quality children's program, and I enjoyed caring for some of Vail's earliest toddlers and preschoolers. Among these little friends were Gretchen and Stephanie Miller, Jody Boyd, John Tweedy, and Nancy and Ted Kindel's daughters.

When I left the East Coast and headed to Colorado, I wanted to work in my field of study, but I was clearly ready for the high altitude social life that was to come in Vail. Since this was the carefree 1960s, the fun began nightly after work and went on until the wee hours. Happy Hours

were obligatory at the Red Lion, The Casino, La Cave, or Donovan's Copper Bar and often continued at a private party somewhere in the village. It was during this time that Bill Whiteford, owner of The Casino, offered dance lessons to the "locals" so that we could properly entertain the tourists who came to Vail and insure that they enjoyed their visit.

My girlfriends and I particularly liked spending time with members of Vail's early Ski Patrol. We would stop in at their hut on the summit to "warm up" even if we were not cold. We would laugh and flirt and had not a care in the world except to make sure that we did not miss the next social event.

It was during these wonderful social times that I made friendships that have lasted nearly 50 years. Among these are Jebbie Brown, Marka Moser, George Knox, Nancy Miller, and perhaps my favorite of all, former ski patrolman Jim Clark. Jane Langmaid and Robin Apple were close sidekicks throughout my days in Vail, and they remain my best friends to this day here in New England.

I cherish the time in Vail. These years allowed me to "sow some wild oats." I met Steve Stoner my husband of 43 years in Denver, and we skied

12

together in Vail prior to returning to New England, where we have raised three children and five grandchildren.

The early days were carefree and magical. The village was small, and everyone knew everyone else. For those of us who were there, it was and always will be a time like no other.

BJ Smith

Garrett and I arrived in Vail in October of 1967. We had purchased a VW Bus that June and had it fitted with a camper package to drive 25,000 miles to Alaska, Nova Scotia, and Florida. On our return, we thought we would try skiing for the winter. We parked in a dirt lot and walked up Bridge Street to the Deli looking for jobs. Joe Langmaid's daughter sent us to Vail Ski Rentals where Joe hired Garrett for the winter. We found a place to live in Vail East Condominiums for $250 above Joan and Jack Carnie. Garrett made $2 per hour.

I tried out for the Ski School and was hired, but just for Christmas. In those years they just let you go in January, as business was slow. I worked for Joan Carnie for $1 per hour cleaning short-term rentals. We absolutely loved being part of Vail. By summer, we adored the place. The next year, I took a teaching job at Battle Mountain High School in Minturn's Maloit Park. On weekends I taught Denver kids to ski. After two years, Ski School gave me a contract to teach, and I quit the school district. In the summers I taught tennis in Bill Wright's children's program. We soon found that one job was not enough and added property management to what we were doing. Later, we bought the LionsHead Liquor Store and added the Picnic Basket.

I always feel upset when people talk about how Vail is not the same. The beauty that brought us here is still here. True, I-70 is an interstate highway, but we wouldn't have been able to stay without it. Garrett and I feel like the luckiest people on earth, still doing the things we love, which we learned by driving into a dirt parking lot in 1967.

Bunny Langmaid

We heard about Vail when Joe was working in the family lumber business. Dick Hauserman appeared with all kinds of plans about a ski resort, and it sounded great. We watched his movies, and Joe decided to go out to look it over. He came back very enthusiastic. Of course, there was nothing to see but beautiful scenery; nobody was there. Betty Seibert told us how to get there. We decided to get involved and went to Aspen first, rented a house, and lived there a year and a half. I tried to learn to ski better. It was 1961. Blanche Hauserman was an old friend of ours, and that's how we had met Dick. The arrangement Dick made with Pete Seibert was that he'd open a ski rental and ski shop. Blanche and I did the retail. She had skied in Sun Valley and knew all the retailers. I didn't know anything. I was along for the ride. We were all doing things we'd never done before. I was very mediocre, but was enthusiastic and wanted to learn how to ski.

When Vail was to open, we realized we should be living there and rented a house at the foot of the mountain. It had no water, but we could get water from Mill Creek. At the same time, the Hausermans rented one of Jack Olson's houses across the highway, with water

Scott Carpenter

and electricity. We had our meals over there with anybody else who came along who needed to be fed. Our kids were grown up. Charlie was living in the east; Jane was in high school and went briefly to college. The kids thought it was great in Vail; Jane had so much fun. Charlie moved here eventually, and he has never looked back. I think the men involved with opening Vail took a dim view of the shop. Our effort to make it a cozy place with a fire going and serving cookies, tea, and hot chocolate made it a little more unusual. We did our buying in Aspen when some of the reps came there; we would meet them and order: Bogner, White Stag, and Meggi sweaters. She designed the Vail ski instructor parka. We opened when Vail opened the mountain at Christmas. They had to put newspapers in their ski boots it was so cold. The US Ski Team was there, and business was great. At the end of the year we'd sold just about everything we'd bought. We started collecting a few things so we could keep the store opened; we had a three-year exclusive. We gathered flat rocks from the creek and painted the Vail logo on them and tried to sell them as souvenirs. Idiotic things we did. And I think people bought them.

The nicest part of all for me was in the summer when we explored the mountains in our 4-wheel-drive Scout. We had a Labrador and hiked up the mountain for picnics. One of the things I remember from early summer days was a weekend when the Bishops were up from Denver, and we had a handicap tennis tournament in Minturn. Another weekend, men from Denver were shooting guns off our balcony at cans across the creek. There was nobody there, of course.

Beaver Dam Road went just beyond our house and stopped. They were doing roadwork and had to close it. We put our Scout across the creek, and Joe put planks across, we walked across the planks, got the car, and drove to Minturn to grocery shop. Then we carried the groceries across the creek to our house.

I was interested in flowers and remember collecting all the flowers that were new to us. I kept a 5-year diary and never put much in it except what the weather was and what was growing. I don't know where those diaries are. In winter, I'd walk down to the village and open the shop. If we had extra help, we'd go skiing. I must admit that I was more interested in skiing than shopkeeping. Hausermans gave Joe and me a birthday party in the ski shop – and broadcaster Lowell Thomas was there.

Most evenings we were exhausted, and we collapsed. Joe would have a drink and go to sleep in the armchair. No TV and no radio. Unless there was a party going on, then everybody went. Leonard Bernstein came in the shop once. Ted Kindel was in town skiing before he moved here; he came in and said somebody had stolen his ski poles; I loaned him our ski poles. He said that people were so hospitable he and his family would stay in Vail. The interest of the whole community was more on Vail succeeding than on the individual businesses. It was just a great community spirit. Pete Seibert had serious doubts that we women could succeed in our business. We felt he kind of wished we would go away.

We found friends very easily because there were so few of us. My best friends were Marge Burdick and Barbara Parker. We had a little tent, and we'd camp overnight. It was a wonderful thing for me to come here; it opened up so much for me. In the off-season, we would drive and see the rest of the country. I feel that life in the East was very limited and boring; I'd do this again in a minute. Women were seen as equal in those early days. One thing I remember is

Herbie Baldwin

how formal everything in the East seemed in comparison. I was used to formality, white gloves and going to the city. In Vail, kids were calling me Bunny, and I was 50 when Vail opened. There was the time Gordon Brittan asked me to collect money for the hospital – Renie Gorsuch and I did it, but she did most of the work. Kindels had a surprise birthday party for Joe and me at the St. Moritz restaurant. Musician Peanuts Hucko played the Happy Birthday song. They gave Joe a helmet to wear in a DH veteran's race, with poems on it. Morgan Douglas painted it and then borrowed it; I don't think he gave it back.

The first Christmas we were working so hard we hadn't had a chance to put our Christmas tree up. I remember Ed Talmadge was up from Denver, came in the shop, and asked where he could get a Christmas tree. We said, "Take ours, we don't have time." We would have Christmas Eve dinner with the Hausermans or with our niece Nancy who married Gaynor Miller, and people who lived in Vail and didn't have family would gather. We'd move furniture and have our table in the living room. Barbara Parker was wonderful. Nancy Kindel and I used to talk for hours. Generally, I don't feel there was much difference between the women and the men.

Blanche and I got out and let Dick have the store; after that, he was in charge. Then I went skiing. I really loved skiing and was anxious to learn powder skiing. I remember going down the bowls in deep powder and having Blanche yell, "Turn, turn, turn." I had an awfully good time, and I was no kid.

The first year, there were no telephones. The Lodge had six lines, and we were given one of the lines. Then it was taken away from us; I was told Roger Brown needed it. I don't often get upset, but I was wild. I got in the Scout and drove down to The Lodge and went in Bob Parker's office and screamed, what was he doing taking the phone away from us? Not having a telephone at that point absolutely killed me. I was so anxious because a dear aunt was dying, and I felt so out of touch. Happily, I won that battle.

I just felt great pleasure in the fact that we had done it and had the opportunity to stumble into this Vail opportunity. It was because of the Hausermans, and we enjoyed every bit of it. No regrets.

Elaine speaking: This March, Bunny celebrated her 100th birthday with her family.

CAROL BROWN

I grew up in San Antonio, Texas and attended the University of Texas, Austin where I studied voice and Interior Design. I met my future husband Keith L. Brown there. After practicing law in San Antonio for seven years, we moved to Colorado where he joined Caulkins Oil Company. Together, he and George Caulkins started raising money to start Vail in 1959. My family and I were one of the first families to be involved with Vail. I was here and living in our new house on Mill Creek Circle by opening day 1962. I formed a partnership with Gerry Cohen, also an early Vailite, and we opened the first Interior Design business called Vail Interiors. We did very well, being the only design center in town. Keith built many of the condominiums still in use today, and for many of them I had a corner on the decorating business.

Keith and I built one of the first ski chalets in 1962 and used it every weekend when it was possible to drive the mountain passes. We had many a scary moment going over Loveland and Vail Pass. The children loved it when we had to turn around and spend the night in Georgetown where they could watch TV.

Our social life was quite active, and we knew nearly everyone who moved in or built. It was a fast-growing little community, and we made wonderful friends. Our nightlife was quite busy; we went to The Lodge of Vail, the Red Lion, Gasthof Gramshammer, and Casino Vail (no gambling, just music and food). There were many beautiful parties in private homes.

Mainly, we skied, but several tennis courts and a golf course were built the first few years, and we used them. We also had a horse that we kept in the backyard, and the kids rode him all over town.

Family life was more active than our nightlife, having three children of skiing age and one about to turn four. Our house was built for fun so there were always many guests. I loved my house. Lots of picnics and the 19th hole of the golf course ended up on our deck. Because we were ski-in/ski-out, our place was a convenient landing spot for après ski. Every holiday found us entertaining: Easter egg hunts, Christmas caroling with visits from Santa Claus, and the Gold Peak fireworks were right over our heads. Keith and some of the 'bad boys' in town, would buy the fireworks in Denver, set them up, put the kids under a tarp, and light the fuse. Thank

God no one was ever hurt. We also did many picnics on the mountain, had horse pack trips over the mountains, and even spent one night in an ice hut that had been dug into the mountain. A snowcat pulled us on skis.

All we expected to find here was a little cabin in a small get-away ski area to visit on weekends. Our perspective of Vail changed with its growth as it spread up and down the valley. It was an incredible thing to see. We have loved all of our years in this beautiful

part of the United States. I hope other families have had the fun we did.

CAROL COLLINS

I grew up in Berkeley California, which says something from the start. My group of pals was a bit adventurous. We used to roam freely the undeveloped Berkeley Hills and Tilden Park, and as long as we were home for dinner, all was good. That may be why allowing my son Burton Falk to disappear in Vail for the day with his buddies seemed quite natural. The toads placed in the bathtub were not so natural.

I worked at the Russian River where I babysat Arthur Feidler's children and assisted with recreational activities and overnight hikes to Jenner by the Sea. I think I also worked in the kitchen – training for the Left Bank Restaurant when I came to Vail. I attended Berkeley High School and later grad-uated from Marquette University after moving to Milwaukee when I married. After graduation, I taught fourth grade and then decided to tackle modeling at John Wana-maker. I managed to talk my way into helping present the spring collections, and a dear friend, Betsy Irvine, who now is a Vail owner, taught me how to pivot and turn.

After my father's death and my divorce, I was headed back to Berkeley but found myself thinking of snow in a place I had skied once with a friend. So I set off in a bloody, full-on snowstorm with a very large dog in my very small red 230 SL (a parting gift from my ex), but it broke down about two in the morning just outside of Chicago. A truck driver took Buttercup, my sheep dog, and me to a nearby truck stop where I spent a very interesting evening getting advice, directions, and a protective eye from the lady running the establishment. After sleeping in a booth for the night, I got back on the road and picked up my son from his grandmother's. We arrived in Vail about 10pm, but Burton and Buttercup were restless. They played on Bridge Street to their hearts' content, and I felt very safe. We stayed at the Wedel Inn; little did I know that owners Bob and Diane Lazier would become good friends and that their son Buddy soon would be Burton's partner in crime. If I could find a job, a place to stay, and someone to help me with Burton, we would stay until the season was over, then go "home." The job was hostessing at The Lodge. I found a one-bedroom condominium from Decland O'Donnell who gave me an allowance to buy furniture and childcare from Trish De Ferro, a schoolteacher who agreed to babysit at night while I worked.

Two occupations that stand out were working at the Left Bank where I learned how to properly open a very good bottle of wine, debone trout, and give owners Luc and Liz Meyer headaches. Raised in that atmosphere, Burton believed dinner to be two orders of escargot and a salad. He later told me he believed Luc meant it when he said if Burton did not behave chef would put him in the stew. Shirkie Evens was the sous chef and used to take home leftover cuts of meat that "were not fit" for guests and create wonderful lunches for us the next day or late-night snacks after work. We would ski to his house, have a great dining experience with a little wine, then go to work. Sometimes there were overnights – all the staff would participate and Burton would be there as well. He also attended our luncheon staff parties on the mountain where Luc presided. In those days, dinner guests did not necessarily finish their very expensive wine. We saved these treasures and, blindfolded, tried to identify what we were sipping, thereby developing very fine palates. I remember one evening Shirkie and Luc put tobacco in my Diet Cola. The next day I retaliated by turning a hose on Luc in the kitchen through the patio Dutch door. I returned to good graces on my way to work soon after by finding little Nicolas Meyer toddling across the international bridge – he had escaped from his playpen in the office. Imagine the look on Liz's face when I arrived for work with her treasure under my arm. Later, when I was working for the ski school, Liz did ask me to return to the restaurant and take her position as hostess when she was very pregnant with Hugo. I guess all was forgiven.

My next job was ski school. I was encouraged to apply even though I was not then, nor am I now, a proficient skier. They were desperate. Later, Ski School Director Bob Gagne, told me that they thought they could teach me to ski, but they were wrong – I did, however, pass certification. That was a palm sweating time as I looked down an icy mogul field thinking, "You only have to do this once." As I passed by Serge Couté, I heard him yell to Donovan, "I thought you said she couldn't ski." When I was hired, there was one stipulation from me and that was that they allow Burton to come to work with me. To my surprise, I got an OK. He skied with Jebbie Brown, who created the young locals' program, or with me. Feeling right at home, he would frequently ski away from the group only to catch up after taking a few brisk runs on his own. If he was a bit chilled, he would head for Gold Peak where he charged his hot chocolate to the ski school, warm up, then head back up the mountain to find his class. By the time he was four years old he could ski every run on the mountain proficiently. Burton and I also were allowed Christmas vacation. I might have been the only mother in ski school with the privilege, and John Donovan went along with my "Mothers-don't-work-on-Christmas" ideology. One day, Bob Gagne asked me why my private lesson clients always requested me, as they skied better than I. I told him they did not know that because I made them ski first, they took long lunches with wine, and after that nobody cared about much.

It was small, cozy, safe, beautiful, and everyone knew one another. It felt like a large family. I thought it would be wonderful to be part of the town's growth and transformation. After the first winter here, Burton and I headed "home" and explored places to live with family and friends. Returning to Vail in the summer, I was so happy to experience a small village in the mountains where we could step out our front door and go hiking. I felt it was a safe place to raise a child and that the outdoor atmosphere would be good for a family without a father. I knew it would

grow, but felt like a pioneer knowing we would grow right along with it, and because it was small, we might have something to say along the way and be part of the metamorphosis. I was able in Vail to find a career where I could excel, a beginning for me in the beginning of Vail. I remarried and had a wonderful daughter, Lindsay Duddy.

My social life in the early days might have been a bit different from my other lady friends, as I believe I was the only divorced woman in town with a child. I toted Burton around everywhere until he was old enough to "hang out" on his own with other young children who felt the mountain was their back yard. If I went out to dinner, he came too. One time there was a fish fry and pig roast on Gore Creek near what is now the east end of the golf course. A sign was put up announcing the event asking everyone to bring something. A couple passing through showed up with lanterns that were placed along the path and over the bridge to the campsite. A few others came with their horses. Burton fished, "rode" the horses, and played in the creek. It seemed so healthy and was taking place just 10 minutes from where we lived. I used to drive my car up Mill Creek to the top of the Benchmark for twilight campfire dinners. No lights and all those stars. It seemed like the top of the world, and it was our "backyard."

Hiking is near and dear to my heart. When I took Burton hiking, we would rub aspen powder on our faces to keep from getting sunburned just like the Indians. I was a good sport and played broomball, soccer, and softball with the ski schoolgirls. I think Marie-Claire Moritz was captain for both teams. I remember traveling to Aspen for a very important softball game where we were expected to lose mightily, but we ended the games "cleaning their clocks." Later on I played tennis with Bill Wright. Once in the Gore Range on my own, I saw a storm coming in and started jogging to get to lower ground. Lightning struck close by as I raced around a blind corner almost running into a bear that was running as well. I think fear was in both our eyes as we came to a screeching halt, more lightning, and he bolted into the woods.

We would gather after work at the Nu Gnu and the Casino. After taking tap lessons, a friend of mine and I entered the Halloween "talent contest." Our prize was complimentary "cocktails" for the rest of the evening.

Family life was like summer camp. We jeeped quite a bit, exploring the backcountry, and I marveled at Burton taking naps while on some jeep trail like the very bumpy run to Holy Cross City. We used to jeep the old Stage Coach Run starting in Squaw Creek toward Fulford. I remember asking an old Range Rider how the stage got around a very steep hairpin turn right before a stage stop. He told me it didn't – just fell over, and they would pick it up again.

Once when camping in the Piney, cooking steaks over the campfire, a Basque sheepherder came riding out of the woods with his bandolier slung across his chest, his rifle tucked in his scabbard, and a six-shooter at his hip. We were a little nervous, and my friend asked if I thought we were safe. I said he was more interested in a dinner that was not mutton. Sure enough, after a few hand signals regarding the feast and a ride for Burton on his horse, we all had a fine meal, and he rode into the woods.

During our hikes, Burton became an expert in detecting specialized movement in the grass, jumping in, and coming up with a snake – every time. If he and I did not go to California for Christmas, we decorated the largest tree we could fit in the condominium, and I would cook for a fairly large crowd. Everyone would bring something. We had presents and Santa Claus, Christmas music and singing. It was a happy occasion.

That first trip to Vail was on a whim. I loved mountains; why not try new mountains and a new life? Maybe, after a divorce I did not want to go back; I wanted to move forward. The mountains seemed masculine, and I was lacking a masculine influence for my son so I thought this would be good for both of us. It was a thought, became an adventure, then a home. I do miss the small town atmos-

phere. There is nothing like a gathering of old friends who shared the adventures of growing with Vail. We have a tremendous bond that cannot be understood or shared out loud.

CAROL FITZSIMMONS

Before arriving in Vail, I didn't know what Vail was about. But once there, I felt very comfortable and knew I had found home. I was born and raised in Fresno, California; attended Stephens College in Columbia, Missouri and Fresno State College. I came to Vail for a week in October 1965 to visit a friend I grew up with and never left. John and Cissy Dobson were about to open the Covered Bridge Store. I helped them with the opening and then managed it for them. I also worked a short time at Lady Vail Salon and at the First-Bank of Vail.

I stayed in Vail because of all the wonderful, fun, and sincere people. Vail was also where I met Corky Fitzsimmons, who became my best friend and husband. As the years went by our family and friends became our social life – and I enjoyed many sports, like camping, fishing, boating, and water sports with them.

I have moved away from the Vail scene and live 40 miles to the west. Our business is in Eagle County (Corky's Gas & Car Wash), and we still see and visit with many "old" friends there. Vail was a great place to "grow up," and I would do it again in a heartbeat.

CAROLYN TEEPLE SWANEPOEL

The Teeples came to Vail in 1964 when the resort in northern Michigan where we were teaching skiing closed, due to a second January thaw. On the spur of the moment, we jumped the next flight to Denver and headed to the new ski resort in the West that everyone was talking about. We arrived early the next morning in Vail, still wearing our instructor jackets

with the PSIA pin displayed prominently above our nametags. That was what Morrie Shepard, Vail's first ski school director, had spotted when he skied up to us on our second day and said, "We're really short of instructors here. Would you two consider staying and teaching for us?" And that was the beginning.

We joined the 24 or so other instructors that made up the

elite Vail Ski School in those days: instructors such as Ted Kindel, Rod Slifer, Serge Couté, and Tom Jacobson.

There was no employee housing in Vail in 1964. The only place we could find was one of four motel rooms leaning against the green Gambles Store, now the Two Elk Gallery, in Minturn. Linoleum floors and a space heater were the best the valley had to offer. Worse yet, the owners closed the motel March 1 until summer arrived. When that happened, we packed our bags and were at Mid Vail saying goodbye when one of the instructors said, "Hey, Carolyn. Why don't you ski down to the Short Swing (now the Vail Athletic Club) and apply for a job? They just fired the third manager this year."

I raced down Riva Ridge and straight to the Short Swing to find the owner. That night was the first night Grant and I "managed" the Short Swing Lodge, home to the youngest, single Vail Resort employees and a few guests who stumbled by. With this kind of permanence, a fellow ski instructor flew from Michigan and brought our young son, Grant Guy, Jr. Son Granger arrived a couple of years later, and the boys began living a magical childhood where everyone knew whose child was whose, knew the names of all the dogs, and the four-digit telephone numbers.

Kids were free to roam and safe in Vail in those days. No one thought of locking his or her car or doors. Kids roamed the streets or rode their bikes, stopping for peanut butter/jelly sandwiches in the back room at Gorsuch's store, they jumped into Gore Creek with their dogs, and showed up at mealtimes with most of the other kids in town who could all fit around one big table. The gang was Johnny, Jeffey, Davey, Rhett, Buddy, Mikey Smith, Kira, and a little redheaded Nottingham girl. They went to school in one big room over the Vail Fire Department.

By 1968, I made the cut to represent Vail on the U.S. 8th Interski Team – the first time women were members. There can be fewer proud highlights in one's life than representing your country in a worldwide athletic competition. I remember thinking, "I always knew I could do anything I put my mind to, but after Interski—I was sure of it." The experience was life changing.

When people ask me why I moved to Vail, I have to tell them it was the sheer exuberance of building a new town. It seemed easy; there was great freedom. Everyone worked hard, and we had so much fun. We needed anyone with talent or skills in those days, so everyone became a "Vail ambassador." If the village needed something, Vail Associates was right there to help. If VA needed a boost, the village turned out. There was no sense of remote corporate ownership. It seemed we all shared a common goal – a happy future. We thought, felt, and operated for each other.

In those early days we had no TV, no newspapers, and the only radio I listened to was a short-wave that brought in a military station somewhere. We amused ourselves – and we got really good at it. We partied on the ski mountain, ice skated on the outdoor rink made by the volunteer fire department, sang

23

with the piano player under the Ore House, tuned our own skis, hung out at Donovan's -- and built and worked and played. I think we were the best at charades in the country. As long as the Casino was open, there was plenty of entertainment.

The stories of those days are legend and are told when "old timers" get together. There are books written about the vital men who brought a vision into reality, another group who put money behind that vision, but the REAL Vail was the adventurous men and women who left homes, friends, and businesses to come here and put the spirit into it.

I think we had the best of times in this valley. We were the generation, with no prior experience, who created a town, a set of rules, built schools and hospitals, and raised children to become solid citizens. We created an enticing way of life called Vail that had started with a sheep meadow. And we're still alive to tell about it. I doubt it could happen again ever – anywhere.

CELIA ROBERTS

No question, what brought me to Colorado was its beauty. I didn't even know what or where Vail was, only that I had wanted to move to Colorado ever since I came out on vacation from Kentucky with my family in the mid-50s. When a sweet dear Kentucky man, a skier himself, I fell in love with in graduate school found out a job could be waiting for me out in Vail, he was so thrilled with the idea, that I packed my pale blue VW squareback to the brim and headed west, not realizing that I was leaving the love of my life behind. Obviously, my path was leading me where I was meant to be, somewhere other than marriage, one of the few options available for women back in the '60s. I fell in love again, this time with the mountains.

My first memory of Vail was on a sunny day in early March of 1969. I was late for my first day of desk clerking at the Wedel Inn. The consequences of running at high altitude after having lived at sea level for two years were unknown to me. I thought my lungs were going to bust wide open. The job suited, however, thanks to Kathy and Pierre Losereit, who had become friends at a hotel job in the Bahamas while I was escaping the life of a bored, unhappy mathematics teacher in Florida.

Another memory from that first winter was when I noticed a lot of activity at the top of Bridge Street. Being as small as I was, I managed to wiggle my way to the front of the crowd lining a roped-off area at the bottom of the chairlift and watched in amazement as racers came tearing down the mountain at breakneck speeds to the deafening shouts of this throng of enthusiasts. The buzz was about someone named Jean Claude Killy. An unknown to me, it was still great fun, and the next weekend I went back for more, only to find out that it had been a special international race and would not be repeated there for years to come. Certainly, this didn't dampen my love for Vail. Although I never became a great lover of the sport and often felt I didn't quite fit into the bar scene, I always enjoyed hanging out and listening to Sam Stevenson sing and play guitar in the little bar behind La Cave.

My skiing days were blessed with a free pass to the mountain, thanks to my job with the Vail Trail newspaper. At one point, I had an assignment to photograph Gerald Ford and his entourage on the mountain, which led to one of my most embarrassing moments in this thriving little town of dirt streets and no bus station. Needless to say, my skiing was not up to par. After a face plant and much floundering in the snow, I was rescued by one of those awesome men on the Vail Ski Patrol. From then on, I was crazy about one or another of them. Never a ski instructor, always a ski patrolman.

This particular time in Vail was very significant to me. Vail Trail newspaper owner George Knox, Sr. recognized my love of photography, put me in charge of the darkroom, and offered me double-paged spreads of my black and white images. So here's to you, George, Sr. With your encouragement I was able to find my true passion in life as a photographer. With the encouragement of so many dear friends, I continued down that long-sought-after path as owner of Reflections Gallery on Gore Creek Drive.

25

CELINE KRUEGER

Celine grew up in Valparaiso, Indiana and had five siblings. She went to nursing school and worked in a Chicago Hospital in her early 20s. Mother worked the night shift and went to the beach after her shift with her wonderful nurse friends. In the winter, they skied in Michigan on weekends off. She met Ben Krueger while skiing on Boyne Mountain. On a ridge, she called down below that she was coming, and ran over his skis. That night a whole group of them dined and wined together.

So, their relationship started on a ski hill! I think Ben was in the military at the time, and he was not always home. They wrote letters to each other. After Ben and Celine got married, they moved to Denver to be closer to skiing. Dad had a job on a golf course. Celine continued her career as a nurse in Denver. They had sons Berne, John, and Karl before moving to the Vail valley.

Celine and Ben were on their way to a job interview in Aspen one October day. They stopped in Vail to see what was going on and Ben had an interview right there about building and operating the Vail Golf Course. By the end of the ski day, they got the job and never made it to Aspen. They moved to Vail in April of that year to start work on the Vail Golf Course. Their first home was in Buffehr Creek. Celine had stopped working as a nurse when she had her children. She was devoted to being a mother.

The Christmas Fair was one of her biggest events to organize. Most of my childhood, I helped take a donation of 25 cents at the door. The Christmas Fair started out filling the gymnasium of Red Sandstone School. Money raised from the fair went back into school programs. Celine also volunteered at the community rummage sale for many years.

Celine was an artist. She really got involved in her art after all four kids were in college. It was her passion, and she worked hard to get into national shows.

Ben and Celine put their roots down here. They raised their family in West Vail. loved their friends, and felt connected to the community. I don't think our parents ever thought of going back to the midwest to live. They had made Colorado and Vail their

26

permanent home.

Vi Brown was Celine's best friend. Vi lived at the end of the street and had three children. How wonderful that these ladies met and supported each other. Mother was an avid hiker and was a member of the Happy Hiker group. Besides skiing and hiking, Celine liked to golf and do water aerobics.

Ben and Celine's four children continue to live in the valley with their families.

—Memories of mother by Celynn

Chance Earle

It was time to leave the East coast behind me. I was originally thinking of moving to Aspen, but Vail came along first with a job and lodging. In the summer of 1969, I arrived in Vail and started work at the Vail Village Inn coffee shop. I lived in the dormitory upstairs with about 12 other girls who worked at The Lodge at Vail. My waitress skills were nonexistent. George Ward hired me, and it was on-the-job-training. I had to get up early for the breakfast shift. Later, I moved on to work at Donovan's Copper Bar and at Pepi Sports. Besides the coffee shop,

I worked at the Outback Restaurant at the Vail Village Inn. Vail Associates hired me to book private lessons at the Vail Ski School. When it came to nightlife, I have to say, "Those were the days." When I wasn't working, I skied and later took up golf.

I met my husband, Frank Earle, and we now live in Friday Harbor, Washington.

I didn't have any particular expectations about moving to Vail. I was just looking for a new adventure. You could say that coming to Vail in 1969 was about, "Hurry up and pack it all in."

CHRISTIE (BLANCHE HAUSERMAN) HILL

Christie Hill (known as Blanche Hauserman in Vail's early years) was one of the first women to arrive for Vail's opening in September, 1962 with her husband, Dick Hauserman. Blanche had a well-travelled and unique life. She was raised in Boston and later moved to North Conway, New Hampshire, where she fell in love with skiing and met and married Austrian skier Benno Rybizka. She moved to Mont Tremblant in Canada and on to Sun Valley, Idaho. John Fripp, former ski school director at Mont Tremblant remembers her well, "Blanche Rybizka? She was a real dish. She was on the front page of Life magazine." During that time, Blanche Christian (as she had been known during her

modeling career) travelled the world to model ski wear. She graced the cover of Life twice but considered herself a skier, not a model. Blanche was a good friend of Peter Seibert, who later convinced her to come and be part of Vail's new frontier. She had a vision for Vail and was dedicated to making it work. Friends still talk of her elegance, enthusiasm, and crisp sense of humor.

Although Christie gives much credit to her

husband during the early years of Vail, she was his partner and an independent businesswoman as well. Although Dick created the Vail logo, Christie was crucial in designing the famous Vail ski instructor parka, suggesting that the distinctive diagonal stripe across the chest and back mimic the sashes that Queen's guards wear in England. She still lives in the same apartment above the original Vail Blanche, at the base of the Vista Bahn at the top of Bridge Street.

I moved to Vail because I am an adventuress, and I have skied all my life. Peter Seibert came to me when they were building Vail. I knew him and Bob Parker from the East, and they convinced me to come here and open a store. I had done a lot of magazine covers, so I wasn't just known in the ski world. I knew an awful lot of people, so when they were trying to raise money for Vail, they asked me to help.

I was the only skier in my family. I had been modeling and was good friends with Toni Frissell (the fashion photographer), and she did a couple of big pictures for me in Vogue magazine. I wasn't known in the fashion industry, so the photographers wanted to know who I was, and that is how I got started. Dick Hauserman and I met and married before we came to Vail. He worked in his family's business, the Hauserman Company, and was tired of it. I suggested we go do something else. When we first came to Vail, he had nothing to do, but since he was a salesman, he really got into promoting Vail. I believe that, without Dick, there would be no Vail. He used to stop people on the streets and tell them to come into town. He was a huge salesman for the fledgling resort in the Rockies.

When I first arrived, there was no town. I can't remember exactly the feeling when I saw the place, but I knew we wanted to build something. I knew this part of the country. Dick wasn't a skier, and he didn't learn to ski until after we were married. It was a tradeoff; but he wanted me to golf. So I told him, "I'll learn to golf if you learn to ski."

We stayed at Jack Olson's until my place was completed. Jack lived in Minturn, but he had a little house across the road just to the west in Vail. Dick had to go back East, and I stayed in the house by myself while Dick was gone. The house had mice, and I was alone. When I heard them running around at night, I took a blanket and pinned

it tightly around my neck so they couldn't get to me. I'd sit with a flashlight to see where the hole was so I could stuff it, and they wouldn't get to me.

Vail was in the middle of nowhere. Pete Seibert took me out on a snowcat on the mountain and asked, "What do you think of it?" I replied, "It's flat." He surmised, "That's what most skiers want, and this will bring in the skiers." He was right, of course, because there are more average skiers than expert skiers, and this mountain could give many more skiers the ski experience. Pete also took me to the top of the mountain and showed me the back bowls. I used to ski a lot and also taught skiing. My first reaction about the skiing here remained: this was a flat mountain, that's all. We didn't have any steep runs back then.

My building (Vail Blanche, with the apartment upstairs) was the first commercial building in Vail. Vail Blanche was right downstairs from my residence and was completed around 1963. I spent 1962 planning for the opening with my partner, Bunny Langmaid, whom I had known from Boston. There were very few women in Vail at the time. Those who were here soon became friends. I don't feel that I gave up anything moving to Vail. There was nothing difficult at all about it; it was an adventure. I thought it was wonderful, and I never thought of leaving. Of course, there were hard times. For example, early on, we had to get water straight out of the creek. First I'd first brush my teeth then wash my face. Then we poured it in the toilet tank and put up a sign that said, "Don't flush unless necessary." The only toilet that really worked well at all belonged to Eileen and Fitzhugh Scott.

We realized the dream of Vail was coming together that first Christmas. Because there was no snow, the Ute Indians had been invited to do a snow dance. The fact that there was no snow actually made us happy because we were still building the gondola, and the Vail Blanche building was connected to it. Every day was a challenge, and opening the store that first day was quite remarkable. It was also the first day we put water through the pipes in the house above the shop. The pipes broke, and water came down through the electric lights into the shop. Pepi Gramshammer was in the shop, and he always helped me because I did the ski boots. The water poured right on top of him! There weren't many customers, fortunately. In fact, we had so few customers that I used to deliver their shoes or whatever they bought to their hotel.

Many of the wives helped in the shop. Camille Bishop and Heather Slifer worked there, as did Anne Staufer. It was one of the only places to work. Bunny and I were very busy running the shop, cleaning and doing everything ourselves, but I skied every day. Bunny and I put a sign on the door that said, "Gone skiing." We got up around 5 am and did the things you had to do here, like carrying the water, and then opened at 9 am. We'd ski and come back to the shop around 2:30 or 3 and stay open until 6 or 7pm. We were always exhausted.

As the population grew, people had parties. People like the Parkers would have you over in the evening for a little party, which meant we got together to have some drinks. Drinking was not too much of a problem because we couldn't afford it. During the summers, we'd fish and hike. I did everything with Bunny and Joe.

Larry Burdick came the first year and started building the Red Lion. He went back to Kalamazoo and brought back his wife, Marge. He was a wonderful man, the son of a banker, and had skied in Europe. When Larry designed the Red Lion, he gave it a European look. There were often skiers with broken legs coming off the mountain after a day of skiing. We'd have them lined up in the middle of the road on pallets in front of the

Red Lion. Dr. Steinberg would come by and examine them, and I'd give them a shot of brandy to keep them going.

There was a very simple grocery store in Minturn. I taught the man who ran it about food, told him about Pepperidge Farm, and convinced him to bring in a variety of products. The only locals around Minturn worked around the railroad or the mines. I remember an older man who owned part of the Eagle River and did not want people fishing on his easement. He put up a little sign that said,

"Anyone who steps over this line will be shot into hell."

Nobody cared who anyone was. We all worked hard. In my opinion, it was the women who made this town. The women built Vail. Without them, we wouldn't have the schools or the community. I'm not the kind to remember the inconveniences, because I came to pioneer. Of course, there were inconveniences, but you didn't expect to have what you had before. This is home. I've never thought of going anywhere else.

— CWP

CONNIE KNIGHT

Arriving from Florida with my two young children, my mother, and two Persian cats in a new station wagon that kept stalling because of the altitude, we came through Dowd Junction and each one of us said, "Ahhhh," when we saw the quaint alpine village called Vail. We had checked out Denver, Colorado Springs, Boulder and Aspen, but without realizing it Vail was just what we were looking for. We rented an A-frame house in East Vail for $75 a week. Mice and chipmunks occupied with authority, which was worrisome in the middle of the night because the bathroom was downstairs.

We called one of the chipmunks "Jimmy" after my son who seldom came when he was called. One day, Jimmy showed up with surveying stakes in his hand. I gasped. When he saw my face, he said, "Don't worry, Mommy. I'll put them back." They were CDOT stakes marking where I-70 would go. We still laugh today at the last wide curve coming down Vail Pass as Jimmy's doing.

Jimmy and Paul Johnston Jr. used to find loot at the Nu Gnu (the nightclub Paul's father owned) that had slipped from guys' pockets when they sat in the booths.

My mother talked me into buying a condominium rather than renting. "I'm quite sure you'll get your money back, and I wouldn't be surprised if you make some money," she astutely advised. So I bought a two-bedroom, two-bath condo at the Vorlaufer. It was the brilliant orange shag carpet and avocado appliances that sold me. There's a plaque in her memory on the bench across from the Vorlaufer on Vail Valley Drive.

For a never-ever skier, looking up at Golden Peak was frightening so I signed up for a ski lesson. "Make one turn and come down to me," the instructor said. I did. The 190cm ski bindings didn't release. "Don't worry," said the doctor. "When you can put your foot in your boot and bang it (on the heel like we all did back then), probably in three days, you'll be okay." Ha! Three months later, after hobbling around leaning on my children's ski poles, I ventured back on the hill.

People still question if I'm legit when I tell them I came here in 1968. "I never saw you at Donovan's," they said. With two kids, a mother, a bum knee, and two cats, how could I be guzzling at the bar? Blake Lynch agreed to take care of our cats when we took a family trip to California. Blake kept them in his loft attractively carpeted in deep red shag. Since the cats were what breeders call chinchilla, white with black tips, the carpet sure looked more like a chinchilla than red shag by the time we got back, but Blake has yet to complain to me.

The kids' ski passes were a mere 16 bucks if bought through the school, located above the clinic. When they came home complaining of sore arms, I queried them. They simply said they were given inoculations at the clinic. No big deal for them, and I don't recall permission slips from parents.

I learned I could get a free day ski pass if I helped pack down snow on the steep runs on the front of the mountain. The ski corporation wanted the passersby on Highway 6 to see just how fabulous our pristine snow and ski conditions were.

I usually knew where my kids were - either ice skating under Chair 6 or sledding down Bridge Street on plastic or cardboard. Mary Lou Davis, who has a great sense of humor and a prosthetic leg, didn't lose her cool when it detached and went flying down Bridge Street. Instead of hollering, "Ski, Ski," as we did before bindings had brakes, she shouted, "Leg, Leg!"

Baking was a huge challenge and still is at high altitude. Not that it ever was my forté, but for Lynne's first birthday in Vail, getting the frosting to stay put was nearly impossible. I kept running down the block to the Deli to buy more confectioners' sugar. Photos document the disaster, but a sweet disaster at that.

There weren't separate queues for singles in the early days, so the "trick" to skiing was scouting out the lift lines. Only when you spotted a good-looking guy, did you shout, "Single?" I tried it at Chair 6 and by the time we reached the top, the guy asked me to dinner. "Are you married?" I asked. "Hey, I only asked you to dinner," he mouthed as he skied away in a hurry. "PMS" - we always went to Pepi's,

32

Mickey's, and Sheika's for nightlife. And I remember traipsing through the mud across the Covered Bridge to the Vail Village Inn for the Melodrama. Dates were easy to come by, and memories of doing the Charleston on a dance floor covered with peanuts where the Left Bank now sits are indelible. Those were the days when the ratio was seven men to every woman. We were so lucky to be here.

DAPHNE SLEVIN

My grandfather was the governor of Burma, and I was born there. My father was in the Indian army, and when war came, my mother, sister, and I went to England, where I was educated. Then I worked in a very boring secretarial job in London until 1962. I had a friend in Canada who had a connection with Vail, so it seemed the right time to go and live in the States. I wrote a letter and was hired at The Lodge at Vail. Little did I know they could not get anybody to work.

I had thoughts of St. Moritz as I daydreamed on the bus to Denver. An Austrian from The Lodge drove me to Vail – through the town of Dillon, no reservoir yet, and we ate in Georgetown. No snow, Dec 5 1962 – Year 1. It was a construction camp with mud, and The Lodge was still being built. There was a cookhouse trailer in front where everybody ate. Everything was way behind schedule. I was by myself, and it was getting dark and looked so strange to me. They put me up in Dick Hauserman's rental apartment. Snow came in January that year. In Denver, they didn't know much about Vail at all, but we got publicity because astronauts had put money in Crested Butte.

The next morning, I woke up and looked out and up the mountain – then I could see what it was about. That was pretty spectacular. I had never skied, and learning to ski was part of the attraction. No employee housing, they never got around to doing it. That first year, they moved us to wherever they had a little space. We lived in The Lodge, but the trouble with that was that it didn't have heat or running water. You had to run to Fitzhugh Scott's house for the bathroom.

They opened on December 15. VA owned everything including The Lodge because nobody else would build one. They wanted a grand lodge, but nobody would do it. This was in the middle of nowhere, over two mountain passes, small roads, and no town close by. The tourist center was Denver, and it was a long way away. Nobody knew if this place was going to go or not, and it very nearly didn't. I worked in the reservation office and helped at the Front Desk. I wrote letters, so I suppose I was the manager's secretary. There was very little snow that first year. In fact, we drove up to Mid Vail in a VW Beetle on December 10. They were testing the lift. We were the first ones on Lift 4 and went to the top. I didn't have any winter clothes and only little boots. We got off to look over at the Back Bowls – the snow did not come over my ankles. The US Ski Team came and trained at Vail that winter. They had the army coming in with baskets putting snow under the trees, no machinery then.

It was a great hiding place for crooks and a great place to work if you didn't want anybody to find you. Shootouts and wild things were going on. One of the bellboys wanted to kill the chef; he got drunk but didn't have a gun. The head of ski patrol was a deputy. They wrestled the bellboy to the ground and drove him off to Eagle. One of the 10 Most Wanted on the FBI list worked as a dishwasher. It was the Wild West. I was a cocktail waitress, too, because you needed to have two or three jobs.

Anne & Joe Staufer arrived in January; Rod and Heather Slifer were newlyweds; Isabel came with the Kansas City Ski Club and met Manfred (Schober). Bunny Langmaid, Blanche, Barbara Parker. Gaynor and Joann Miller were some of the people with businesses. Gretta was here quite a lot with Bill Whiteford. Suzie

Kuehn (Shepard); Hemmye and Irene Westbye. Roger and Barbara Brown. After ski season, I decided I did not want to be here anymore. Socially it wasn't for me. I had a cousin at Berkeley, so I went to San Francisco and loved it there.

By September, I realized I had to go back to Vail to collect my stuff; I came back to find that Joe Staufer had persuaded VA to open The Lodge in summer. They did it with a skeleton staff that included Jim Slevin. He was there because Dick Hauserman was building the Plaza Building and persuaded Jim to open something – open a restaurant! He did, and they talked me into staying. It was a fun atmosphere. They had horses where Manor Vail is, and we rode where the golf course is. We went fishing. Then we'd do our various shifts. Joe had a special weekend deal for $15 a room for two nights, two dinners, two breakfasts, and a gondola ride.

Jim Slevin and I got to be close. Then Peter Seibert came to me and asked me to work for him in the winter. I had to decide if I should stay one more winter. I worked for Pete as his secretary up Bridge St. I was living in a trailer with three other girls. Jim and I got married, and he opened La Cave New Year's Eve 1963. He paid a year's liquor license for one night. You could dance, and it was the first discotheque in Colorado. My sister sent two 45rpm records by a new group in England that was causing a stir – The Beatles. "She Loves Me" and "I Want To Hold Your Hand." We had a combined restaurant/nightclub and stayed open till two in the morning. It was a lot of work, and we didn't have much time to ski; that's why I never became a good skier. I even remember sitting in our apartment and throwing all the bills up in the air, catching one, and saying that this was the lucky guy who was going to get paid. People were so nice and helped each other out – no cutthroat stuff; not too much greed. Developers weren't there yet.

It was such a gamble in those days. Jim had produced a couple of plays in New York, and they'd lost money. Dick Hauserman invited him to visit, and he stayed. Weird coincidences. People were arriving and staying – like the Morettis. It was becoming more interesting. Employees were always very hard to come by, especially in the restaurant business. We built Golden Peak House in 1967 with the Morettis and opened the Copper Bar because we couldn't get anyone to come to La Cave underground for lunch. Breakfast and Lunch – plus nighttime. Donovan was our bartender, and he was so good at it. He asked to buy the bar, and that's how Donovan's came to be. I opened Kaleidoscope with Anne Staufer; we had no idea what we were doing. Personally, the thing I would say about coming to the States (or maybe it was the Vail experience) was that it enabled me to do all these amazing things that I could never in a zillion years have done in England, ever. Women with no business experience. Then we started the Children's Corner in the same building when I realized there was big potential. We were the first and only one; yuppies were having children later in life and had more money. They were willing to spend money on children's ski clothes and not just dress them up in old ski pants.

Nobody in my family came over here except my sister who worked at the Copper Bar. My family would have said, "You can't possibly do that." But somehow we weren't scared to open a business.

Interstate 70 and the tunnel were being built. Wild things – we went to Minturn for breakfast when La Cave closed at 2 o'clock in the morning – to a place called Jeff's, I think. It was the original Saloon. All the early people will tell you that they wouldn't have missed those early years for anything. People gave lovely parties, and everybody was invited. Halloween was always a big fun thing. It all seemed to be centered on going to bars and having a wild time and drinking. We worked very hard, too. That was our social outlet. You didn't just jump in your car and go to Denver. You stayed overnight, loading up with food at the supermarket. Best parties were at the Casino, the Kindels', and Sheika gave great parties. It was always fun to go up to the Murchisons' house. Was there an elite group? No, not in those early years.

Here's a story: Jim went to the Vail Village Inn one evening after work. He must have been really drunk and had the idea of going into the pool. So he took off all his clothes and jumped into the VVI pool. A stranger sitting next to him did exactly the same thing.

We had a snoopy postmistress who knew everything. Someone got the mail from Minturn and brought it over. We sent out wedding invitations, and she would say to people, "Have you had your invitation to the Slevin wedding yet?" So we invited everybody. We wanted to get married October 3, but people said to us, "You can't get married October 3; that's the opening of the grouse season." We changed it to Friday, October 2. On October 3, we went up on the gondola, took our dog, took our guns, and hunted grouse. Our dog was hopeless because he was gun-shy. About a week or so later, Blanche and Dick organized the honeymoon. There were 10 or 12 of us on horseback, and we went up to Pitkin Lake. Donovan was shooting grouse from the saddle. We came down the same day on horses. And that was how it was.

DENYSE ROGERS MCCOY

Arriving in Vail on an October evening when I was 19 years old, I was totally enchanted as the snow fell softly. Those were the days when the Left Bank was considered to be on the edge of town, the Copper Bar and Pepi's were après hot spots, and Jo Jo Lyles sang in the basement of the Clock Tower Lounge. I fell in love with the moments, the skiing, the people, and the magic of a tiny village in the middle of nowhere…. It became the only world I would call home.

As I look back, I remember being one of a hundred or so who came to ski for one season and never left. I stayed that spring and into the next summer with eyes wide open and a feeling of the wonderment I was becoming a part of.

With the spring came mud season…literally. Living in Avon in Roybal's Trailer Court where the Westin Resort now sits, there was nothing but great views and the elk herd that shared our space, a post office on the creek, and a farmhouse now called Restaurant Mirabelle. We fished and hunted for our bounty then…it seemed the proper thing to do.

Then came the summer with all of her glory. The '60s had bred a bit of hippie from the western coast and a strong bond with the land, horses, and the feeling I had been here before. I felt that I belonged to a greater dream that was to come. And so we lived every moment, listening to 8-track tapes and partaking of the rodeos that came to town, located in Bighorn in East Vail. I worked as a hand for $50 a month including room and board at the old cabin at Piney Lake. I skied and played hard, working three jobs at a time just to be able to stay. I loved this valley and the crazy people who called it home.

My first job in Vail was at the Schober Ski Shop with Manfred and Isabel, then Aux Ducs de Savoie Pastry Shop with André and Josephine, and then onto being the first Checkpoint Charlie. I had the pleasure of a "European internship" with Sheika at Pepi's Bar and learned countless swear words in many dialects. Everyday People with Judy Evans gave me the skill to size up a jean fit in a second and wear the infamous Ms. Vail crown while vacuuming the shop at closing time. I worked in bars and restaurants up and down Bridge Street.

The '60s and '70s were filled with the true spirit and much dedication from each first "Vailite" woman, or "Vail Chibbie"… all contributing to the making of the dream that has evolved into what we are today. We should all be proud of the part we played in the making of a destination resort and home to our children. I still hear the echoes of laughter and delights of skiing those perfect snow days.

DIANA DONOVAN

I'm an Army brat and proud of it. I was born in Ft. Lewis, Washington, where the 10th Mountain Division was also born, so my mother says I am a "10th Mountain Baby." When I was six weeks old we moved to the Hotel Colorado, in Glenwood Springs, while Dad focused on training troops at Camp Hale. Over the next couple decades I hopped around the country, as Army Brats do, and spent time in Minnesota on our family's dairy farm, getting my pigtails caught in the milking machine motor, time in Georgia where I fell in love with archaeology, time in Texas where I came face-to-face with a rattlesnake, and even crossed the Atlantic via the USS Callahan to "help" my father coordinate efforts to prevent Germany from possibly invading Austria. I attended 13 different schools between 1st and 12th grades. My dad retired from the Army at the same time I graduated from the University of Minnesota in 1964 with a BA in anthropology. As planned, we moved to Evergreen, Colorado to be close to an army hospital and return to the beauty of the wilderness.

Bob and Barbara Parker had been family friends for a very long time. I saw a prototype of the first gondola in their yard in Denver and heard about the new project but thought nothing more of it. During a family visit, I asked Barbara if she thought I could get a job in Vail. She told me that the only available jobs would not give me "more than $1.50 an hour." She went on to say that, "Living is very expensive; the only thing available is a horrid hole with four in a room, at $2.50 a night and food on top of that would be $3.25 to $4 daily." I would have to buy a ski pass for another $100. I carefully figured that I could make the same as my current job of drugstore clerk and still have time and a few dollars for skiing. I had absolutely no expectations beyond a job for the winter that allowed me to have fun skiing. John Donovan may have lived in the basement of Parkers' that winter, but I didn't know it. I lived in the house with them. When I first saw him, his face was sunburned, he had on an ugly maroon coat over a down parka, and a faded hat. He invited me out, asking, "Can I buy you a cup of tea at the Red Lion?"

Barbara put me in touch with Gaynor and Joann Miller who owned the Night Latch, a dormitory where the Mountain Haus now stands. They offered me a front desk job. I gave my notice, and in the middle of January 1965, loaded Mom's "great" Kneissel wood skis with bear trap bindings and my bamboo poles from Austria into my '55 Chevy and headed to Vail for the winter. I drove by way of Kenosha Pass as I was afraid my car would not make it over Loveland Pass.

I soon "bent" my Kneissel wood skis on my favorite run, Lodgepole. After examining the direction of the protruding splinters, the only way I was making it down the hill was skiing backwards. I was lucky to find used Head skis, and, fortunately, Mom's leather buckled boots lasted several years.

That first winter I had the requisite three jobs: front desk/secretarial at the Night Latch, babysitting for The Lodge at Vail manager, and seamstress for Sport Haus that preceded Gorsuch. Perhaps as a result of working three jobs, I managed to shorten a pair of fancy wool pants overnight for a customer. The only problem was I shortened one leg twice. The second winter I was working at the Night Latch, the US Ski Team came into town over Christmas. They piled into the dormitory rooms – Jimmy Heuga, Billy Kidd, Moose Barrows, and the rest of the ski team, sharing a few rooms and fewer showers.

I started a children's day camp with Ginny Crowley and worked a bit for Vail Resorts, Vail Recreation District, and Vail Resort Association while continuing with my three main jobs. There was the odd job that surfaced. I remember putting on a Wonder Woman costume and skiing with other "Super Heroes" for a promotional movie. Another time, I earned $50 for being in a Jeep commercial. The premise was a hip young wife and husband dropping off their teenage son for a rock concert. I played the hip young wife. The commercial had critical flaws - I was barely older than my "son," whom we dropped off on Bear Tree ski run as he plodded into the woods for his rock show – Hollywood magic.

From 1967 on, I did all the office work and bookkeeping for our businesses including Donovan's Copper Bar followed by Vail Honeywagon, the local trash removal company.

When you own your own business you are the permanent on-call person, but I realized early on not to learn how to fix a drink or drive a big truck so I never had to do those two jobs. When the kitchen help did not show up one time, I managed by myself to put out a record number of lunches for Donovan's with Kerry in a pack on my back. I made evergreen garlands for winter decorations around the windows to save money. St. Patrick's Day was crazy at the bar. We served green beer, of course, and John would bring home the money for me to wash as it was all soaked in green beer by the time the day was over. I would have hundreds of "one dollar bills" spread out around the house to dry.

If Vail was a family, then the Copper Bar was its living room. Our bar was the first business started with money made in Vail, not brought in from previous successes. Out-of-town moms called to leave messages for their kids; we installed a TV so we could all share the moon walk; we had lock-ins if a powder day was imminent, and when John returned from Denver after the birth of our first son, the bar cheered. In his words, "Like Notre Dame had just scored a touchdown." We opened Golden Gate Restaurant, the first golf course restaurant located on the first hole at the base of Golden Peak. We also owned an Italian/pizza place on Wall Street. I baked key lime pies and made bulgur wheat salads for the restaurant. It later became the Hong Kong Café.

When I first met John he had a haphazard way of doing business paperwork. He paid a bill and tossed the invoice in the trash. He put the day's receipts, uncounted, in a zippered First Bank of Eagle bank bag for once-a-week pickup by an armored truck because Vail had no bank. I accused him of marrying me because I was good at detailed, time-consuming paperwork. We figured in the off-season we lost the same amount of money whether open or closed, so we never closed Donovan's for a single day the 16 years it existed. Beers were three for a dollar or 35 cents each, and almost everyone had a house charge. I added those little numbers up on a hand-operated, pull-the-handle-down, adding machine and sent out handwritten bills monthly. I still have the list of people who owe bar bills and a couple bad checks. We eventually closed the bar due to a lease dispute. My husband's skiing accident and the loss of the bar were life-altering events, but I was so busy holding things together that it took years before it all sank in.

My other work was a deep involvement in town government. My husband was on the first town council in 1966. I was appointed to the Sign Committee and served the most consecutive years on the Planning Commission. I feel very good about what I did and how I influenced the town in its formative years.

John was a ski school supervisor and had to be there, but he never said he was going to work. Instead, he'd say, "I'm going skiing." When he went to the bar, he never called that work either. He bought the bar in the fall of '66 from Jim Slevin. John said we only needed to make enough money to have fun. He spent his time surrounded by people, so we usually chose family time over "parties" on the rare occasions free time came our way. In the summer and fall, we would share the "harvest" of the day with other sportsmen and cook dinner at someone's house. It seemed we were always meeting to protect and fight for our water and wilderness or organize a fundraiser for environmental and community causes. We stopped a timber sale in what became Eagles Nest Wilderness by suing the US Forest Service and winning. We stopped I-70 from cutting through the proposed wilderness in a series of tunnels and destroying Main Gore Creek. We fought the Denver Water Board to protect the water Vail needed and keep water flowing in Gore Creek. We served on boards and laid sod on sports fields.

One party we always attended was the end-of-season Ski Patrol party, otherwise known as the Farmers' Party. Everyone dressed in farmer garb, and animals were often in attendance. John chose this event in 1967, which was held at the Copper Bar, to announce we were getting married that fall. While everyone cheered, I tried to think when he had proposed. He had not. I'm still waiting.

When we married in 1967 at the Roman Catholic Church in Minturn, the Irish Rovers and a dance troupe sang as though they were a church choir, although it was not planned that way. This resulted in a Protestant version of the Lord's Prayer in a Catholic service. It was perfect. We had a reception attended by almost everyone in Vail: maids to mayors. The only person we consciously did not invite was the manager of the Red Lion who had kicked our St. Bernard, Bandit, out of the bar a few weeks earlier. Some guests left their sheep herds to attend and arrived on horseback. The flowers came from Glenwood Springs and the

5-tier wedding cake from Leadville. We had a second party at the Copper Bar and ordered enough liquor for the party plus several more weeks. When we checked the next day, the liquor had been consumed.

I remember a Halloween party at the Nu Gnu dressed as a very pregnant nun and accompanied by a "priest." The annual melodramas were hysterical with an original script written by John Dobson, our mayor, with popular locals playing the leads. The Diamond J on Highway 6 near Eagle had huge steaks, good food, and you could talk with local ranchers who hardly knew where Vail was.

I have had a vegetable and flower garden in Vail since 1968, a challenge because of short summers and cold nights. Prior to that, I harvested rhubarb and asparagus from old homesteads in the valley and made jelly from wild berries. I got to know John in the fall of 1965 when he learned I was an experienced driver of rough roads and an "outdoor" girl. I was the one who drove his old Land Rover on four-wheel drive roads to drop the hunters off on some hill and pick them up hours later at the bottom. The top of Mill Creek was a favorite place with the pickup at the bottom of Marvin's ravine on Vail Pass (named for chubby Marvin Clark who once desperately and embarrassingly rode his jacket down the snowy, steep ravine). We spent the summer and fall outdoors - horseback riding, horseback camping, and hunting/fishing. I did what John did and loved all of it, except golf. We never said what we were going to do tomorrow; we just did it. We had three children - John, Matt, and daughter Kerry.

And in the winter, we skied. That was why we had come, and we never forgot that motivation. John was often one of the packers on the hill, which meant they skied around all day to side-step and pack steep areas. My job was to ski ahead and yell when it was clear for them to jump every lip. They referred to skiing as "what they did between jumps."

I forgot to leave before I met John Donovan and realized I loved him, the life that was Vail, and the surrounding wilderness. No one I knew foresaw the level of success we would build for Vail. I was not conscious that we were actually building anything. We just went day-by-day, doing the right thing, and happened to build a town. Financial stability was a goal but never getting rich. It was an adventure filled with positive energy and delightful folks who had chosen to come here. I believe that

wanting Vail to be a place we could be happy in, while making a living, remains the "unidentified" undercurrent of its success and that it remains the essence of Vail 50 years later. Because of the geography and a shared love of skiing, you got to know everybody.

41

Diane Lazier

I came to Vail the very first year the resort was open for skiing. Our first week in Vail was the coldest single week ever. It reached 50 below zero and was never above 20 below. By the third day, we were staying in Minturn where there wasn't another car that would start. Ours had a crank, so Bob parked on a hill and eventually got it to turn over. Anybody who needed rides pushed it down the hill. We had to pour hot water on the tires because

they were frozen to the ground.

My new husband, Bob Lazier, and I missed that first summer of building. We had met and married through auto racing. He was so different from anything I had known. After a winter ski bumming in Alta Utah, Bob came back with a broken leg, shattered; he had jumped and landed in a tree and had a peg in his leg. He came back the day of my sorority prom with shoulder-length hair and tanned. We married in 1961. He brought home the Hal Shelton rendering of the Vail ski area and put it above our bed so we would remember not to spend any money on anything before Vail, which was to be our honeymoon.

I would do almost anything to be with Bob; we enjoyed every second. I will tell you, skiing was a ball, and the people were fun. So we headed to Aspen in a Euro model Morris Minor woody station wagon with a crank to collect $100 that someone owed him. As we drove over the pass, there was a full moon that night. It was so cold when we looked at the mountain that everything sparkled, you could see the runs, so impressive, "This is the rendering." We pulled into the filling station and overheard twin sisters say, "I'll never work for that Charlie Gersbach again." We said, "Ah, two jobs available." We went into town and applied for a job with him, got it, and spent our first night there. I didn't go to Aspen for seven years.

The first time we drove into Minturn was in daylight. The RR shacks north of Turntable Restaurant didn't have doors. They had tarps or blankets; I remember looking through the frosted window and seeing a child standing there. There were two buildings and a few homes dotted the town.

We skied every day all day and worked at night. The following year, I did double duty - dinners in dining room and bar when I turned 21. We lived in Gus's motel with a kitchenette in Minturn. At that time, we were the only married young couple, each with one job, and we skied all the time the first year; after that, we realized two jobs were the only way to make it work.

We worked evenings, when people did crazy things. There was a redheaded ski instructor who bit me on the butt and ended up with 14 drinks on his head. There was the time I flambéed the lady in the dining room; the busboy had been drinking and was out of it; it barely grazed her. I feel guilty to this day about taking lobster from the freezer, and I would bring customers baskets of bread until the lobster was thawed. One lobster slipped off the plate and onto the floor, the people were turned away, but the other table saw it. I picked it up, put it on the plate, took it in the kitchen and boiled it. The people were laughing hysterically. You worked harder during the holidays. I was mostly at the Vail Village Inn and one summer at The Lodge. My best friend was Susie Eldridge, who had a terrific sense of humor.

For the off-season, we went to California and planned trips to Tahiti and Las Vegas. Sailing was the plan, but we ran out of money. When we left California we had $35. If we stayed in Vail we would have $30, because the trip cost $5 in gas. It was a good day if I couldn't stretch my fingers around the dollars in tips. We built The Cornice and paid $7000 for the smallest piece of property in Vail. The Night Latch was so bad that the boys could watch the girls from one bathroom to the next and through the walls. When we built the 8-plex next door, we rented upper floors for $150 for two people; downstairs was $125. That was the same summer we moved into The Lodge for the summer, and Bob worked there for a while. I can remember walking up the stairs in November 1963, when President Kennedy was shot.

Once we decided we were going to stay, we borrowed $5000 from our folks, then we were able to build and move into The Cornice. On my 21st birthday we were staining the building, and I got so high from it. We built a building every year for 14 years: Cornice, Wedel Inn, part 1 and part 2; Arcade Building where The Emporium is on Wall St. (named because it had the first bank). We had been together all the time; the biggest challenge to the marriage was that all of a sudden I didn't come first. There were a lot of black-sheep-in-the-family in Vail. I was an only child - very pampered, very conservative; I came with a husband who was an orphan, adopted. Most were younger and not married. I never wanted to leave. Once here, you literally fall in love with it. I think the hardest thing was not being in communication with the rest of the world. Sometimes you could only get the radio at night, only Minnesota stations and no radio in Minturn.

We went home and got the Porsche spod-

ster and brought materials in it; it was almost impossible to do. On that trip to San Francisco and Haight Ashbury in 1963, I saw that it was so different from the life I had lived. We finished the Tivoli Lodge and had three children in three years. The first child was born in 1967. It didn't change my life much. He was born, and we moved to Fitz Scott's duplex and stayed the summer. We were building the Tivoli. Vail changed me; my dream had been to get my Master's and teach Humanities in a small town somewhere. All I got was the small town. Horseback riding was also a dream, but the horse threw me and broke my back. We just rolled with the punches, no conscious effort to come to Vail, it just happened; no conscious effort to stay in Vail, we just did. I never felt inequality; I've never run into that because the men in my life never allowed that to happen. My father and mother both had me believe there was nothing I couldn't do.

43

DONNA BUCKLEY

Until I decided to "go west" I had lived my entire life in upstate New York, starting in Ellicotville – home of the Holiday Valley Ski area - and later Rochester, where I taught elementary school. I graduated from SUNY at Oswego with a BA in Education and a minor in psychology. I headed west at 24 to get my Master's in Guidance at the University of New Mexico. A funny thing happened on my way to Albuquerque: I visited Vail. A friend in Denver drove me up to see the new ski town. I had read about it in ski magazines and was excited to see it. We had lunch on Pepi's deck, and I thought I had never seen a more beautiful place in my life. It was the natural beauty – mountains, gold aspens, blue sky, and flowers. I was blown away. We went back to Denver and in the paper I saw an ad that changed my life: "Wanted – live-in babysitter in Vail; heated pool, lots of ski time."

Totally on a lark, I called and later that week interviewed with Bob and Diane Lazier, owners of the Tivoli Lodge and parents of two children, Buddy age 2 and Wendy Sue age 3 months. Diane needed help. They were so natural and friendly; I really liked them and the kids. Thank goodness they liked me as well and offered me the job. I went back to Denver and in a couple of days headed up to Vail in my trusty Corvair, which broke down on Vail Pass. I arrived at the Tivoli in the Conoco tow truck. Welcome to Vail, Colorado.

Unlike others who came to Vail, I had none of the worries about housing – I was moving into the Tivoli penthouse. I had very few expenses, got a ski pass, and a paycheck. I should have paid them. Bob and Diane helped me to make friends, eased me into the schedules of Buddy and Wendy, and made me feel more like some long-lost relative than a stranger. To say the least, it was a great situation and one that I stayed in for two years. It wasn't a life of wild parties, but it was just a short walk to the Nu Gnu, The Red Lion, or Bobby Macs. With Packy Walker at the front desk you never knew what to expect, but you could be sure it would be outrageous. Graduate school was erased from my plans.

That was the Vail I found when I arrived in 1969 – friendly, helpful people living in a special place. After only skiing in the East, I loved the wide-open trails of Vail, the sunshine, and the incredible snow – not the ice I was used to. The girls here were not "Snow Bunnies." They looked great and skied even better. I wanted to try the Back Bowls, and not knowing, did a big no-no. I went by myself and, impossible as it may sound, had a collision with the only other person on the hill. He did not stop and left me to pick up the pieces of my skiing yard sale. I never did that again.

I had another life-changing experience that ultimately was responsible for my staying here. My good friend, Liz, who was then married to Chupa Nelson, thought she would play matchmaker and arranged a blind date for me with one of Chupa's fellow soccer players, also a ski patrolman. He was known as "Buckwheat," but his real name was Bob Buckley. Like many blind dates, it wasn't a huge success – a potluck dinner with a bunch of ski patrol couples who all knew each other and the inside jokes. Nothing says fun like an evening of watching slides of people you don't know, and everyone's laughing but you. Fortunately, there was a second date, and a third. From our first potluck to our engagement was a mere three months. Since I had no relatives here, Bob Lazier had a talk with "Buckwheat " to make sure he was prepared for the financial aspects of being married. Our wedding was the following February. That March, I was working at The Krismar for Peggy Rosenquist. At the end of one workday, after packing up many beautiful things to be shipped, I discovered that not only had I sent off the crystal, but my new wedding band had slipped off and was on its way to an unsuspecting customer. The marriage betting pool had us a very long shot. I'm happy to say that we are celebrating our 40th anniversary with our three children, Brian, John, and Amanda. I can't thank Liz enough for introducing me to the love of my life. I made the transition from single Vail girl to married Vail woman, and it was the best possible place to raise a family. We decided to stay because it was already home, Bob had a great job and where else could we have this quality of life. There was a great sense of freedom and opportunities for the kids.

45

DONNA MEYER

I am a third-generation Coloradan. I grew up in Denver, went to school there, and then college in California. I rode horses, showed at the National Western Stock Show, and hunted to the hounds. I married and had three children. My life besides my family was volunteering and raising money for non-profits.

I did a bit of politicking, too. Marnie Jump, Gretta Whiteford Parks, and I campaigned for a Congressional and Senate seat organizing a door-to-door statewide campaign. The three of us were co-chairs of the First Ski Ball at the New United Bank - it was a Twist Party.

Marge Burdick

What brought me to Vail was our investment in 1961 in a new great mountain. In 1962, we spent weekends at The Lodge. We purchased a condo when Vail Trails East was built. Later, we moved to Manor Vail and then built our own house on the golf course. When the weekends grew to four days a week, we moved into the house permanently in 1966.

In 1962, we all skied and partied together. We wore black stretch pants and Pucci blouses. We ate lunch every Saturday and Sunday at The Red Lion, the only bar. I loved the rye bread rolls. In 1964 when the Casino opened, we partied on Saturday nights and went to the church service there on Sunday mornings. The Jean Harlow party on Halloween at the Casino in 1965 was great as was the line dancing. I partook of lots of picnics and lunches on the Murchison's Deck above Vail Village. I remember getting a ride into the village once on the back of Mary Ann Caldwell's skis after lunch. Tea at Marge and Larry Burdick's was the best! I guess it was the rum in the tea and the great friends. The summers meant tennis, hiking, and picnics.

The best part of beginning a small town is that everyone is involved in business or volunteering. I do believe a community is not a community without cultural events, and Vail has made that happen. The buildings are larger now, but the past to the present has not changed, in my opinion. It has only grown in the numbers of people. We were a small giving group of people and now we are a more populated giving community.

Doris Bailey

We were reading Bob Parker's brilliant hype about Vail in SKI magazine after Dick Bailey and I married in 1962. Hal Shelton did those magnificent watercolors of the Back Bowls and front of Vail Mountain. We just thought it sounded magical. We had never skied anywhere but in the East. Dick and I decided we

would come to Vail for that first season. The Cleveland Ski Club was going to do Vail for the first week and Aspen the second. We wanted to do that but couldn't afford the plane fare. I imagine it was February 1963; we rode the train with two bachelors, pulled into Denver, and got on a Continental Trailways bus; I had been in the west before but when we came over Vail Pass – it was magic, soft pillows of brilliant white snow and blue skies. My jaw fell open and stayed that way all the way to downtown Vail and The Lodge, which had opened with 65 rooms. We stayed there. We bought the room with breakfast and dinner; every night they had a cocktail party. Bob Parker and Pete Seibert were at all of those wearing ascots, which Dick also wore. You had no choice in The Lodge at Vail; it was quite dressy.

The skiing was unbelievable, and the evenings were magic. We rode the gondola to Mid Vail and then the chair. It was so exciting; after we got over the cliffs we broke out of cloud seven days straight, and there was the blue sky. It was like a magician was there creating this whole thing to make sure we liked it. We'd get off and the picnic tables had six fresh inches of snow every morning. The memory is like it was yesterday.

During that week, we visited with Ottie Kuehn, who sold film at The Rucksack. I don't think four people could stand in front of the counter; that's how big The Rucksack was then. Ottie had one story after another – like shooting Kodiak bears in Alaska.

The Red Lion was the size of the bar in the front and dining room. I skied the Back Bowls on my wood Northland skis. Then, the next week we got on the bus to go to Aspen, and Aspen had not had one inch of that snow; the streets were mud. In 1962, America was just learning that there was a sport called skiing. Vail's timing was impeccable. We also flew to Jackson Hole with friends – took a look and thought, "Vail, Vail, Vail."

During that first visit, we saw a little house where Bishop Park is with a sign that read, "Fitzhugh Scott, Architect." Vail Bridge Chalet. Fitz built it. He and Eileen lived in it at first, and they had the only telephone, toilet, office. We stayed in the chalet, which had a massive moss rock fireplace. Fitz also had a house on Mill Creek Circle. He was a quality guy. Everything was black, white, and red, checks, red carpet. It was just fun. Dick had sent a letter asking about work. Fitz called and wanted to meet in Milwaukee. As it turned out, he wanted Dick to come out and run his office. We owned a TV and a sofa; that was about it. Imagine our surprise when we plugged in our TV set, and it didn't work.

It was the skiing that made us pursue the possibility, never dreaming that we'd spend a lifetime here. We were newlyweds and figured, what the heck, if we can get jobs out there, let's go. It was an adventure. We came to Vail for the skiing; it sure wasn't like eastern skiing. I was 26 and not planning to get married. Our decision was two-fold: we would be involved in building a community and skiing. We realized that when we met Fitz. What a guy, what he envisioned, a sweetheart.

There was an excitement to early Vail, when you talked to Parker and Seibert, their enthusiasm was boundless, and you wanted to be part of a life like this. I came from a conservative place; most people still live there. My mother thought it was great, but most thought we were nuts. She later moved here and lived 20 years.

About four nights a week, we went to cocktail parties – the same 40 people, each other's houses. Bob Parker, Gaynor Miller, and John Donovan had just started the Vail Resort Association. I told Bob, "I have some degrees, but I can't do anything in this town that I have training for. Do you have anything?" Bob said, "Yes." Daphne Slevin and Barbara Parker were working at VRA. Parker said, "We need to expand this, and we need a full-time person." So I went to work there along with Irene Westbye. It was 1964-65. VRA was a fun job. They took away the telephone console and put in a PBX switchboard. I hired my sister, Shirley Ward, and Patti Steinle; Marvel's daughter, Linda; Susan Herzog Bristol, who had worked for the Bauhaus; and Lois Bernstein. By then, we were in Gold Peak House.

Great memories of the VRA were meetings with Pepi, Joe Staufer, Jim Slevin – oh, the fights, "No, goddammit, we can't be that way. No." They were practically fistfights in the old Rathskellar (later Golden Ski). The fun part of VRA was a manual typewriter. Every time we got a letter, my job was to respond to it. So I did; and I wrote these really long letters; and of course, we didn't have correction fluid. I tried so hard to write perfect letters. Telephones – the original phones in VRA were called consoles, a telephone with buttons. We had a button to every lodge and ski shop. VA would call and give us the morning ski report, and we called every business. I kept statistics by hand.

When Merv Lapin suggested I buy a Lifetime Ski Pass, I said, "Merv, we live here; we ski for free." It was a great time. Merv was a waiter at the Red Lion, then at the Clock Tower. George Knox, Sr. came to start the Vail Trail and rented the other side; he was so much fun to be with.

We had the movie theater in Minturn, with benches and seats that broke. Gaynor Miller would make a brandy milk punch using the blenders we all took. We watched Super Bowl and all the big football days. Ten or 20 of us would rent a room at the Harrison Motel – we'd watch and drink. Vail grew pretty quickly. The first couple of summers Bridge Street was still unpaved. Dick Hauserman had the ears of a werewolf and could hear a car come off Hwy 6. He would run up and accost these cars with his stack of pictures of the trout you could catch, the weasels, marmots, fox, and deer. He would not let people go through that town without seeing those pictures. He was so great at it. People were just enchanted, and nine times out of 10, they would stay at the Plaza Lodge that night for $10.

I remember a certain unnamed person getting caught by the postmistress as he went through the transom in the post office. He was the nosiest man I've ever known; he used to go and read the mail. She came in early one morning and found him dangling in the transom window, caught. He'd already read the mail and sealed them all back up.

Every morning you'd see that northernmost porch of the Plaza Building where the ski patrol had been the night before, and half of them were still there. Once, someone came home and found his girlfriend in bed with another man. He took an axe and chased him naked up toward the mountain – oh, maybe he had some boxers on. The ski patrolmen saw this. It's a great story whatever way you tell it. The good news is that the lover was fast, and he feared for his life.

We were now a municipality, so we had to buy land to become Home Rule and needed 40 tax-paying residents. Some owned businesses as corporations, and that didn't count.

VA sold us that lot farthest west on Forest Road. We put in $2000 and that was a lot of money. We had become a town.

VA decided they were going to move their ticket office one day. Dick, Rod, and I went into the Deli (the morning after a big party – Phil and John always gave us greasy chili and milk because their chili was the magic fix after a party). It was starting to pour snow when Hauserman came running into the Deli, "C'mon everybody, we need help. We're trying to move the ticket office, and we don't have enough manpower." They were moving it from the top of Bridge Street to the west and north. I remember going right back in the Deli and having more chili.

Leonard Ruder was as important to the beginning of this mountain as were Seibert,

Parker, and Earl Eaton. He was a magician with earth equipment. That's why they named Ruder's Run after he died. He mowed the lawn to set the towers. And the genius with the towers was Earl Eaton. It was an art figuring out how to cut the ski trails.

The bug for Vail got my sister, too. "Shirley wants to quit college and come to Vail," mom called me to say. "I don't know what to do." So she came here, and I remember that she and Dick ate vanilla ice cream from morning to night together.

49

EDIE FRICKE

I think of my life in three phases. Phase one was when I moved to Colorado Springs from Wisconsin for seven years of advanced hairstylist training and heard that Vail was happening. I was a skier and belonged to a ski club.

"I'm going to move my salon to Vail," I said. I came to Vail, found a spot in the downstairs of the Plaza Building in the fall of 1964, and called it the Plaza Salon. I was so in love with skiing and had found a way to make it part of my life.

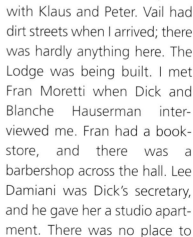

A restaurant was next, and that's how Alpenrose was born. I did that for 20 years, with Klaus and Peter. Vail had dirt streets when I arrived; there was hardly anything here. The Lodge was being built. I met Fran Moretti when Dick and Blanche Hauserman interviewed me. Fran had a bookstore, and there was a barbershop across the hall. Lee Damiani was Dick's secretary, and he gave her a studio apartment. There was no place to live, so I shared with Lee at first. Then I moved to a three-bedroom apartment in the Texas Townhouses with two other gals. I sold my salon in Colorado Springs and was able to buy a condo at Vail Trails East. It was one great big studio, and it was wonderful. The Kindels lived above me. I moved to the Lady Vail space and put in a much bigger salon. I sold the condo in 1966-67. The next big project for me was building a house.

I'm from a family of eight children, the youngest girl. When I went to Glacier National Park some years before Vail, that was my "leaving home." My mother thought it was wonderful that I came to Vail. Once I became established, I worked hard to make my living. From the very beginning I knew I would probably not leave Vail. I loved the whole idea of being a pioneer at a new ski area. I thought it was a great opportunity, and I was ready to do something like that. I knew it was going to be tough. That first summer, I had to work three days in the Springs and three days in Vail to pay the bills. At first, everyone wanted Vail to have a country club atmosphere, but no one could make a living with that idea. We had to contribute money to help with dirt streets. With everyone taking part, Vail became a town.

Most of us who were in Vail then were 25 to 35 years old. We were single and met all the time in the Vail Village Inn. There was a bar and fireplace that we gathered around and sang. My single friends and I, Marilyn Fleischer, Hemmye Westbye, Irene Westbye, Daphne and Jim Slevin, and Charles Gersbach, did a lot of dancing. Bill Whiteford put in a disco at the Casino, and his wife Bettan taught us the latest dances. She was marvelous.

I did Jackie Kennedy's hair, and we talked about Appalachia.

"If you want to see Appalachia," I said, "Just go to Minturn." I was told she went to the Catholic Church in Minturn the next day. The celebrities were lovely people. There was no class structure in town those first years. I felt out of place at parties sometimes, but I was always invited. The only negative thing I heard was, "You shouldn't come here if you don't have money." Some thought the idea of a "company town" was not their thing. They were independent enough to be on their own.

I met Klaus in 1966 through my massage therapist. I'd advertised for one, interviewed her at the Brown Palace, and she said she'd do it. She lived with me, worked at the Gondola Boutique and for me. I met Klaus in September, about the time that Marie-Claire and Walter Moritz were starting their restaurant, and Klaus and Walter were going to be partners. We married and went to Europe for our honeymoon. When we came back, Sheika needed a chef, and Klaus started the Gourmet Room at Pepi's.

I'd do it all over again, no regrets.

EILEEN SCOTT

My mother was Eileen Scott. She arrived in the Vail Valley with her husband, Fitzhugh Scott. My father was a practicing architect in Milwaukee, and they both skied Vail Mountain by snowcat before the lifts were built.

They were instrumental in finding and entertaining investors during the early stages of the resort's development. They built

Fitzhugh Scott

the first building at the area around 1963, which was used as an office for Vail Associates with an apartment upstairs for themselves. He designed many of the early homes and businesses in Vail. As Vail grew, they moved into their new home on Mill Creek Circle.

I know my mother loved her years in Vail. She made many wonderful friends, and she so thoroughly enjoyed skiing, and all the other activities that the Vail community and the mountains offered.

— KIT STRANG

ELAINE KELTON

I did not know how to ski. I grew up in Philadelphia and went to an all girls' school then attended Smith College. (You'd think by then I would have realized the world was co-ed). A year in New York City left me well positioned for retail and the fashion industry. My idea of camping out was "no room service." Vail eventually had lots of "room service," and we had fun getting to that point.

Gerry White and I knew each other growing up; he had gone to Williams College and I to Smith. We married in 1963 and moved west - living the first 10 months in Jackson Hole as we pursued a dream of "ranching and cowboying," only to discover that one would be hardpressed to make a living at it. Fishing and climbing guide friends had told us about Vail and were headed back there to work on ski patrol. Our jobs ended, we packed the GMC pick-up, and a friend drove the VW Bug.

As we traveled from Denver up Loveland Pass

on Route 6, those heart-pounding steep drops of the Seven Sisters left us in awe. Crystal-blue skies turned to dusk, and an early fall snowstorm had one of us walking in front of the VW to keep us on the road.

We descended Vail Pass past meadows that were dark and open. Then, we saw lights at the Vail Village Inn. Turning at The Lodge at Vail sign, we passed a gas station alive with people, cars, and music. Turns out it was a wild game dinner benefiting the Vail Country Day School (the game had been shot locally.) We were the only room sold that night at The Lodge. We felt as if we had taken a huge step forward.

Breakfast, with views up Vail Mountain, was seductively spectacular. Exploration and job hunting were next. Someone told us to find "Lazier," so we scoped out the Wedel Inn. The guy on the roof was Bob Lazier, who, with his wife, was building their lodge. He invited me up two stories on a ladder. When I reached the top, he laughed and said, "Bravo." We have been neighbors and friends ever since.

VA was hiring, and we found their office in the Plaza Building. Pete Seibert and Bob Parker interviewed us and hired me as social director for The Lodge. Job description: fill the Golden Ski with customers using rented movies on low bar nights. Gerry became the bellman at The Lodge and line manager in the cafeteria.

That first season seduced us. Vail's community was welcoming, and there was a sense of democracy. Men and women worked hard, played hard, and were accepted on the basis of their skills. A glass ceiling didn't exist, but a level of fun did. Vail was contagious in its desire to succeed. We knew our success was tied to that.

Within days snow fell, and the trailer at what is now Potato Patch was warm and homey. About 25 trailers were parked there as employee housing; the Village was a commute.

The ski season started, and employees arrived. The Lodge provided family for its workers, and with neither TV nor decent radio reception, we set up Monopoly games in the back halls; management studiously ignored them. The rented movies were a success, more so than my ability to pace the congenial drinking.

Christmas Week came, along with the Newman Family from Chicago: three kids in navy double-breasted coats and a suitcase for every day's stay (14). Pearl Newman Rieger and her family, still dear friends, have a presence and a house in Vail 48 years later.

We were in love with Vail, the sense of community and adventure. Dirt streets, no I-70, no supermarket, no doctor, no vet, and no library, but there was magic and a community with a shared goal.

By March I had learned to ski, spent the year in a trailer at Potato Patch, had a multitude of house guests sleeping on the trailer floor, acquired Stormy, a tri-color Collie, made friends who are still in my life, played lots of Monopoly, and became pregnant, due the following fall.

In September, we rented a duplex in the Bighorn area. Our only neighbors, John and Laurie McBride, were building The Clock Tower. East Vail was miles out of town and had a different weather system. Courtney arrived three weeks early; Dr. Steinberg sent us to Denver.

Gerry was now assistant manager at the Christiania Lodge for Ted and Nancy Kindel, who were an awesome team training us for the hotel business. By mid-winter he had assumed the management position there, and we knew that a ski lodge was our goal. That opportunity opened up when a commercial lot at the base of Gold Peak became available, and we enthusiastically jumped in. Design, planning, and funding for the construction were incredible. The banking community in Denver was unaccustomed to not being granted the deed of sale as basis for a loan. VA would not give the deed until construction was completed. Vail began its growth spurt, and the Denver bankers gave in, acknowledging Vail's presence.

The following June we broke ground, and the Rams-Horn Lodge was built in 120 days. We opened for Christmas 1967 with an Opening Party that in-

Art Kelton

cluded the town. Paul Johnston and Bill and Sally Hanlon from Crested Butte, were in the process of opening the Nu Gnu, a nightclub under the Post Office. Typical of "The Vail Way," they were told to stop by and introduce themselves. Paul arrived, head shaved, elegantly attired in the first and only red satin-lined black wool cape I had ever seen on a man. I was smitten. He re-set the dress standards for Vail; my parents loved his style.

Vanessa was born that February. As our family and community grew, we became increasingly involved with their needs: education and the structure of the town. Vail was exploring its direction; we all wanted to gain our independence and extricate the fledgling Vail from its

company-owned status. Out of the many meetings in The Lodge cafeteria, the petition vote passed, and Vail incorporated in 1966. Everyone took on a piece of the responsibility for what Vail needed, and we all took steps to make each a reality.

New businesses opened, but we still hung "Gone Skiing" signs on powder days. Our guests at the Rams-Horn became our families for Christmas, Easter, and every holiday in between. They knew the "White girls" on a first-name basis.

Ashley arrived in 1970, to complete the trio. These three girls grew with the town, knowing the community as their second parents. They skied, skated, and took part in new activities. They started their schooling with Mrs. Gagne at Montessori School in the basement of the Rams-Horn Lodge. Sammye Meadows came to work our Front Desk, adding whimsy to each day as she shepherded our group.

The overriding direction of Vail was to be the best: World Class. VA provided the greatest skiing experience on a one-of-a-kind mountain, and we all provided the support systems: lodging, shops, restaurants, services, a town government, and schools. We have done a great job.

Vail has been, and is, a unique experience. It is not often that anyone has an opportunity to "grow a town," especially one whose world-class reputation means that when you say, "I am from Vail," a story and a connection follow.

53

Elizabeth Eber

I grew up in Deerfield, Massachusetts, and Martha's Vineyard. My studies brought me to the University of Denver. My first job after my degree was as editor for an educational reference book company in Denver; then I worked as a writer and established a connection to Vail.

I first visited Vail on my honeymoon in 1968. We stayed at Pepi and Sheika Gramshammer's lodge. I sunburned my face to a crisp and spent the honeymoon swollen like Porky Pig - how romantic. But even though my eyes were reduced to little slits, that didn't stop me from skiing the back bowls in three feet of powder. The second day in Vail, my husband challenged me to a NASTAR race: whoever lost would carry the other person's skis to and from the lift every day. I did not carry the skis.

My first job in Vail was as a hostess at Mickey's Lounge. Aside from seating patrons, I was to offer them Mickey's recordings for purchase by placing them in a stack on their table. I received a commission for whatever I sold. Only problem, the cocktail waitresses were also allowed to sell them, as long as they got there first. The more the competition raged, the more the waitresses' resentment for me grew. I kept asking our manager if he could do something about it, but he ignored me. I finally drew up a written plan (after all, I had been a professional planner…) to divide up the territory and thereby eliminate the competition. I left the job before it was implemented, but I did earn the manager's respect, an excellent job recommendation, and the friendship of those cocktail waitresses. In addition to my other work, I wrote a ski column on technique, as well as travel articles for the newspaper. I also wrote feature articles for magazines.

What kept me in Vail was skiing, the environment, the healthy lifestyle, and the close and long-lasting friendships with Vail locals. I skied avidly, biked, jogged, and worked out. For entertainment, my girlfriends and I said that all you had to do if you wanted to be taken out to dinner, was walk down the Bridge Street Slalom after skiing. It never failed, and we never failed to just "dine and dash."

My expectations before moving to Vail were the same as my reasons for staying: skiing, the environment, and the healthy lifestyle. When I walk outside, I see the sky full of stars, and as the sun dawns, the blazing Gore Range. In the evening, I can't take my eyes off those mountains, pink in alpenglow. I've shared deepening friendships and have become comfortable living in the mountains. I love the changes that have come with Vail's growth, but I am also nostalgic for the wild days of youth.

The beauty and healthy lifestyle are still like glue to me. I don't anticipate trying to break that bond anytime soon. Beneath the veil of Vail, I have found my place.

Elizabeth Wilt

Growing up as an Air Force "brat," I moved to new locations every three years. When I was in high school, Dad was stationed in Colorado Springs where I first learned to ski and also got my first job at the Broadmoor Hotel, working for the social coordinator. In reality, it was a babysitting job, but it turned out to be pretty neat. I then headed off to college. I completed three years of studies at CU in Boulder and decided to take a semester off and ski Vail. The semester turned into three and a half years before I took a break from Vail and returned to get my degree. When as I graduated, I ran back to Vail to continue my life.

On my ski vacation, I tried to think of a reason not to move to Vail for a while. I couldn't think of one, other than the fact that I was still in college. The rest is history. I came without many expectations, given that my arrival was an idea that I formulated after a great ski day. I met happy, healthy people and decided this was the place to be for a season in between semesters.

After arriving in Vail, I roamed the town (Bridge Street) looking for a job. Only minutes after I started my search, someone told me that they needed help at Pepi Sports. I went there and met Pidge Coventry, who hired me to join the crew. A couple of years later, I had an aspiration to become a waitress, so John Kaemmer hired me at the Clock Tower. I loved working there for what must have been six years. I skied most days and didn't have to show up for work until 4pm to do the "prep" for dinner. I eventually worked for Vail Associates, starting out in "Office Services."

My roommates always knew the party spots and after a day of skiing, après ski was the best. My social life was not that big. The 'early' fun experiences were, for instance, jeeping with Packy Walker and about a dozen others that squeezed into his jeep. Perhaps my more 'infamous' moments were a product of years of participation in the annual "Great Race." Our team leader was Pat Jackson who, after the race, led us on to the Ore House where we fell off the bar stools in the guise of trying to appear sober.

Back in my Clock Tower days, I always knew or recognized the faces on Bridge Street. As years passed, newer and younger crowds moved into Vail, but really didn't know how to explore the valley and shape our village the way we did. Even though the faces have changed throughout the years, a lot of the "old timers" are still around, and our stories of the early years will stay with us forever.

Wander through the aspen trees. Take a look at the Gore Range at sunset. Look at that blue sky and breathe deeply. Where else would you want to be?

55

ELLA KNOX

Ella Mae McWhorter Knox, born March 25, 1911 and died in June 2008, arrived in Vail in 1962 from Colorado Springs with husband George Sr. and sons George Jr. and Allen. George and Ella had been involved in business ventures before moving to the new resort. George, an advertising man, decided Vail needed a publication to promote the new ski village, and the idea of The Vail Trail became a reality. The newspaper served the community with news and advertising. Ella used her talents as a wonderful cook to bake her famous pies that were sold at local eateries including the Clock Tower Restaurant.

Ella had many talents: mother, wife, gardener, and gourmet cook. She could take an ordinary head of lettuce, a few herbs and spices, and make a feast. She also wrote a popular newspaper column, "Green Thumb Ella," where she explained how to grow beautiful flowers, plants, and anything green at high altitude. She was extremely active in the Christian Science Church in Vail and her beloved Republican Party. She kept photos of President Ronald Reagan at her Intermountain home. Ella never failed to try to make a democrat into a republican, nor was she afraid to express her political or religious views to anyone.

Social life was a whirlwind of fun in the early days of Vail. George and she entertained and were entertained by their many new friends: Marge and Larry Burdick, Pepi and Sheika Gramshammer, Betty and Jerry Ford, and many more of Vail's first pioneers. Ella often told stories of gatherings at the Burdick's Red Lion Inn. Ella gave up skiing in her 40s but managed to keep her love of the mountain. She kept busy with young employees at The Vail Trail acting as a second mother and grandmother, mentoring the next generation of Vail. Although there was a 40-year age difference with most of them, they invited Ella to their weddings. She babysat for their babies.

Ella loved Vail. She loved her family that multiplied here with her sons, their wives, and grandchildren. She made Vail her home. In the early years, Ella belonged to a ladies' ski club and a hiking club. She could put together any jigsaw puzzle given to her. Ella was never boring and kept her life full and interesting. She worked at The Vail Trail with son Allen after her husband's death. She was head of the subscription department and learned how to work a computer to update her subscriptions.

Ella enjoyed skiing and spending hours in her garden. She kept fit by walking her little dogs. She was an active parent in her sons' and their families' lives and was very proud of her boys, George, Jr. and Allen, and the proud grandmother of four grandchildren and five great grandchildren. The Vail matriarch had many stories, loved a little gossip, and knew the details of all the people who came to Vail: how many times they had been married, who had changed their names, and tidbits about who they used to be. She was one of the most intelligent people I have ever had the pleasure of knowing and one of the most interesting. Her interests never ceased to amaze me, and her knowledge of so many things was incredible. I remember Ella loved to study the stars and planets and donated her telescope to Battle Mountain High School. She was also interested in geology, had a rock collection, and was a terrific card player.

Her baked brownies were the best things in the world, and she was "green and organic" before it was cool to be so. As a young Vail Trail reporter, I met Ella when she was 69. We had an instant connection, and I always felt she was my contemporary with a twist of humor and an edge. We didn't always agree, but her sage advice and what I learned from this amazing lady keep her close to my heart every day. Ella was an original - one of Vail's finest ladies and a true pioneer.

— FROM A FRIEND, JACKIE HIGGINS

ELLEN JACOBSON

I studied back East and worked at Massachusetts General Hospital as a Neurosurgery Research Technician from 1960-1962. I met and married Tom Jacobson, a ski instructor, in 1964, and his brother suggested we move to Vail. My husband had been an instructor at Alta in Utah. I think I did every kind of work in Vail. I sold lift tickets for three years, was the Vail Resort Association for the summer of 1965, worked in Dr. Garrick's office on Bridge Street, the Post Office for three summers, and at Diversions Needlepoint. There were not that many job opportunities, so I did whatever could.

I came for the skiing, of course, and we had an active social life. The first few winters, almost everyone in town had to be invited to parties just to have enough people. We often had parties at Rod Slifer's home; he was assistant Ski School director at the time. Morrie Shepherd was the director. The parties were raucous with quite a few single ski instructors present. As Tom began teaching only private lessons, most of his students asked us to dinner or invited us to parties. Our winter social life consisted of many evenings out on the town. One of our favorite restaurants was the Red Lion where we both always ordered--- the Gold Brick Sundae.

Tom fished right in front of our house on West Forest Road. When he had caught two, he would whistle and I would get the frying pan ready. I skied as often as possible. My season pass through VA cost $5, and who could pass that up? I also gardened and began my lifelong interest in collecting wild mushrooms. My best friend was June Simonton, and we spent hours digging for antique bottles in the old Leadville dump.

We had one child, Michael, and traveled to see our families when we could. One of our favorite pastimes was four-wheeling on the weekends. We bought a Korean War Willys from Steve Boyd and promptly named it True Grit. We visited Holy Cross City when the buildings still stood and the tables inside were set with dishes and silverware. I really had no expectations of life in Vail before we arrived because there wasn't much there, only The Lodge, the Vail Village Inn, and most of Bridge Street. There was no library, clinic, church, newspaper, or TV, and one gas station. The doctor was in Glenwood, the supermarket was in Minturn, and the high school was in Red Cliff. There was a sawmill and a trailer park where Potato Patch is now.

The first winter we were there, 1964-1965, we received 10 feet of snow in 9 days. After the first few fun days, we looked out the window each morning at the steadily falling snowflakes and groaned. Chair 1 was buried, cars were stuck, and we had to have a back-

hoe dig a roofless tunnel to our cabin. Vail chugged on, and somehow everyone made it to work. Tickets got sold, lifts ran, and the skiing was terrific. Gradually the sense of the pioneering community that we had once shared began to disappear.

My best and funniest memories are from the years I sold lift tickets. Rixie Flewelling was the ticket supervisor; the first ticket booth, which was recycled as Checkpoint Charlie, held the two ticket sellers AND the ski school person. Rixie ruled with an iron and very creative fist and was absolutely determined to foil ticket cheaters and lax lift operators. The first winter we were there, she drafted our houseguest, Terry, stuck a season pass on him with a picture of the Schober's Afghan Hound, Jezebel, printed on it and told Terry to go skiing. Alas, for Vail, Terry did not get caught. Tickets were $6.50 for a full day of skiing then.

Erika McCall

so many I'd forgotten, so many I really miss.

My husband Dale, son Trevor, and I arrived in Vail October 1969. Dale and I had decided in 1968 that we wanted to get away from corporate life In Kansas City and head west. We lived in Aurora while Dale worked on short films for educational and/or marketing purposes. During this time, he met Dean Canada whose brother, Stuart, was managing the All Seasons Club condominiums in Vail. Dean mentioned to Dale that the Vail Resort Association was looking for an Executive Director with public relations experience. We had heard about Vail but had never been to the resort. We had our first introduction on a glorious September weekend when Dale interviewed for the newly created position.

I will never forget the first time we came down Vail Pass on the old winding US 6 into the valley, which was decked out in the most glorious fall colors. What a beautiful place. Yes, we wanted to live here, and Dale got the job. In October 1969, housing was extremely hard to come by. We felt very lucky when a condo in East Vail became available. What a view, and what clean air.

My past work experience did not exactly fit into the scheme of things in Vail, but I "aimed high" for an office job, which materialized in the position of secretary to Don Elisha, manager of The Lodge at Vail. My main occupation was to follow up on convention leads that came from the VRA and to try to convince convention coordinators to come to The Lodge at Vail. This job, which I really enjoyed, ultimately caused my leaving The Lodge due to some VRA members' assumption of "a conflict of interest" because of my husband's position at the VRA. That was never the case. When I gave Don Elisha my four-week notice of resignation, he "fired" me on the spot. Oh well, I went over to Pepi's porch and celebrated with Sheika, Pepi, Roger Staub, and some others. What a nice day it turned out to be.

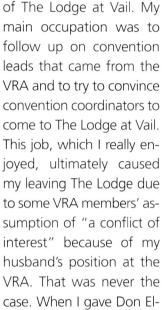

My next job was with Gaynor Miller, developer of the Mountain Haus, which was barely out of the ground at that time. Gaynor had his rather small office in the Golden Peak House. Up to this day, whenever I go to a Mexican restaurant, I am reminded of the smells that emanated from Los Amigos restaurant above. Gaynor soon merged with Vail Properties, headed by Dudley Abbott, developer of the

Sandstone 70 condominium complex. That's where I met my good friend, Jo Brown, and her husband, Ernie.

In the meantime, my husband was trying to increase business for Vail, especially summer groups. He felt lucky to have "old-timer" sisters Doris Bailey and Shirley Ward, as well as Brooke Franzgen, Judy Gold, Patty Steinle, Susan Bristol, and Stella Cruz on his staff. Groups usually wanted to have entertainment for their dinners, but in those "early days" there just wasn't much locally available that could be presented at group functions. So, Dale suggested that I get a German folk dance group going, which could perform for group entertainment. To my great surprise, a notice in the Vail Trail resulted in enough people to form a dance group, among them my good friends Jo and Ernie Brown, Don Chaplin, Ginny Burns, and Marka Moser. With the expert assistance of Dave Pratt and his accordion, we found music and instructions, and the "Bavailians" were born. With the help of a community-minded and inexpensive seamstress, we ladies got rather nice dirndls in Vail colors – blue and white – and the "buben" danced first in knickers and eventually in lederhosen. We had barely mastered our first dance when we had a request for a performance. But, we only had that ONE dance down pat, not enough to fill an evening, so we added an alphorn blowing contest with small prizes for the best blowers. It was always fun to watch people who were so sure of being able to coax a sound out of "that thing" fail miserably.

One memorable evening happened at Manor Vail when one-third of our dance group had come down with "Vail crud" and did not show up for a performance for which we had been paid the goodly amount of $100 by a convention group, who rightfully expected some fun for its $100. So we asked members of the audience to fill in, pairing them with a healthy "Bavailian" and telling them to just "do the same" as the dancers in front of them. It was pretty hilarious; everybody had fun though, the evening was saved, and no complaints were heard.

Aside from working with the dance group, I taught German at Colorado Mountain College. When I was first approached, I had lunch with a representative from CMC at the Red Lion deck. I remember having a pleasant lunch that I wanted to finish off with a nice cup of coffee. When the coffee was served, the cup seemed a bit heavy, and when I drank from it, I found out why. It was full of nickels, dimes, and quarters! One of the waitresses had used that cup to

60

stash her tips. After I got a fresh cup of coffee, I figured the tip money was "served" to me, so it was mine. The waitress was livid when she found out that I had the audacity to "take her money" and pay my lunch ticket with it. And yes, there was enough to cover the bill – and a tip for her fellow waitress. She was later overheard saying, "And she is the wife of the head of the VRA."

Going back to teaching German - 11 people showed up for my first class. I remember a very pregnant Isabel Schober, who stood most of the time, because sitting was too uncomfortable,

and – are you ready – Packy Walker! However, Packy didn't last very long. One night he brought me the most gorgeous apple and announced that he loved the class but that he was needed at Donovan's.

Life was good. We felt blessed and a little smug about living "in God's country." Most people knew everybody else in town and "newcomers," like us, had no problem making friends. I have fond memories of those years in the Vail Valley and of raising our son in such a wonderful place.

EVE ELIAS

My husband, Richard "Dick" Elias, brought me to Vail in the summer of 1967 for a job interview with Manor Vail Lodge. I fell in love with the pristine beauty and could not think of a better place for us to raise our daughters ages 12-3: Noella, Christa, Lisa, and Josette. We were in our late thirties and young enough to make the change. Of course I had some trepidation coming from a city, but I knew no city could give my kids what this small town had to offer...a beautiful childhood. My husband accepted the job, and I joined him in the summer of 1968.

That first winter, I quickly learned to keep a full supply of candles, firewood, blankets, and to use the TV as part of the decor. I could drive my 1962 Buick Le Sabre over Loveland Pass,

Battle Mountain Pass, and through Glenwood Canyon like nobody's business. My sporting life ended fairly early due to a very severe ski injury that changed my life. That was sad, as I loved to ski with my girls and especially my youngest, Josette, as she would wiz by me. For our first Christmas, we had a small tree, or rather a large branch, and the electricity went out. We celebrated by candlelight, and it is still a cherished memory for all of us and one of our best Christmas celebrations. That holiday, Chris Biggs (Nancy Biggs' son) gave my daughter Christa a white kitten that we named Missy. That kitten grew up and shared our life in Vail and reminded us of that first Christmas.

I enjoyed those summers when Randy Milhoan, Dan Telleen, and Jim Cotter started the SummerVail Art Workshops, where I took classes in silversmithing and pottery at the Anholtz property. The kids could participate, but they prefered playing and exploring on the old homestead and wading in the creek in the secret spot that had been dammed by a large tree and was unusually warm. I taught them how to fish with a branch, a safety pin, and a worm. Those summers were some of my fondest memories. I admit I was not as social as I could have been, but enjoying those times with my kids was the most important to me.

My first job was at Bloomberg's Jewelry store in the old Lazier building. I became an early female entrepreneur with Dairy Depot and ventured into the vending machine business, opened the first Kosher Deli and later Eve's Fragrance & Cosmetic Boutique. My work became my social life were I met many people from all

over the world, some famous, and made many friendships. I loved those years and our pioneer spirit. That is what made Vail, and for me that is what it has sadly lost. Vail gave me many things, but most of all it gave my children a special spirit and quality of life. In those years, without a phone or television, it kept our family close and gave us quality time. I treasure that and would not trade anything for it. I feel very fortunate to have had that opportunity.

EVI NOTT

My Colorado connection came with studies at University of Colorado where I graduated in Zoology and Chemistry. I was born and raised near San Francisco and returned for post-graduate studies at UC San Francisco School of Medicine. I later came to Vail with three young daughters. My then-husband, Robert, was recruited by Pete Seibert to establish a Real Estate Department for Vail Associates, Inc. We

wanted to escape the increasing pollution of the Bay area and raise our daughters in the pristine environment of the Rocky Mountains.

I co-founded with Susan Hanson the Vail Nature Center, preserving a piece of land destined for a huge development along Gore Creek. Thanks to the influence of Vail Symposium speaker, Robert Redford, and his message of environmental conservation and preservation plus the support of town manager, Terry Minger, and councilman, Gerry White, our proposal to renovate Mrs. Anholtz's gutted homestead was approved.

I was an avid skier, especially on powder days and participated on a team with Meredith Ogilby and Lizette Rayor Lamb in the Vail Mountain Winter Triathlon for several years. I was relegated to the speed skating portion, a new adventure for me. I have belonged to a book group in Vail established many years ago. I enjoyed many hikes up Vail Mountain with our daughters as well as "mushroom-

ing" with Ellie Caulkins in "secret" alpine glades near the ski runs. Mahaney Stables was a frequent destination for us as well.

I really had no idea what to expect before coming to Vail. Once here, trying to keep Vail Village's surrounding areas from massive development was a huge challenge that involved several of us – including Suzi Anderson and Diana Donovan. Preserving the Nature Center property as well as the sage meadow at Booth Creek at the east entrance to Vail were significant victories.

FLO STEINBERG

I have tried to reproduce how my Mom would respond to a query about women in Vail but will likely lack her zing. I gleaned the bulk of the impressions from my Dad and added some of my own memories.
— FLO'S DAUGHTER KRIS

Almost in her own words…

We arrived in Vail when it was three years old. On looking back, I note the preponderance of men vs. women, the social mixing of people of many ages except a lack

of the very young and the very old, and the fact that I made many more friends in this new life than I had in stodgy New Jersey. The town was intimate in size and brought people together. I have fond memories of learning to ski and then going on to become a "senior (no kidding) racer."

I enjoyed being involved in politics as a member of the sign review board and the TV advisory board. I enjoyed writing "Flo's Flotsam" for the Vail Trail but resented the paltry pay. The challenges of early Vail included the arduous trip over Loveland Pass to get to Denver, the mud in spring, and the dust in summer. I felt isolated at times because my husband Tom worked seven days a week at first. This likely facilitated my friendships, however.

There were ample opportunities for mischief. I fought with town manager Terry Minger over 'unnecessary' stop signs and removed one myself, with the assistance of my son Erik. I grew tired of the prolonged presence of the construction trailer in Ford Park, long after the construction season was over, so I spray painted it with helpful comments, with the assistance of Kris. I may have pointed out the presence of the "hemp" plant in the office of the chief of police, or maybe I planted it there. Who knows?

I loved to shop. Tom and I also took up jogging. The whole family volunteered during the construction of the Vail Trail path. Once we felt we had some ownership in the trail, we monitored it to frustrate destructive bikers who created unsanctioned paths off the trail (more subterfuge). We had to create our own entertainment. The solution was "the cocktail party." These gatherings crossed socioeconomic lines and were a great equalizer. The wildest I recall was Tom's yearly bash for the ski patrol. I put an end to them when a patrolman and his "date" used our bed briefly. Maybe I am not so liberal after all.

Remember the early Rummage Sale? We worked for days sorting clothes and gossiping. I was known to donate an item of one of my kids who went on to buy it back, all in the interest of charity, of course. Before the Bank of Vail arrived I did not enjoy my task of driving the clinic cash receipts to the bank in Eagle. That road was grim before the interstate opened, particularly in winter. The plus side of helping in the clinic was recruiting new doctors and their wives. We met scores of bright young people who stayed for one or two years on their paths to bigger careers. I encouraged Tom to get involved in the council. I believe Pete Burnett grew tired of me when we protested the dumping of snowplow snow over the banks of Gore Creek into the water. That was stopped, to the benefit of the environment. I hope this information gives you a sense of what a gift it was to pioneer in our little town.

— FLO (KRIS)

Kris remembers:
I arrived in Vail reluctantly in 1965, wishing I could remain an 11-year-old in suburban New Jersey forever. But I soon caught on and became one of the tribe of kids roaming the miniature town. Some of my fondest memories are moving the Vail Country Day School from the firehouse to the clinic (present hospital site) by turning our desks upside down in the snowy streets, putting our books on the top (bottom), and sledding them to the new location. I also recall playing War (a kind of mass chase game) in the Lodge at Vail, and having the chef pursue one of the Seibert boys with a cleaver. I often think I imagined these things until my brother, Erik, confirms them.

Tom's recollections of Flo:

Flo was the last of nine children of a coal mining family in Pennsylvania during the Depression. She became a nurse and then moved back into New York, where she'd worked as a hatcheck girl in a famous bar, exposed to the big city atmosphere.

In those years, she studied Greek, discovered opera, and was in a chorus on Broadway. In 1951, I was an intern and was introduced to the scrub nurse on a case. That was it as far as I was concerned. We had both skied growing up and wanted to work where there was skiing. I found an ad in the AMA Journal in the summer 1964 – "new ski area is looking for a physician." We found out it was Vail and went to a public meeting where Pepi Gramshammer represented the new resort. We accepted in September '65. Flo was happy. Our kids were 11 and 12. My office was across from the Mill Creek Building. Occasionally, she'd come in to help. At night, I drove the ambulance, and Flo went with me.

Out here you had a diverse population: from millionaires to drunken ski instructors. She enjoyed them all equally. Flo was outspoken, as everybody knows. When she developed breast cancer, she let people know what was going on. She was a private person, but it was one of the things she had the guts to do. Fortunately for her, the breast cancer did not involve glands, no chemo, and no radiation. I think it made her much more serious than she had been before facing death. She started early with the Vail Community Players. Flo liked good clothing, good food, and good wine. She brought her own to the Vail Mountain School benefits; she brown bagged it. We skied a little bit together but I was working all the time; I'd go up with ski patrol early in the morning and wait for the hospital to call me. Flo did local racing and won women's downhill in her age group. She also loved to run, and we started running with Terry Minger.

We came here the same year Knox came and started the paper; later, she started a column called Flo's Flotsam talking about local problems, making suggestions. She did it for free but thought that as popular as it had become, she ought to be paid a little bit. She was so particular about her writing, spending hours writing and rewriting. Flo became a strong and active environmentalist as a result of living in Vail.

GAYLE HOLDERER

I graduated with a BS degree in Recreation Administration from the University of Minnesota by finishing my final paper on a typewriter at a bar table at the Ore House the day the paper had to be postmarked. Other than lifeguarding during the summers in Minnesota, Vail is where it all started and what a way to break in my new recreation degree.

I had met up with Sharon Ringsby (now Evancho) in Incline Village, Nevada, where she was spending a summer. I stayed when Sharon returned to Vail, but not for long. "Gayle from Vail" is what the locals nicknamed me when I first arrived. I am now a practicing attorney and still love resort living. Vail is one of the loves of my life and my home away from home. Aside from arriving in my 1965 yellow Ford Mustang, I had dreams of white powder, great adventures, new friends, and excitement.

By my second evening in town, Beetle had hired me as the new hostess at the Ore House. This was just the beginning of a long career in the restaurant field. The bartenders were very protective of me, and the patrons at the door didn't have a chance of getting out of hand. Nothing was better than hanging out with Andy McMasters, Ronnie Anderson, Jack Gould, and Pat Jackson (at different times, of course). I remember the Christmas parties we had (I was in charge of the Christmas tree and never the food), a stop at the Tuck 'em Inn on the Mountain for some wine and cheese, Donovan's après ski, JoJo Lyles at the Clock Tower Lounge, a winter living in the actual Clock Tower, summer rodeos, July 4th parades, living with Pat Jackson and our roommate Charles Cornelius on the side of the mountain, the old covered bridge, plus Everyday People clothing store and Judy (and Shirkey) Evans. The good friends I made and have kept and treasured over the years along with the fine memories have kept me coming back to Vail.

Every day in Vail was a party. It was a combination of Vail life, work life, sporting life, daily life, mountain life, and when I put that altogether it made up a lot of social life. In other words, I was fortunate to be able to ski, hike, work, play, and hang out with people I enjoyed being with. Skiing was "numero uno," but when the tourists got too thick a few of us headed to the woods on our cross-country skis or hit the Jacuzzis or hotel swimming pools.

My nightlife was my working life much of the time; this was a good thing because I enjoyed it. I would usually run into locals at one time or another during a shift, and we'd plan to rendezvous later. After work we went to the Clock Tower and listened to JoJo Lyles strum his guitar and sing. Every once in a while, Judy Collins visited her brother Davey and popped in to sing. Dancing at the Nu Gnu or heading to the Slope for an adventure-packed movie were among our favorite pastimes.

The worker-bees were my family. Many of us didn't make much money (75 cents/hr. plus tips). When I arrived in Vail I lived at Poor Richards, an employee dormitory. Shortly thereafter, I met Joann Carhart and moved into her three-bedroom Sandstone 70 condo (she talked her father into buying her a condominium) with roommates. This was absolutely great, and my "immediate Vail family" was born. Joann has remained a dear friend.

The night I arrived at the Ore House to work, there was a large sign on the front door that read, "CLOSED UNTIL WE FEEL LIKE OPENING." The front door was locked. When I entered through the back door, all of the employees, including Beetle, were inside drinking. Ralph and Vince Ferraro were in the midst of preparing a feast with all of the trimmings for our crew. The Ore House never did open that night.

When I first started dating Andy McMasters, he went to Sun Valley, Idaho, to shoot a movie with Warren Miller and was gone for what seemed like "forever" to me. I kept making threats to Beetle that I was going to leave my job to go join Andy. The night he returned, Andy walked into the Ore House surprising me. Beetle gave us a bottle of wine and told me/us to "get out of here,' meaning the Ore House, and asked another employee to finish my shift.

Joann Carhart always hosted the traditional Christmas Eve celebration, and it was never at the traditional time. We worked long hours during the holidays. So, our party lasted from 11pm until about 2am. We always made sure that every attendee received a gift of some sort and there was plenty of food to go around. We never knew who was going to be asleep under the Christmas tree when we woke up in the morning. Steve McDowell was the one who started that fine holiday tradition.

I had absolutely no expectations of life in Vail before I arrived. This allowed me to enjoy every bit of the Vail experience. In my mind, there was nothing not to love, and it only got better.

Georgene Burton

Once upon a time, there was a Vail.

When Vail opened, I was in Red Feather Lakes, Colorado in a little cabin on the shore of one of its seven lakes. It was beautiful and quiet. I wasn't looking for anything. My husband was a cadet from the Air Force Academy and a pilot stationed overseas.

A friend called and said I needed to ski at Vail. I took my multi-grooved, 10-year-old skis and headed out. I was a certified instructor, but they wouldn't let me teach at Vail until I bought a more up-to-date pair of skis. I always felt that if the skis turned both ways that was all you needed. I had won the US Junior Nationals at Winter Park in 1952 after breaking my leg in multiple places. I was told I would lose my leg if I broke it again, so I switched to being a race official and worked for 10 years at that including the 1960 Olympics. I had been a weekend skier out of Denver, who joined the Eskimo Ski Club, bought my skis and boots for $10, and rode the ski train to Winter Park every weekend. I was a product of the 10th Mountain Division's joy of skiing as they came

back from the war and hit the slopes.

At that time there were 10 paying people on Vail Mountain, and the powder never ran out. In fact, by spring we were looking for snow that was awful just for the fun of it. Bad snow was extremely hard, if not impossible, to find. There was no one living on top of the mountain, so we would stay up top with a few patrolman and ski down in the moonlight. One night, two jet fighters flew over so low that as we came along the ridge, we could see their helmets silhouetted against the evening sky, which was just beginning to change to a beautiful orange. Other times, after the mountain had closed for the day, we would start the lifts just for us and night ski. Who knew? I also remember that when you skied out to Minturn, there was this little dog who chased you by his house. It was a trick to get by that dog. In all, it was a dynamic, fun-filled, and safe world.

The ski patrol were men to match the mountains and a hoot and holler every day. If there was trouble, you were glad they were there. The people in town could be counted on when needed, checking back on the mountain to help out any way they could. There was Dr. Gaul driving the ambulance, Dr. Eck heading for an accident up Piney Creek in the back of a speeding patrol car, and Dr. Steinberg riding along with a child in trouble to Denver.

Vail ski school decided we weren't very polished, so they had us take dance lessons to be a bit more social. This was fine until the ski patrol got wind of it, and you can just imagine what followed. Old cow towns couldn't hold a candle to us when the patrol started rocking. There was a ball and dance, and we were invited. My husband was in full military dress, and I wore a ball gown. We had dressy clothes because we were often invited to presidential ceremonies as the military backdrop. As we arrived that evening, it was fun to see everyone with snow boots on under the ball gowns slopping along in the snow. Under it all, we were the same, living in a world of snow boots, powder forever, and ball gowns but with no place to buy underwear. How close to heaven do you want to be? Vail was heaven for me because my life at the time was centered around Vietnam and the war. It was so nice not to have to be aware of what the defense condition was for the day. At Vail you could shut the world out. It was my salvation - the powder, the healing of nature, the camaraderie, little ermines sticking their heads out and playing tag under Lift 4 just as you came over the cliffs, and such a joy being in the quiet of nature. There is nothing that compares to making the first tracks in the back bowls with a cou-

ple of friends and no one else around.

The four-lane highway changed the valley. The animals are gone. I can remember when the so-called hunters found the deer and elk at Dowd Junction and shot them like fish in a barrel. People started standing guard there because the "hunters" wouldn't shoot them in front of people. Earlier, if you shined a light off the road at night, there would be pairs of eyes shining right back at you. To appreciate the mere numbers, you had to have been here. Whole hillsides of elk and deer and porcupines trucking down the trails.

I started the first children's nursery in Vail's Mill Creek Court building – called Pooh Vale - because I needed to work and take care of my daughter. One thing I received was an education in building. I came to work one morning and found a tower over the drug store. The work had been done overnight by cutting a hole in the roof and putting on a tower. Very effective, quick, not entirely acceptable, although I liked their style.

As the children grew we added a summer program including swimming and gymnastics. My daughter, then two years old, would go to the Lodge pool and swim her little heart out. Bill Brown added a small ski hill for us in front of the gondola. I painted the Pooh animals as a ski terrain garden for the children. We had to get a release from Disney in order to use those animals. The kids would go under Tigger, then around the honey jars and Pooh. My daughter grew up riding in a little red sled. In fact, you could have survived with a little red sled and a pair of skis in Vail at that time because you parked the car for the winter and didn't dig it out until spring.

One George Washington weekend my daughter, who knew how to ski by then, decided to cut the lift lines with her friend. They told the people in line that they had lost their class and had to catch up. Everyone let them pass. When I heard of this, I contacted the head of the ski school and asked him to call her in and inform her that if she ever cut the line or ducked a rope she would then ski a whole day without the benefit of a lift. It worked. About that time Vail started to change. VA informed me that they were taking over my toddler ski school, ski garden, painted Pooh animals and all. They wanted me to take care of the babies because I was licensed, qualified, and a fully certified ski instructor. My daughter was five, and I wasn't interested in the babies because she was a skiing toddler. So we took off to travel and camp in Europe. We drove to New York City

and hopped on the SS France line, and another adventure began.

I love the deep blue skies of Colorado, the Rocky Mountains, snowy peaks, aspens, columbines, sparkling rivers, and the animals. And I loved Vail the way it was.

GINNY CROWLEY

I met Charlie my first week in Denver (September 1962), and we started dating. I had a job teaching English in Cherry Creek Middle School. He had heard of a new ski area, and we took a day trip with Tom Burnham, Charlie's roommate, to check it out. Charlie decided to join Tom, who needed a hand running Vail's taxi service: a horse-drawn sleigh.

We arrived in Vail on New Year's Eve, 1963. After the holidays, no one in town needed a taxi so Charlie got a job at the Red Lion, and I continued to teach in Cherry Creek and drive up each weekend. We lived in "Sin City," the trailer park in Potato Patch, and shared a 3-bedroom trailer with Larry Benway and Tom Burnham. This was before the Eisenhower

Tunnel and new Vail Pass construction; the trip took four to five hours depending on weather. I shared the ride with another "commuter," and we'd leave right after work on Friday nights arriving just as things were starting to hop at the VVI. We'd leave about 3 am Monday morning to get back to our jobs because it felt safer driving Loveland Pass in the mornings. We were snowed in a couple of times, and I'm not sure my principal at the CCMS believed my excuses on those occasions. We began to talk about staying in Vail to see how the summer construction business might work out. I got a job at Minturn Middle/High School at Maloit Park, scheduled for completion in the fall.

We married in February 1964, and I don't think we ever had another discussion about leaving Vail for the real world. On weekends I worked at Bill Whiteford's snow bar at Mid Vail. He built a snow surround and served hamburgers and malts to ski-up traffic. It was a terrific job.... for my two-hour shift I got $7/hour, a lift ticket, all I could eat, and the boss was never around to mess things up. During the summer, I worked at The Lodge at Vail for Joe Staufer.

I taught English one year at Minturn Middle School. It was a very frustrating experience as the county seat and the population base were in Eagle. The school district officials had very little concern for the mostly Hispanic student population. The school was still held in Red Cliff, and we endured hair-raising trips during snowstorms. The school in Minturn was completed in January of 1965 - the water fountains started falling off the walls in February.

Memorable students included Robert and Gerald Gallegos and Jessie Edeen.

In 1965 a position opened up as "Head Teacher" at Vail Country Day School, and it was my job to supplement the curriculum. I soon realized that a more cohesive and challenging program was needed. As luck would have it, I rode up the chairlift one day with the Colorado Superintendent of Schools who became my advisor and opened up the resources of the Colorado Department of Education. Mine might have been one of the best ski-bum jobs in town because the school's PE program consisted of skiing every afternoon.

Some of the other teachers were JoElla Gormley, Jean Saubert, Anneliese Freeman's sister Hanni Megel, Judy Gagne, and Judy (Marshall) Nelson.

I was given the opportunity to open a shop in a small space being built to keep snow from sliding off the roof onto passersby. Byron Brown Real Estate was in the front half, and my business, the Gaslight Candle Shop, came into existence in the back. John Amato gave me the space rent-free - just one of the many generous things he did in the Vail community. I moved the store to the Wall Street Arcade a couple of years later. I operated the candle shop for about five years, taking Nona Wilke in as a partner until we sold the shop.

I don't remember any discussion about leaving. We were having fun, working hard, and, as many pioneers have found, learning a lot. We had opportunities unlike those in the real world. I remember John Donovan demonstrating why he'd never go back to Chicago (one night rather late in Donovan's) and watching him do a very good imitation of a commuter on a train holding onto a hand strap and struggling to keep his balance. Maybe the balance part was because of the lateness of the hour, but that said it all about the grind of the real world that we all were trying to avoid. We adopted our daughter Katie (Kayti), and three years later our son, Matt, was born.

The Liquor Store provided employee housing. We got to know many locals because a bell was located at the entrance so that they could get their "roadie." I won't name those who were frequent users of this system because they have mostly gone on to respectable jobs in the area. The bars were the source of an evening's entertainment. Donovan's, La Cave, Red Lion, The Slope and Vail Village Inn, where on our first night in Vail I encountered Diane Lazier waiting tables. She had been my sorority sister at the University of Minnesota. It was such a small town that we were all friends and partied together. Closer friends were Mike and Barbara Loken, Tom and Nancy Burnham, Hemmie and Irene Westbye, Gaynor and Nancy Miller, Jim Austin, Barbie Bowes, Lynne Langmaid, Bonnie and Steve Hyland, and Evi Nott.

We swam at the VVI pool, hiked and explored our surroundings, and I remember trips to Piney Lake that felt like we were on an expedition - it was so far away and difficult to reach. We can't forget the Il Cornuti Bar. Miss Bo Peep and Dave Garton climbed the antler chandeliers in the Casino, but not together. It wasn't a festive weekend unless someone

dropped their pants in one of the bars...we were easily entertained. The Irish Rovers sang at the Casino until the wee hours, and the sounds of the Gibson Jazz Festival were more soothing - remember, we lived right across the street. Jebbie Brown taught almost every kid in town to swim and ski. Ginny Holmes was a second mother to the same kids.

We really had no expectations in the beginning but quickly realized that the founders of the town had some unique visions that we wanted to be part of. Our hopes to stay were solidified when Charlie got a full-time job with the Liquor Store at Vail in 1966. We became partners in that operation and later opened two additional liquor stores. We spend winters in Denver now, but while we were in Vail we lived in 14 different homes, never leaving the Town of Vail.

GRETTA PARKS

I want to thank George Caulkins for bringing Ellie to Vail. He sold Vail all over the world, and he deserves credit. On my way to Vail, I found my way to Denver from Michigan. That's when I became involved in the early days of development. My husband was in the oil business, and we came to Vail because we loved skiing. Pete Seibert asked us to come.

I had gone to Austria and France after the end of WW2 and that developed my interest in ski development. My husband and I had learned to ski in Austria and were looking for "more." We saw the Vail terrain on a snowcat, and it was like heaven. It was a chance to be in the world of skiing that we had known in Europe.

That first year, my oldest son went to school in Seiberts' basement. Billy did that for one wonderful winter. The Gondola Boutique was the first shop; we opened on the afternoon Kennedy was shot. We lived above the shop, expanded to a ski shop, then opened upstairs as Cyrano's Restaurant. I remember the early days of unpaved streets, everybody's children and dogs, and you knew where everyone was.

My cousin was Larry Burdick. I called him and said, "There's an empty lot right across from me," and that's how the Red Lion got started. I grew up in rural Michigan, and other than working in a couple boutiques, I sailed all the time as a teenager. In Vail, we built the Gondola Chalet and lived upstairs. It wasn't really a challenge. Lorraine Higbie, who had come from Vermont, was a partner of mine in that business. Higbies were very involved in the development of Vail. I built the building, and we had the first beauty shop with Edie Fricke running it. She was wonderful; we put in a couple of chairs, and business boomed.

There were no concerts or entertainment, really. The weather was beautiful in summer, so the entertainment was out your own back door, hiking and riding, picnics. We never had Christmas, Thanksgiving, or Easter on the actual day – everybody was working seven days a week; we celebrated in the off-season. There was always conversation at the Deli and Rucksack, places to gather informally. I was happy just being here on those unpaved streets.

Betty Seibert and I would meet Pepi on a March day and go on top of the mountain to ski with no one there. Friends? I have the fondest recollections of Betty Seibert, some friends from Germany taught skiing here, Suzie Shepard is one of my dear friends, and so was Nancy Kindel. I miss the spirit that was part of the town in those days.

— CWP

73

GULLVI LINNEA BLUME

I missed Sweden and found Vail. Born in Sweden, I flew as a stewardess for United Airlines, and married Fred Blume in 1960. It was the snow and skiing that brought me to Vail. My work by then was massage therapy. What kept me here were the summers, skiing, and the friends we made. I loved the mushroom hunts. I modeled some for benefits and fundraisers. Helga Pulis and I made a commercial.

We were lucky to get three lifetime ski passes, so we did a lot of skiing. Besides time on the snow, I liked hiking and horseback riding in town. At night, it was fun to go over to Sheika's, the Nu Gnu, and the Blue Cow.

My expectations of the area were that there would be beautiful mountains and great snow. I totally fell in love with Vail and consider it home.

74

HARRIET MAZER

In the fall of 1970, while I was working the graveyard shift in a South Lake Tahoe restaurant, a drunken chef raved about a great new ski resort in Colorado. I had become a ski fanatic in Utah, and it just sounded like a fun thing to do. I deemed it much better than going back to Salt Lake and becoming a schoolteacher.

I was born in Kyoto, Japan, and traveled with my father in the Air Force for 16 years: Turkey, Norway, South Dakota, Montana, and

Utah. I graduated with a BS degree from the University of Utah. Skied incessantly from junior high school through university years. Once in Vail, I started as a hostess at KFC, then got a temp job during Christmas at Donovan's Copper Bar and made more money in dimes in one night than a paycheck at KFC. Donovan hired me full time and talked me into trying out for ski school. I worked at Los Amigos in the summer with a fine man, George Ward, and still maintain friendships with the other waitresses from those days.

I fell in love with the ski patrol fellows who frequented Donovan's every night after the mountain closed - the joy of skiing, and the fun of play. I shared a couple of drinks after ski school with friends, sometimes lots of drinks. Now, would you call that a social life? I skied every day, and tried to learn to play golf and played some tennis in the summer. I raced on Donovan's Ski Team. For family life

I would have to say, "Not so lucky there."

What I expected before arriving in Vail was exactly what I got: skiing, plus a life full of energy and freedom to do what I wanted. I still miss the sense of adventure my friends and I shared - like celebrating St. Patrick's Day on the porch at Donovan's, skiing powder, winning ski races, spring skiing, going to Mexico at the end of the season, wine and cheese on top of mountain, and skiing in a blizzard. It was a great life for my 20s.

HELGA PULIS

The Women of Vail. In contrast to so many of them, I did not come to Vail as a "Swinging Single." I had been married for seven years and had two children. My stories, therefore, will include my family, my/our goals, and it certainly will differ greatly when it comes to my Vail social life.

I was born in Schlesien, in the eastern block of Germany, now Poland. WWII took its toll on my childhood, shattering my security of home and family. Living in Vail replaced many of those voids. I earned a teaching degree and moved to England for a brief time, to practice English, before immigrating to this country in 1956. To backtrack a bit, in 1941, my husband Warren's family acquired a ranch in the Gore Valley and built a cabin on what is now

Cabin Circle on the Vail Golf Course. Long before Vail was an internationally recognized resort, Warren and his two older brothers, Don and Jay, hunted, fished, and hiked in the area. Warren proposed to me on the ranch property in the summer of 1957, and we were married in November of that year. We soon followed my husband's dream of living in the mountains, specifically, on the ranch in Vail. The thought of being able to live there year-round and make a living seemed unthinkable. Though it seemed a bit crazy, we both felt excited and confident about the plan. Looking back, trading the secure life of suburbia and university employment wasn't a big hardship; adventure has always been in our blood.

We left the state of Washington and drove

for two days on icy roads, a U-Haul in tow, two restless preschoolers sharing the passenger seat next to the driver, and me, a seven-month pregnant woman, taking up the entire back seat, before arriving in Vail Village on February 19, 1964. Between not being able to breathe, and being cold and tired, I wondered, "What kind of a 'dream come true' is this?"

In the beginning, Vail was known as a ski resort only. Most ski instructors had come from Austria, some from Germany. "Funny Talkers" they were called but, oh, how handsome they looked in their blue uniforms. As a whole, they added a very European flavor to our community. Many of them stayed year round, starting construction companies and being instrumental in Vail's growth.

Back then, everyone seemed young. We were a spirited, idealistic, exuberant, and crazy bunch. Our extremely diverse backgrounds made for a most interesting mix of people, and our common interests created an everlasting bond between us. Life in the mountains was not easy in those days. I remember getting royally stuck in snow banks time after time. Father Stone, our Catholic priest, came to my rescue once. We plowed our own driveways and shoveled our own roofs. Even worse was mud season with the unpaved road to our house and the muddy parking lots of Vail Village. We were always ready to help each other out of a ditch or out of a pickle.

It soon became clear that, in order to survive in a seasonal resort, we had to find sources of additional income. Most worked several jobs to make ends meet. I remember we needed three bank refusals before we could qualify for a Vet-

eran's Administration loan to build our first home. No problem getting those refusals. Banks simply did not want to make risky loans in the mountains, especially in unknown places like Vail. Even JC Penney turned down our credit card application.

We built our first Vail home in the summer of 1964. Warren and I had chosen a charming location on our family property, located halfway between Vail Village and Bighorn, now East Vail. Tucked against the mountain and into a grove of aspen trees, we were the only home seen for miles from Hwy 6. With the Gore Range framed in every window, what more could one wish for? Earlier that spring I had given birth to our third daughter, Piney. Like her two sisters, Vali and Fawn, we had named her after the area we had learned to love.

We were totally isolated and had to maintain our own one-mile country road and, more than once, were snowed in completely. We often had to park our jeep with snowplow attachment by what is now the Pulis Bridge. In that case, Warren and our oldest daughter, Vali, then six years old, would have to ski out. With ski poles and his briefcase under one arm, holding onto Vali with the other, a backpack for groceries on his back, Warren and Vali skied to work and school. All the while, I kept the fires going at home. Our house was self-contained. We had our own septic tank, a well, a large propane gas tank, and no television for the first five years. I can't say we felt isolated; nature compensated us in abundance, and we had no problems entertaining ourselves. I always have believed that boredom stimulates creativity and our girls developed plenty of that. They all became avid

Moon walk celebration

readers before kindergarten. We were known to give the best, and the scariest puppet shows at the children's birthday parties, and the cast included Warren and me.

Much has changed since we built our first home. The road is now paved. We relocated, building our second home further to the east on Sunburst Drive. Soon Vail was on the map, and tourism changed our little village forever. Those early years in Vail built the foundation of our close family bonds, now carried into the next generation. "Yes, it takes a village" and I have to say, Vail raised our daughters as much as we did.

In 1967, my husband and I opened The Valley Forge, an arts and crafts shop, across from the Red Lion Inn, later relocated to the Casino Building. We had bought the freshly rezoned "Commercial Condominium," which had previously been the "Hand Maid Shop," owned by Freddy Felton. By adding a second story, we were able to open Vail's first art gallery. Our new location incorporated the old, run-down Continental Trailways bus station. We gutted it all.

We early Women of Vail made it our responsibility to help establish the vital amenities needed to attract not only visitors and part-time residents, but also new local families like our-

selves. If we realized a need, we took it upon ourselves to do something about it. In that sense, we women led a very active and fascinating life. Volunteering was a big part of who we were. The nice thing about that...it is very contagious! Some of my most favorite laughs and memories go back to my volunteering times. Many a close and lasting friendship has evolved from those days.

You can't live in Vail and not ski, right? There once were four Superchickens: Barbara Parker, Marilyn Elisha, Marianne Clark, and me. We were four moms, who had been deserted by their husbands and children's addiction to skiing. Never having skied before and deadly afraid of those slippery slopes, we approached VA's, Vice President of Marketing, Bob Parker, begging for help and got it. We were assigned Ski School supervisors to take us under their wings. I am convinced we changed their entire philosophy about how to teach women. Not in our wildest dreams did we expect instructors like Ludwig Kurz, Hadley Gray, Johnny Mueller, and Bob Gagne, to name a few. Our elite club became so popular, it eventually was divided into two groups. The second one, with the most improved chickens, graduated to The Easy Riders. Our foursome, however, stayed faithful to the Chicks...and not by choice.

As Vail changed, so did we. Warren and I have relocated to a lower altitude and less severe winter weather, an hour's drive west from Vail. However, our hearts will always remain in the Vail Valley. It gave our family the roots I never had. I will always cherish the memories, the camaraderie, and lasting friendships that we as a family formed in Vail.

ILA BUCKLEY

Once upon a time on a cold and snowy night, I arrived in Paradise 81657. The trips over Loveland Pass and Vail Pass were very trying after a four-day drive from the East coast, where I had been a schoolteacher in central New York State. I checked into the Holiday Inn and then meandered into the pub where I met Don Lilly, Stan Anderson, and Don Nash. They asked me what my name was and I said, "My name is Sue, how do you do?" Big mistake, because they continued to call me Sue for several months.

My first job was at the Deli where I worked for Phil Lamantia and his wife, Judi, a college friend from Western State in Gunnison. Judi and I later became partners in the popcorn wagons, which we parked on the Deli patio. I continued to work at the Deli part-time and as a ski instructor for Vail Ski School. Those early days required that most of us had to work three jobs in order to survive.

When John Kaemmer opened Pistachio's restaurant in the old La Cave location, I worked for him as an assistant cook. It was there that I firmed up my love of the restaurant business. My dream was to own my own restaurant some day. Bob Finlay, the real estate guy, approached me with an offer to buy the Silver Buckle in West Vail. I consulted with John Kaemmer and former boss Bob Newell, manager of Holly Vail, where I had worked as a Holly Dolly for a few years. John told me that the Silver Buckle had a very bad reputation, and it would take a great deal to change the image from the fist-a-cuffs bar to a respectable eatery. Fortunately, I was very naive and continued with my dream and opened Torino's.

Living in Vail in those days was very difficult, and it took a special group of people to persevere. There is a bond among us now that is obvious when we get together at the Pioneer reunions. The camaraderie is strong, and the knowledge that we chose these friends and this town to live in and enjoy is remarkable. We came from a variety of places and assorted backgrounds to live in this Paradise Found.

Those were the days my friend, I thought they'd never end.

Irene Westbye McConnaughy

I was born and raised in southern British Columbia, Canada. After high school I moved to Vancouver and attended business college and then went to work. During that time, I started skiing and fell in love with it from my first day out. I loved skiing so much I decided to take a winter off from the business world to work and ski at a resort in the US, much to the dismay of my parents.

First, I went to Alta, Utah, but snow was scarce at the beginning of the season. Frustrated, three other ski bums and I hopped in a pickup truck in early January of 1963 with our meager belongings and drove east until we found snow. Our first stop was Aspen, but it wasn't that appealing to us; snow conditions weren't great there either. One companion had a friend working at the new ski resort at Vail. He called, and she said, "Come on over, there are lots of jobs, and this is an exciting new ski resort." I don't think we had any particular expectations about Vail; we just wanted to ski. Within two days we had jobs, a season ski pass, places to live, and three meals a day in the cafeteria in The Lodge at Vail.

I was fortunate to be hired as Peter Seibert's secretary. Vail Associates offices were in three guest rooms in The Lodge at Vail. Peter Seibert and Bob Parker each had an office, and the third was an accounting office. The snow finally came in mid-January, thanks to help from the Ute In-

dian tribe's snow dance on Vail Mountain. Working with Peter Seibert was a delight. He and I would meet at the office about 9 am. If it had snowed the night before, Pete would say, "How about if we meet back in the office around 2 or so, and go ski some powder this morning?" I lived in Vail during the winter those first three years. The second and third winters, I worked for the newly formed Vail Resort Association and the Christiania Lodge. Soon, I was in Vail year-round and opened the Gourmet Wine and Cheese Shop in the Lazier Building on Wall Street.

Nightlife was limited those first few years. The Rathskellar in The Lodge at Vail was a favorite hangout as was the bar at the Red Lion. I skied many days every winter. The back bowls were my favorite and where I eventually learned to perfect my powder skiing technique. Back then, you could ski the bowls several days after a powder storm and still find untracked snow. Lift lines were almost non-existent, and the sheer size of Vail Mountain amazed me. Skiing Riva Ridge from top to bottom was a great way to end a day of skiing.

Standing on top of Vail Mountain and looking out at the Gore Range and surrounding scenery still fills me with the sense that I am a very lucky woman to have found this place. Vail is my forever home.

ISABEL SCHOBER

I was 26 when I came to ski at the new Colorado resort with the Kansas City Ski Club in 1963. I met my second husband in a ski class. They switched me to Manfred Schober's class, and he took me down Tourist Trap. I wasn't a good skier, barely intermediate. He said it was my fault when I fell. Everything came off, and he said, "I told you to follow." I replied, "Please don't just stand there, help me up." He offered to buy me a drink, and that's where we started. The ski trip ended, but I came back and got a job at Vail Blanche working for Blanche Hauserman and Bunny Langmaid. They later fired me for not dusting.

I lived in George Mallinckrodt's cabin on the creek, and on weekends the ski patrollers and ski instructors would stay in the extra bedroom and living room where there were bunk beds. They brought their own linens and paid me $5 for each bed. We had great jug wine parties on the weekend.

I wrote to my mother, "Please send some of my clothes, and cancel my date for the dance, mom – I'm staying here." I was in love and Manfred, and we got married. We bought a condo in All Seasons and opened our own ski shop in the Golden Peak building. We later built the Bell Tower building and leased the downstairs to Hermann Staufer for the Lancelot restaurant.

I have two sons who went to school first at Pete Seibert's house, then the Kindels', then above the Fire House. I had a full-time babysitter for Rhett and a playpen in the shop; we had a classy Afghan hound dog named Jezebel that stayed next to the playpen. Jebbie Brown taught Rhett to ski.

I remember a Christmas in July party at Rod and Heather Slifer's in Buffehr Creek, and we asked, "Who would live way out here? They must be out of their minds." There was a tree, a turkey, and somebody walked across the back of the sofa; they broke the sofa, and fell into the fireplace. Everybody was young at heart. We didn't have a lot of responsibility, and it was inexpensive to live here. In order to have a party you had to invite everybody, and everybody came. My best friends were Anne Staufer and Daphne Slevin. We played poker and charades. It was hysterical with some of the Austrian guys; they would do the gestures, but they would say the words anyway. I remember Nancy Kindel outside making snow angels, and Heather Slifer playing in the snow.

There were people who didn't want TV, didn't want the roads paved, and some developers wanted to keep it their own private ski club. Everybody opened up ma-and-pa businesses. Customers expected the owner to be at the restaurant when they went for dinner. Some of the women were more responsible than the men.

The Lost Boy event was a near tragedy when a child got lost on the mountain. Fortunately, the next morning the boy came walking in from the back bowl now named after him. But that night, women made sandwiches, and we took them to patrol HQ to feed the searchers. Father Stone picked up those who skied all the way to Minturn, meeting them with a bottle of liquor to warm them up.

Bill Whiteford had a bar called Il Cornuti bar – it means cuckold in Italian – and a jukebox with a screen. He had shuffleboard in that bar, and we all played. There were women's tournaments. Irish singers came. The world's greatest jazz band played for three days over a weekend and only stopped for two hours in the middle of the night. Everybody was there all day, left and got a couple hours of sleep, then went back and listened to more jazz.

One of the things that made it easy for me was that I'd lived in a lot of places in my life and I had had to make new friends and make a new life a number of times. Everybody was struggling and hoping to make ends meet. Maybe it was easier for some because they had more backup money. For others, everything was on

credit. Donovan had a tab at the Copper Bar, then he cut everyone off. I was one of the few who could still run a tab there. The funny thing is, I never bought my own drinks. I remember the Village Players Melodramas. John Dobson wrote melodramas, and we all played in them. He started writing charitable pieces for the hospital: take offs on things going on in Vail, politics, making fun. Merv Lapin and George Ward acted – generally, it was the same group of hams. Rehearsals were at John and Cissy's house. We all wanted to add things to the plays, but John used to say, "Now, Isabel, we can't say that."

I was never a dyed-in-the-wool mother, never a carpool mom. The boys were polite, nice, good athletes, but I hated to talk to the teachers. In third grade, Lance fell asleep all the time, and his teacher complained that I needed to take him to the doctor. "Is it possible that he's bored?" I asked. I started giving him coffee with his milk in the morning, or coke. I guess it worked because it was the end of that.

It took so long to get to Denver; that twisty road by Georgetown, where you couldn't even get up the hill sometimes and had to spend the night. I couldn't look. Manfred would say, "You have to look out the window and see how close we are to the edge." It wasn't pleasant. One night, after we had built the Schober building, I had a dinner party and the electricity went out, so I had all the candles going. The lamb roast wasn't finished. Blanche was the only one with a gas oven. Francis Brofos and the guys took the roast and put it in Blanche's oven to finish cooking.

The Austrians and Germans did very well,

worked hard, and had gone to hotel-restaurant management schools in Europe. Some did it on their personality, like Sheika. She learned business and worked hard. I used to ride with her to Denver to pick up the liquor for the bar in an old station wagon. I think it was that we were willing to take a chance in a new place. It was definitely a risk, but we didn't know that. I had a business, husband, kids, friends here – that's why I stayed. You got involved in skiing, horseback riding, and hiking to those high lakes. I had great friends in Kansas City, did all the right stuff, social, arts league, and philharmonic, and I had a closet full of evening gowns. Now I have a closet full of slacks. I didn't come to Vail because of a man; I met him here instead. The pioneer in me still wants things to be personal and easier. I was never a conformist. Individuality was my strength.

I have memories of the good old days of dirt, Gore Drive, no TV, few phones, sheep meandering through town on the way to the slopes to graze, and the road bridge across the creek making it easy for Clare Elliot to catch ski thieves. Barbara Parker and I started the Vail Art Club; I was secretary-treasurer and still have the checkbook, but no money though. We even had a wonderful Japanese art teacher who came to teach us woodcut printing techniques.

Oh, the grand opening--- my Mom and I stayed in a new house on Willow Circle and went up the gondola to Mid Vail for the celebration. Vail had just had the Indian dancers in full regalia up there to dance for snow, and it started snowing shortly afterward, so we were very impressed, and the pioneer VA directors stopped sweating. Vail opened, and then it was up to us. We made our own world really.

JANE LANGMAID SMITH LANCY

In 1961, my parents and I moved from Massachusetts to Aspen so my father could work for a ski rental shop and gain experience before settling permanently in Vail. I spent my senior year at Aspen High School. After graduation, we moved to Vail and rented a house on Mill Creek Circle while our house was being built on Beaver Dam Road.

In the fall of 1962, I attended Colorado State University, but during the first Thanksgiving

holiday of skiing in Vail the excitement of being a pioneer in the West was too much to resist, and I decided to leave college. I did, however, return to Boston for a year of secretarial school.

I worked for Byron Brown in his real estate office on Bridge Street and remember watching from the office window as the tourists and locals paraded across the Covered Bridge and up the street to go skiing. I was envious of them, but I needed to work for a living some of the time. I skied on my days off. In the early days, there was only a gondola and Chair 4, plus the back bowls. So we were somewhat limited to "Rams Horn," "Swingsville," and then "Riva Ridge" at the end of the day. Vail in the early 1960s was a wonderful experience for everyone who was lucky enough to be there. It was like a big family. We all knew each other and were there for the same reason - to make Vail a success. At night, we got together at the Vail Village Inn for après ski until Bill Whiteford opened the "Casino," and that became the "in" place.

Being young and only interested in having a good time, I do not have any historical stories of Vail's early days. However, I can share a couple from my mother, Bunny Langmaid. During the winter of '62, the temperature dipped to 40 below zero, and we had to cover all the windows with quilts. That first year, the United States Ski Team trained in Vail. My mother re-calls moving into their house on Beaver Dam Road, and the only means of communication were six telephone extensions at the Lodge, one of which they had extended to our house. One day, the phone did not work so she hopped into the Scout and raced down to Bob Parker's office at The Lodge. She was told that the phone extension had been given to Roger Brown. With my mother's warm personality and beauty, she persisted and got the phone extension back.

I consider my years at Vail some of the happiest and most exciting years of my life. It was special to see a village grow from the ground up and be part of it. In 1968, I married and moved back to Massachusetts. I have two children, and my son learned to ski during our trips to visit my parents. While skiing in Vail, he fell in love with an Australian girl, and they now have two children. Vail has now influenced four generations of my family.

83

JANET BOYD TYLER

My mother was Janet White Boyd Tyler, who first came to Vail in 1964 or 1965. As the story goes, some men owed my father about $5,000 but didn't have the cash. My dad was in the DJ Basin oil play in north-eastern Colorado, and I suspect they were, too. The men said, "We don't have any money, but we do have a lot in that new ski town they're building in the mountains, um, we think it's called Vail." My father was not in any way a skier, but my mother was an avid skier. He said, "No way," but then my mom got wind of the offer, and suddenly we had a lot in Vail. When we built the house the following year, everyone said, "Why are you building way out there?" (Forest Road, between Vail Village and LionsHead). The home is still there---one of the few "Vail originals."

Janet came to Vail to ski. That's it: ski. It was her life. Beginning in 1965 or so, we traveled to Vail at least once a year from the East Coast, usually during spring vacation. If the snow got skied out on the runs we headed for the trees---for Janet, being here was all about skiing. Whenever I visited my mom, the first order of the day was: skiing. Always. Policy!

When she was living "on the hill" there was a rash of burglaries, and she knew that "that nice Tim Tyler" owned the house on Beaver Dam Road below her. She called him in Denver to see if he wanted her to keep an eye on his place, maybe turn on a light. Well, more than that was turned on. I had the honor of being her Maid of Honor when she married Tim the day after Thanksgiving (he was so nervous, he carved the Thanksgiving turkey upside down). Good friend, Don Simonton, married them at the Interfaith Chapel. Janet loved being in Vail. She would have never left, I think, except that she and Tim had an active life in Denver. Vail was always essential to them both.

"Social" was the essence of this lively woman. She had the ability to spark any gathering, just by showing up. Entertaining was like breathing for her. She gathered people in from all worlds and made them feel they were the center of the universe; ask anyone who spent time around her. And she was very well connected. She knew how to network before that term was invented and

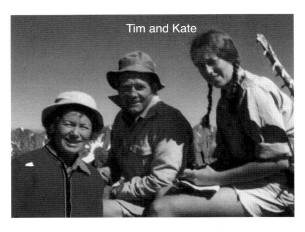

Tim and Kate

loved to introduce people to others whom she felt they should know. Janet loved parties, dancing, conversation, and ideas. She loved people. Tired from a day of skiing? Got the after-dinner slow-downs? Too bad. Janet was just as likely to head downtown to go dancing. Or to listen to Mickey play piano at The Lodge. Heavens…life is short.

On the slopes, we seldom went inside. On nice days, Janet always packed a picnic, and we'd find a place in the trees somewhere for midday refreshment. Christmas was as follows: Stocking. Breakfast. Skiing until 3pm. Only then did we open our presents. It never mattered how Janet felt: she went skiing. She also hiked, played tennis, swam, and was active in any way possible.

Janet's happiness in being wife to Tim Tyler was easy to see. They were a true pair, a real match. They skied avidly, socialized with new and old friends, traveled, entertained, and enjoyed each other. We had group birthdays in December since four of us celebrated birthdays that month. I think Mom knew Vail was a perfect fit for her. She loved it here, in the gaze of the Gore Range. Janet didn't mind change---but definitely felt that there were certain traditions in Vail that needed to be maintained. She was willing and able to get involved when it meant making Vail a better place.

Years later, Summit Huts approached Ben Eiseman to help them get their hut system started. He agreed to assist them only if they would name their first hut after his good friend, Janet, who was dying of cancer. Janet's Cabin (where her lifetime ski pass to Vail is buried in the foundation) remains a legacy to her.

— KATE BOYD DERNOCOEUR

JANETTE JANSKE BIER

I was born in Nebraska and attended the University of Nebraska, receiving a BA in Secondary Business Education. In 1964, I taught school there. During that school year, I met Linda Kottmeyer, who wanted to quit her job as a bank teller and move to Vail, Colorado, to become a "ski bum." I was ready. I didn't know what to expect, and when we arrived I was stunned by the beauty and serenity of the Vail Valley.

We drove to Vail the summer of 1965 in my '64 yellow Malibu, sporting two speeding tickets. My first job was cashier at the Deli working for Phil Lamantia. I soon found another job at Casino Vail as a cocktail waitress. I sold lift tickets and babysat for John and Laurie McBride's two small children. Linda and I lived in what was known then as "Chris's Closets." Our social life was centered around friends whom we met at work. We spent a lot of time at Casino Vail because it was the "place to go" in the evening. As I recall, Sheika Gramshammer was in charge of the disco music for dancing.

Linda had told me that she was an experienced skier and would teach me what I needed to know. Well, she took me to the top of the mountain and then took off and left me after a very brief "lesson." I tried to ski, but a patrolman was watching my struggle and took me down in a toboggan. I searched for Linda and found her at the small medical clinic with Dr. Steinberg. She had multiple breaks in her leg. She spent the rest of the season working at the Red Lion Inn as a cashier. Downstairs at the Red Lion was a great place to hang out after skiing, and everyone would write their names up on the ceiling using candles.

I returned to home ground at the end of

85

the season. In 1969, my husband Jim Janske and I came to Vail after spending a year as traveling musicians. We had met shortly after my return to Nebraska. I shared so many stories about Vail that he was intrigued with the idea of spending time or making our home there. We rented a condo in East Vail from Jack Carnie. Jim worked at the Nu Gnu for Paul Johnston, and I worked at the Red Lion for Heinz Heite and Gunther Hofler. The Burdicks owned the Red Lion. It was great fun that year, and I met wonderful people including my dear friend, Sally Johnston. When she came from Boston to see Paul, she wore the latest in fashion—short dresses with beautiful stockings. Judy Gold and I had fun working together at the Red Lion. My favorite dessert was the Gold Brick Sundae—hardened chocolate with nuts on vanilla ice cream.

I was pregnant with my son, Jon, when Jim and I decided to move to Wisconsin, to be close to his family. We later lived in Longmont, Colorado, where daughter Jayme was

born. We eventually moved back to Vail. Life transitioned into single parenting and teaching at Battle Mountain High School. I now live in Redstone, Colorado, and am married to Jeff Bier whom I met at a Vail Reunion. Ironically, Jeff lived in Vail in 1962-63. Friends Chuck and Meredith Ogilby and Helmut Fricker introduced us. For many years, I sang with Helmut at the Christiania. He and his friend, Art, played Alphorns at our wedding.

JEAN KLEIN

I came here to ski with girlfriends and stayed at the Night Latch or Short Swing, $2 and $4. We shared a bed so it only cost a buck. We'd go to Il Cornuti Bar and The Casino at night and might have had something to drink. Pepi's and Cyrano's had just opened.

Dad was a ski jumper in the '30s. We had a cabin at Squaw Valley, and I was the only kid I knew who skied. I remember talking about ski-

ing at my school's Show and Tell. I went to the University of Colorado because of the skiing, and Vail had just opened. There were important names to me in1965: Roger Staub had won a Gold in the '60 Olympics, and Renie Gorsuch was there. I went to the Olympics and recall it made quite an impression on me.

I moved to Vail in the fall of '65. After a big snowfall in November, my friend's mom wanted to buy a condo, and she bought at the "Green Latrine" in Matterhorn. We had great parties. You could get free lift tickets if you went up and packed snow. I got a job and met a ski instructor. I was at a tough time in school, so I got a job at Vail Blanche, but I didn't drop out. I commuted to finish the semester and then dropped out. I was disinherited; my parents were furious. We lived in a trailer park in Sandstone area. The trailer park was on a gradual hill; we lived at the bottom and had water pressure (unlike those that were at the top).

Blanche Hauserman was hysterical. I remember going up to her house, and there were fur throws on her beds. I thought she was so cool and sophisticated. I worked two years at Vail Blanche, and by then, Blanche and Bunny were eager to retire.

I was young and strong, so the ski conditions were okay for me. There was no grooming, no footrests, and the chairlifts were so slow you had a chance to rest, but you had to be tough. I got a pair of handmade boots from Karli Hochtl because we were about the same size. I kept my first skis with screw-on edges. I skied with the same people all the time. In January, there were free lessons for locals. I was in a women's class with Blanche and Ann Taylor. It was interesting being a woman in ski school; we were divided into classes of those who could ski and those who couldn't. I could. I remember buying a pretty parka at Vail Blanche that made me look like a tourist.

Not having kids for a while allowed me to be part of the group. Everybody worked, and we all chipped in. Judy Gagne taught piano, and she was a great cook. My go-to person was Blanche Hauserman. She didn't try to be my mother, but she was that age-group influence and so elegant. My mother was a singer and beautiful; she was like Jane Wyatt, but Blanche was worldly. I was friendly with Fran and Cesare Moretti, too. Another in our group was Shorty Wilcox, who had a special bed because he was 7'2". Fred Schwartz had a toy shop in California and planted trees here. It didn't matter where you came from or who you were. We were quite an assortment of skiers.

We often went to The Lodge for après ski. Ski school had a race with instructors on Fridays and then we'd après with oysters on the half shell, then we'd move on to Pepi's. We would wear our new ski boots into the sauna. The Ski Team came and trained with Jimmie Heuga, Spyder Sabich, and Bob Beattie. I recall someone brought us dinner, but it was still alive - two geese and a turkey, and there were feathers everywhere.

Steve Haber and I got married in Boulder nine days after we met. I wanted a change and figured it was my turn, so I quit school and ran off with a ski instructor. The Steinbergs came to town and lived on Forest Road; they had us over for dinner, and Flo showed me how to use a washing machine. Steve did the cooking, and I made breakfast sometimes. We had our wedding reception at the Red Lion after we came back from Boulder. Larry Burdick bought the champagne, and Roger Staub asked me, "What have you done?" We all wore those Moriarty ski hats; Steve had a pretty Moriarty sweater that I wore for my wedding picture in The Vail Trail. When my daughter was born, I named her after Anneliese Freeman.

It never seemed to be an issue to make ends meet; the trailers cost nothing, and we always got by. At night we went out and rotated where we went. We left the car running for two hours while we were inside a bar. Since there was no TV and no radio, we went to sleep at 8 o'clock. Steve was doing grad work, so we went to Boulder, and I got a job at the phone company. We lived in married student housing, and we were all broke, but it was fun. I came up on weekends and skied. I think I looked at Vail as a temporary thing. All you had to do was put 10 cents together, and you could do something (business). We worked Christmas Eve, and Christmas Day we were back at work. And then suddenly, it was January and the town was empty.

We had a company called Performance Products and added different lines, like goggles and ski pole lines, and just repped the products. The boot thing never made money, but we had fun. Then we manufactured clothes, then a goggle line: Bollé, which we branded.

Before the '68 Olympics, the company paid Killy to use his name. We had rights for North America and the South Pacific for sunglasses. The Argentine army all wore Bollé goggles in the Falkland war.

The Peter Pan story is worth telling. Walter Moritz was at the restaurant, and Marie-Claire Moritz told her boys about Peter Pan. They had a Golden Retriever, and she had instilled in her children that you could do anything you wanted to do. She was visiting me one day and looked over from my house to see her kids coming off the deck trying to fly. There was snow on the ground, fortunately, so nobody got hurt. Even the dog jumped off.

Vail was a little frontier town, and there's always been an employee-housing problem, and then we had trailers for our housing. Every fall we had the hunt parties – elk and venison – to benefit the school. We'd go to each other's houses to learn to cook. George Rau was prominent and he had a house on Forest Road, so we had parties there. Parties were normally small because not many people could fit in a singlewide trailer. Everybody chipped in, and we went to George's.

For summer work, if you had a pickup, a dog, and a broom you could be a contractor. Finally, my mother sent me money as a peace offering (after my disinheritance). I went to the Covered Bridge store and bought an iron. Looking back, I guess Vail has always attracted the captains of industry, a select group of intelligent and interesting people who wanted to do something different, and there was a way to do it in Vail.

— CWP

JEAN NAUMANN

I was born and raised in Denver and graduated from what is now University of Northern Colorado with a degree in Elementary Education. My first teaching position was fourth grade in Lakewood. During that time, I met Bert on a blind date. After dating him a year, I moved to North Conway NH and taught 5th grade for a year. When I returned, Bert and I married and settled in Winter Park. He was a snow and forest ranger for the USFS there. We resided at the Ranger Station for two years while I taught physical education and American History in Granby.

An important story in my life was our move, moving a house, that is. A few years after building our house in East Vail, I-70 was being planned. We fought along with others to keep it from being routed through Red Buffalo Pass and the Eagles Nest Wilderness Area. We won that battle, but it resulted in the interstate being routed through our house! We went through the whole condemnation process and bought back the house without foundation, fireplace, or chimney. Bert Naumann cut the house in half with a chainsaw. We had it moved to a piece of land on the Colorado River between Bond and McCoy, and he put it back together.

The house-cutting story began with a lot that Bert had purchased in Bighorn, East Vail when he was driving from Oregon to Dillon. He was being transferred in the USFS. In 1967, he resigned from the Forest Service so that we could build a house on the property. It took two years for us to complete our abode. During that time we lived in Jay and Graham Utter's home in East Vail.

My first position in Vail was as head teacher at the Vail Country Day School (now Vail Mountain School). In those days, it was a 1-8 grade school with three teachers. That school board turned over grades 1-6 to the public school and then I taught 7-8th grades.

Steve Rieschl invited me to join his Cross Country Ski School that was under contract to Vail Associates before they took it over. When he left, I was made Supervisor. I was involved in the program for more than 30 years. When I first got involved, I needed a supplementary job, so I worked at the Red Lion when the Burdicks owned it. In the summers, I guided backpack trips for the first couple of years for Bill Mounsey, an outfitter for The Wilderness Society. Then, Jim Himmes and Greg Earl invited me to join them as a guide for Meet the Wilderness, an organization that took mostly inner-city teens on backpack trips.

The many wonderful friends I made, the climate, cultural events, libraries, interesting/challenging jobs I had, and the beauty of the area all contributed to my staying here. It is a lifestyle that is ideal for me. My life has revolved to some extent around outdoor activities, early on mostly with friends. Living in the mountains, I've always had a number of out-of-town friends come and stay with me. I alpine skied when I arrived in Vail and replaced it with Telemark skiing. I've also been active in track and backcountry skiing since 1969 and introduced snowshoeing in the VA Nordic program. I have no children, although I just married (Bert died six years ago) a man with children and grandchildren, so I have a new family. My mother lives in Denver and is 94.

I skied in Vail in 1963. When I met Bert, we occasionally skied here and stayed at the Minturn Ranger Station. After living in Winter Park for two years, I had an idea of what ski resort life was like. We already had a few friends here, and I don't recall thinking there would be a great adjustment coming to Vail — just to the effort involved in building our own house while being employed. Also, I was concerned about teaching in a private school with no formal administration, a totally different challenge. I made many of my best friends during those early years. It seemed then that we knew most of the residents of Vail, and there was great camaraderie. As the town and area grew, strangers came, but then amenities grew, too. It seems wherever I go in the county, I run into one or more friends and acquaintances from those early days.

90

JEANNE TILKEMEIER

In February 1963 we stopped by Vail on our way home from our annual Aspen ski trip. After coming out of the back bowl and seeing what looked like midgets skiing where we'd come from, we stopped at The Lodge at Vail to look at a table model of the ski area on display in the lobby. A ski instructor appeared from out of nowhere to explain the layout and said he was also a real estate agent. His name was Jay Utter. He invited us to come up again, from our home on Lookout Mountain west of Denver, to ski with him and look at real estate. Jay and his wife, Graham, did not have kids, so when we arrived one weekend with three, I'm sure they were a bit surprised, but took it all in stride and became close friends. Jay owned a little red cottage in Minturn, and that became our 1963 weekend home for our first winter in Vail.

Our first reaction to Vail was that it would be a good place to invest in property, but we would always spend our ski vacation in Aspen, as we had done, when we lived in California. That idea lasted for about one week after feeling the excitement of the possibility of joining the adventurous pioneers in Vail. We did just that when Jay learned that a Chinese investor got cold feet on the 50-acre easternmost parcel of the Kaitepes Circle K Ranch. We went to look at the property on snowshoes and had to cross Gore Creek over a snow bridge because there were no bridges - or even roads - in that very remote part of the valley. We could not afford the whole 50 acres, but Jay convinced the owner to sell us 13 acres right along the south bank of Gore Creek where Main Gore Drive eventually crossed the Creek. Everyone thought we were crazy for buying way out there in the boondocks, but as soon as the bridge was built we started construction. Roger went to the courthouse in Eagle to inquire about a building permit and was met with the response, "A what?" and the rest is history.

We built four fourplex condo buildings on three acres, finishing with a duplex for ourselves in 1968, and then sold the remaining 10 acres to Art Kelton and Tim Garton. Our plan was to build a fourplex, sell two units, and then move on to the next building. Much to our pleasant surprise, even in that remote part of the Vail valley, it worked.

Our first sale was fun and unusual. Don Lilly had a horse corral where I-70 is now - across from the entrance to Main Gore Drive. He loose pastured his horses about where the East Vail Park is and gathered them on horseback and move them up Main Gore Drive to his corral. We were pioneering the building of some condominiums just south of Gore Creek Bridge on Main Gore Drive and were showing a unit to a person who had just moved to Denver from somewhere in the east. Don was dressed up with hat, boots, and a 6-gun in a fancy holster. As we stepped out the door, Don came by whooping & hollering behind his band of galloping horses. Our customer turned to us and said, "Hot damn -- I'll buy it!" That was our first sale. I'm so thankful to have been part of those early days.

JEANNINE ERICKSON

Even though I am a Colorado native, I didn't start skiing until my mid-20s. I joined the ski club at my place of work, began taking weekend trips and ski lessons, and became hooked. It was in 1964 that I met my future husband who was teaching skiing on weekends in Vail. We skied weekends and holidays and stayed at the "We Ask You Inn," a motel on the north side of Highway 6 in Edwards. Mr. and Mrs. Jenkins owned it. They would always hold a cabin for us along with one or two other "weekend warriors." There were metal shower stalls, and I remember an inscription on one of the stalls: "Beware of Falling Rust." We had a lot of laughs while staying there. It wasn't long before Rod Slifer made us aware of some very desirable lots for sale in nearby Buffehr Creek. We purchased a lot and built one of the four early chalets there. It was basically a "livable shell" and required a lot of inside finish work, which we tried to squeeze in when we were in Vail.

The great skiing and the fascination watching a new ski resort evolve brought us here. Also, many of our friends were skiing and working on ski patrol weekends. Skiing was our main interest with an occasional trip to a Caribbean island for scuba diving. We spent the summers hiking, playing tennis, biking, and trying to finish the chalet we were building.

The lifestyle, the perfect climate, and outdoor sports were the main reasons I chose to live here permanently. There were about a dozen women with whom I became friends, and we had some great times together. Our social life was mainly après ski at the Red Lion, Donovan's Copper Bar, The Slope, the Blue Cow, and Pepi's. A big night on the town was a steak dinner at the Clock Tower, then to the Bear Trap Bar in The Lodge to hear Tom O'Boyle, the pianist. Sometimes we'd go to the Casino or Nu Gnu.

I don't recall having many expectations of life in Vail. It was just fun being here during the early development of a new ski resort. I remember a comment my father made, "Vail will never 'catch on' because it's too far from Denver, and there are two passes to cross." Then came the tunnel, and the rest is history. It became obvious to me as time went on that Vail was going to become a major ski resort. Little did I know how it would surpass my expectations.

JEBBIE BROWN

When the authors asked Jebbie Brown to share her early days in Vail, she showed up with a fat album of photos that told the story of how she spent the '60s. The album is filled with page after page of kids learning to ski, swim, and ride horses. Jebbie is there, too, teaching and supporting children.

My first job in Vail was as a cocktail waitress at the "Golden Ski" in The Lodge at Vail. To get to work, we walked from the "Mallinckrodt House" up Beaver Dam Road, which was an unpaved, muddy, slick mess. We had to wear boots up to our knees, and they often came right off our feet.

I spent many afternoons sitting on the roof sunbathing and drinking Fresca and Bacardi rum. We would then slide down the roof into a gigantic snow pile, which had come off the edge of the roof onto the ground.

When Elaine White had the Montessori School at the Rams-Horn Lodge, I started giving swim lessons at their pool. From there, came the first 3-to-6-year-old ski class. Bob Gagne, our ski school director at the time, allowed me to organize ski classes for the Local Vail Kids. At 9am, the Vail mommies brought the afternoon kindergarten kids to Gold Peak to ski. There

were eight children in the class, and it lasted until 11am. The kids came in for lunch, supervised by one of the moms, and at 11, eight 3- and 4-year-olds arrived for their ski lesson. The moms made sure all the morning skiers got lunch and were ready for the school bus to pick them up for afternoon kindergarten. This bus also dropped off eight morning kindergarten children, who were met by a Vail mommy. They ate lunch and got dressed and ready for their afternoon class from 1 to 3pm. This was the original Tiny Tot ski program in Vail. After a couple of seasons, it got so popular that we had to get another ski instructor to help out. Joanne Savoie and I would go to the Learning Tree preschool on the North Frontage Road and start many of the toddlers out sliding around in the parking lot. From there, we would go out to the Vail Golf Course and have them slide down small hills to get used to sliding with skis on. Kara Heide, Susan Bristol, Drex Douglas, and Jill Napolitan were the other instructors who helped with this ski program.

We had our own race at the Chair 12 Bunny Hill called the Sloppy Slalom. It was an obstacle course, with a limbo bar, hay bales, and an inner tube to slide down in with skis on. They had lots of fun, and there were balloons and prizes for all. Ernst Larese from our Haagen Dazs ice cream store invited everyone for free ice cream cones. Several kids who skied with me went on to race – among them, Sara Schleper and Sacha Gros.

There were many Adventure Trails on Vail Mountain, which were barely wide enough for little kindergarten kids to ski through. A favorite is now called Chaos Canyon. On a snowy powder day, a man saw us duck into that area on our "secret adventure trail" and followed us in. He was not a particularly good skier and fell in some bushes. I believe he broke his leg, and the ski patrol had a difficult time getting a toboggan in there to get him out.

One afternoon, there was a lot of fresh powder, and I decided to ski my group down the International run. The kids loved it, skiing a Black Diamond run. I was so proud of them I told

their parents, and some of them were very upset that I had taken their 5-year-old on such a hard ski run.

I still wonder where the Vail Local Kids parents came up with ski boots and skis for the kids. They were so tiny, and no ski company made kids' equipment back then. Skiing has changed so much.

JIL MACDONALD COOLIDGE

I graduated from Washington State University in English and French, was a PAC-8 cheerleader, and worked as a lifeguard for two summers before coming to Vail. I was married at the time, and we both wanted to improve our skiing and have an adventure. I believe I read an article about Vail in SKI magazine. That was it. While here, I worked for Gorsuch Ltd, Rod Slifer, the Gondola Ski Shop, and did some catalog modeling.

We were completely seduced by Vail and made great friends over a three-year period. Vail was small, our social lives revolved around the friends who worked at the Clock Tower (Phil Minella), The Ore House (Tom, Beetle, John), The Slope, The Lodge (JoJo Lyles), the Deli, plus all the people we worked with at the shops and the Red Lion. We really just skied, drank, and watched a movie once in awhile. My good friends Libby Malo, Betsy

Cropley, and Brigitte Biasca are still in touch. There were so many ski events and extra jobs either waiting tables, bartending, or working event tables that we were pretty active all the time. It was also the beginning of acrobatics and aerials on snow, so pros were in the shops just hanging out. We'd usually end up skiing with them and trying to keep up.

There were cross-country movies on location, which was fun. Steve Rieschl was around then and very actively promoting it. They made the movie "Downhill Racer" one year, so many of us got to be extras and had fun watching Robert Redford. We got paid for having a good time. There were always Olympic athletes coming through, and in those days, people like Jean-Claude Killy, Spyder Sabich, and Billy Kidd were the celebs. I recall going out almost every night to some different bar and being comped for our drinks. Libby usually accompanied me, and we knew the bartenders by name. I doubt we paid for much, but we fed the tip jar. Watching movies at The Slope was my favorite thing. Vail was really a singles' spot, and I was married at the time.

I felt then, and still feel, that Vail is the most exquisite place to ski of anywhere I've been. I had pretty much seen and skied everywhere in the West that I wanted, but those places still pale in my experience in Vail on any given day. I will never forget the laughter, the crazy moments, and the unbelievable antics of some of the residents at the time. Anyone who spent time in The Ore House, The Red Lion, Clock Tower, or the bar at The Lodge knew a good time. There were always stories from the weeks the Kennedys were in. I specifically remember the day I first skied the back bowls, Riva Ridge, and LionsHead.

It was a very heady time of life. I don't think much has surpassed the feeling of living and working in such a wonderful environment.

JIMMIE BEARDSLEY

During and after my schooling, dance was my life in Atlanta, Georgia and San Francisco, California. It was there I met the dashing, intelligent, and 'life of the party' Jack Beardsley, a fellow dancer. We married June 7, 1957 and were blessed with daughters Jamie, Jill, and Janet. His adventuring spirit took him to the skies, flying anything from little tri-pacers and helicopters to 727 jets. I was happy to be a stay-at-home mom and raise the girls while he flew around the world. It shouldn't have come as a surprise when he died as a result of an air crash while working for Air America. The shocker was that there was an insurance snafu that left us "not covered." So, after being 12 years out of the work force with three children to raise, I was suddenly forced to become the breadwinner.

Fortunately, I had a wealth of friends, early lovers of Vail, who were willing to take a chance on giving me a job. Through Lt. Col. George Turner and his wife Janice, who owned a vacation home in Big Horn, I was offered the position of assistant manager of The Rucksack.

We had lived in Vail for about six months when the Fritzlens invited me to a cocktail party, and I met Bobbie Allen. He was the manager of a little nightspot in town and had a small theater group that gave weekly performances. We became "an item" and were included in much of Vail's social life. We all knew each other, and it was a community.

I'm afraid my family life wasn't optimal. From always having been home with my children to always being at work took its toll. When I was offered the position of office manager of the Red Lion Inn, I accepted because it was an opportunity that also (importantly) included allowing my children to come into the restaurant and eat as part of my salary. So, they ate well after spending the afternoons on the slopes and ice skating rink. On many Sundays, we hiked or went on day trips together.

When my husband Jack died we were living in Malibu, drugs were rampant in the schools, and I wanted to get my children away from the "California Experience" so to speak. I had a "movie story" in my head

about what a fun, clean, wholesome life we would have in Vail. It was a new frontier, and some of our best friends were there. We could take long hikes and campouts in the summer, basking in the beauty of nature. My children would learn winter sports and have a healthy life. It was a small community, and I would know they were safe. I soon discovered that they weren't that safe, and all the drugs weren't in California. Having decided early on to raise strong independent-minded women, I worked hard to accomplish that.

The ski season was brutal on the small community. We all worked to exhaustion on a daily basis, always with an eye to the end of the season when the town shut down and we had Vail to ourselves. Not that we didn't appreciate the skiers, we prayed for them to come "in season." Summer was a time to let down, share, and celebrate. I'm happy to say that despite our teen travails and all the resultant angst, the girls are well, and Vail played a part in that.

I feel my real work in Vail came about at a cocktail party at Gerry and Elaine White's home at the Rams-Horn Lodge when someone commented about the people of Bighorn taking up the tennis courts. I took exception to the remark and made it a point to learn about the taxes we paid and where they went. This started me on the "Annex Bighorn Trajectory," and a committee was formed to annex Bighorn into the Town of Vail. I was the Chairman, and we worked hard on seeing this come to pass. Not sure, but I think it almost doubled the size of Vail. Special kudos go to Mayor Dobson, Terry and Judy Minger as well as board members and hardworking citizens of Vail.

The years in Vail were rough and cold, and as majestic and beautiful as the area itself. It was a magical time. I still hold the relationships I made dear to my heart. From time to time, my years in Vail bring a smile, a chuckle or two, and, on occasion, a shudder.

JO BROWN

Our family of six moved to the Vail Valley in August of 1969 after living in Oklahoma, Texas, and eastern Colorado while Ernie worked for Philips Petroleum. We thought we had relocated to heaven on earth.

We left our oldest daughter in college in Texas and enrolled the two teen daughters, Elaine and Barbara, in Battle Mountain High School in Maloit Park. Our 10-year-old son Mike attended school in combination classes held above the clinic. He was Mike Brown in the 4th grade – not to be confused with Byron Brown's Mike Brown in the 2nd grade.

My husband, Ernie, who had been in and around the oil business most of his life, was the first operator of the Gulf Station which

was just being completed in the village. He started and operated the NAPA Auto Supply Store.

We stuffed our family into Dr. Distelhorst's duplex in East Vail after almost giving up finding a place in the valley. Needing to generate income, I went to work for Bishop-Perry replacing Dave Sage in the property management department at our office in Crossroads. Although not licensed at the time, that was the beginning of my real estate career. I seemed destined for real estate, however, as my previous experience had been as legal and real estate secretary and as a scribe in an abstract office.

Because we were starting again, we spent most of our time working, although over the years we spent many hours at high school

97

drama and sporting events. I learned to ski late and was never very good at it. Walking seemed safer for this flatlander although I love winter, snow, the mountains – and trees. There are not many of those in western Kansas.

We moved to a home in Intermountain with many steps, decks to shovel, and no garage. I was not happy about moving out of the Town of Vail. Since we had transferred so often with Phillips Petroleum, it was good for our children and grandchildren to have a place to "come from." Three of our children and six of our grandchildren graduated from high school in Eagle County.

Our years here are everything we wanted them to be, small town atmosphere and real neighborhoods, even though the area has grown so much. We still feel a real connection to those pioneers who came before us.

JOAN CARNIE

I'm from Rochester; Jack Carnie and I met skiing in New York. Jack was in a bar in Denver heading to California to surf when someone told him about the new ski area 100 miles west. He came up, went into the Vail Village Inn, and decided to stay. He reported back to me, "This is the most beautiful place I have ever seen. There's no place to live out here though. Would you mind living in a trailer?" He came back to Rochester, we were married, and came here. Our first visit to Vail together was during the Easter vacation; I fell in love with it. We came again in summer and went horseback riding and fishing.

We moved to Vail in a new truck in November 1963; I'd never ridden in a truck before. Our wedding presents were in the back. The mud was horrible; I'm sure everybody's trailer was full of mud. We moved to a duplex in front of The Lodge at Vail on a road that went straight into The Lodge. We moved again to East Vail and have been there ever since. We

love it there. There were cows in a pasture across the road; and further, horse stables. There was not any traffic on the two-lane road. Jay Utter was the only realtor at the time, and he had a nice vision for East Vail because nothing was there yet. Jack and I got our real estate licenses and worked for him, but he was killed right away. There was going to be a gas station, but people fought it. It is only residential to this day.

Laurie McBride and I started a nursery school in the Plaza Building the first year. I ran it for two more years after she moved to Aspen and called it: The House at Pooh Corner. Dick Hauserman gave us that space without charging any rent. After three years, he said, "Joan, we need this space. Do you mind going to the Mill Creek Court Building?" He gave me the space free again. We had a sleigh and a horse to take the kids on sleigh rides. I earned an early childhood major in college. Then I taught school in Minturn; it was the only school at the time: 3rd and 4th grade. Parents were so involved with education and dedicated to have their children become something. It was a real community there. Perhaps there were 10 kids the first year. I couldn't wait until the next day to have the kids come.

We went to Denver or Leadville or Minturn in the truck to get groceries. Three hours to get here. The snow was so bad on Vail Pass sometimes. I never really had a lot of time to ski except weekends; then my kids were born, then Buddy Werner League. My mom came out, "Aren't you lonely here in these mountains?" She was claustrophobic and didn't understand how I could like it. Friends back East thought I was a pioneer. I had taught for 10 years in a wonderful school system. I took slides back to the school before I left and showed them to the kids. The word "condominium" was a new word. Going west was an exciting experience. I've had a marvelous life here; it's been paradise, coming out and living all my married life in one spot in this gorgeous place. Not many people get a chance to grow up with a community that started from nothing. The snow was deeper then than now. One day, the owners of our trailer said, "We forgot to tell you we are burning all these down today; and they did." We had to find something else.

The McAllisters had a wedding party for us, and everybody in town came. The McAllisters had the best time getting ready for that party, and it was marvelous to meet everybody who lived here. Penny McAllister had been a flight attendant and came to Vail in 1945. John was a Dartmouth graduate and did many of the lifts. They told us about early Vail. The Katipas have a restaurant in Denver with lots of pictures of this valley in the back room. Photos of those times showed a big bread oven in the back yard, and Penny hanging her washing there and baking bread. People sailed on the Black Lakes, the women in long dresses. When the homesteaders had parties, they put the kids upstairs in the houses that were two stories. Mr. Mann (Mann's Ranch Road is named after him) had a house and a pond. He made ice and took it to Minturn by horse and buggy to sell for refrigeration for the lettuce that grew in Beaver Creek. He went to a bar and drank himself under the table, so they put him in the buggy, and the horse brought him back home.

The Happy Hikers got started when Wendy Gustafson and Vi Brown said, "We should go hiking." I made friends with Nancy Reinecke, Barbara Loken, and Ginny Crowley; in 1967, I met Vi Brown and Celine Krueger. We had our kids five years after we got here. It was wonderful raising kids; Pam Garton shared babysitting with us; she's the only one I remember ever taking the boys.

We sledded and swam. Jack kayaked, and we went camping. I'd tie a rope around the kids' waists, and we'd follow along the river so they wouldn't fall in. It was marvelous when they got older, and they were allowed to ride the bus. I knew if anything happened, the bus drivers would watch out for them. If they went into the shops, somebody took care of them. We never got TV; they didn't know what it was until they went to college.

We had meetings where everyone talked about the problems they had. If Jim Slevin's icemaker went out, everybody helped. We knew each other's business. Then, it changed. I guess people became independent. When Jack came out, he was a footpacker on the mountain for day tickets. Then he was on ski patrol for three years; then a ski instructor; finally, a supervisor. He'd been a teacher in Vermont and decided he didn't want to be inside anymore. I remember Bob Parker bringing us poinsettias at Christmas and a ham; the company was family-oriented. I never felt gender bias. It was a new life and very exciting, but gender never came into it. Coming now, it wouldn't be the same – we saw what worked and didn't. Everybody put their hat in the ring and did what they could to make it go. The Vail Interfaith Chapel was a marvelous idea; it was said we shouldn't have a church on every corner because there was valuable real estate. Cissy Dobson had a lot to do with the interfaith concept that worked for every denomination. It was a marvelous innovation. Then Don Simonton was interfaith minister and we all went to that until his higher-up said he had to preach his own doctrine.

We'd go up on Hwy 6 and pick raspberries and up Sandstone Road to pick rhubarb. Our dogs were never on leashes; they ran the whole length of this valley. When we first got here and before we were married, we came

down and took our showers in the Night Latch. I can still see Laurie McBride riding in a wheelbarrow as they came through the Covered Bridge for their wedding. There was singing with the ski patrol and piano playing in the Rathskellar below the Red Lion, and they'd bring pitchers of beer and peanuts, then we'd toss the peanut shells on the floor.

Jay Utter's dream was to make East Vail so beautiful, but when he built the bridges the snow plows couldn't get through so they had to take down the bridges. Houses got moved up and down the valley. You could park wherever you wanted. Jack and I rode our horses, and there was a hitching post. I worked at the boutique, watched the Christiania being built that summer, and I saw the Gore Range disappear, "Wait till the Whitefords come home, and they don't have the view of the Gore Range anymore."

We'd ride horses up Mill Creek and look over the valley. It was such a beautiful summer. We used to drive to the Diamond J near Eagle for steak. They had the brands of the ranchers on the wall. It was so dark driving there because there weren't lights on the road west of Vail. That was the summer of 1963. There were no paved roads in town, just dirt in front of the Red Lion. It was just a small town, and it was hard to get it through your head that people might come.

JOAN FRANCIS

My family was very much into skiing and the outdoor joys of living in Vail. My husband Tom and I were both born and raised in Colorado. Soon after we were married in Denver in 1956, we bought a small cabin near Empire. It was 45 minutes from Denver, and we went up in our spare time - weekends, summer, and vacations. Once the babies came and we wanted to ski with them, it meant driving to Winter Park or Arapahoe Basin; so, when Vail opened up we eyed the possibility of getting a place here so we could ski out our front door.

We bought property from the 2nd Pulis filing and built a house on Homestake Circle. An interesting aside is that Tom had gone to CU with Jay Pulis and had been up to their ranch before anyone dreamed of it as part of a ski area. I can't remember when we came, but it was about 1969, I think. The house was next door to Mitch and Zane Hoyt and Art Kelton - across the street, a stone's throw from Gordon and Thelma Brittan - and in the same block as the Steinbergs, the Donovans, and the Seiberts. What a blessing to have all those full-time residents to socialize with.

I have many memories of 4 o'clock tea at the Brittans - yes, tea, not cocktails. They did it almost daily, and Thelma baked cookies or cakes for guests. It was a grand time to hear about the doings in town. We used to laugh when there were several cars in their driveway in the morning because we knew Gordon (whom we labeled The Godfather when he was hosting those morning meetings) was planning something with the Town leaders. His big project was the hospital, of course, and he once said to me, "Every successful town needs a hospital and a church." He was working on the hospital, and he wanted me to do the church. Well, long story. I helped with that, but Cissy Dobson was the big cheese.

The Hoyts and Art were best friends, and I was grateful that most of our friends were residents, even though many of our Denver friends were commuters as we were, driving up almost every weekend or vacation.

Early memories of restaurants bring up only The Red Lion, Pepi's, and the Left Bank. We were at Pepi's on a Sunday night when Pepi came in and bought drinks for the room. He gleefully told us he had just paid off the mortgage saying, "And to think a poor Austrian boy who loved to ski could come to this country and OWN this. It's wonderful!"

We played lots of tennis in the summer and hiked. We spent many happy times watching something grow from bare land to this incredible international resort.

JOAN HANNAH

I am a farmer from New Hampshire, whose father (Selden Hannah) was a ski area designer and former Olympian. He had consulted Peter Seibert on Vail's design and was responsible for recommending the front side of the mountain to go along with the back bowls.

I was on the US Ski Team from 1959-66 and a medal winner (Bronze in 1962). After ski racing, I became a certified ski instructor at Loon Mountain, New Hampshire. I was selected to be on the 1968 American Demonstration Ski Team in Aspen, Colorado. The US Ski Team were invited to train in Vail when it opened with only the Gondola, Chairs 4 and 5, and a Poma lift at Mid Vail. Here we ran Git-a-long Road in a tuck for downhill training and did other training off Chair 4. After Interski, I looked to the West for a job in ski instruction and chose Vail over Aspen. Sarge Brown kindly found housing for me, and I knew the Swiss Director, Roger Staub.

I came to Vail first with the US Ski Team and liked the atmosphere and down-to-earth attitude, as opposed to the radical ideas of the youth I ran into at Aspen, "Like, I should have my hair long because, man, that's the way I feel." Vail expected a professional look for its ski instructors. I worked in the ski school 26 years and made pottery in the summers down valley.

I liked my job and bought a place in Red Sandstone. The ski school was a great family.

I wasn't a very social person. I mostly had dinners with my customers and joined in all the ski school parties. I was always part of fundraising skiing events.

I continued ski racing in the pro circuit for a couple of years and went to "The Return of the Champions" when it was held, an event where medal winners were invited to make teams with the current US Team members at the US Nationals and compete. I took part in tennis at Vail but found, as a single person, I did not always have a partner - so I spent more time making pottery. For years, I joined Linda Meyers Tikalsky and her husband for a summer backpacking trip. We went to many parts of the West. I joined Jack Eck and other friends for backpacking, also. I often fished in the Eagle River or up in the Piney River. Sometimes, I would join the Malloys on a bicycle trip over the pass or in the winter to cross-country ski to one of the huts. I joined the ski school on their various tours from Vail Pass to the back bowls and those from Vail Mountain to Minturn. Of course, there were the torchlight parades, too. Nightlife was mostly parties with my students and other ski school functions, besides the event gatherings I attended. I remained single but joined my family in New Hampshire a month in the spring and a month in the fall. My mother suffered from a disability from Polio and was unable to visit me in the West, although my father did visit on occasion.

I don't think I had thought much about what life in Vail would be like. I just needed a job with a longer ski season than Loon Mt. At that time, the US Ski Team was purely "amateur," and we did not earn money as racers. It was time for me to earn a living. I realized after a time that a resort was not the best place to find a partner and settle down. I spent all my time with clients, summers at my studio, and the off-season helping my parents. However, I enjoyed what I was doing. I visit Vail once a winter with some of my old racing buddies and see my Vail Village Teaching Team.

Most of my family is in the East so I see them much more often than I did when living in Vail, and that is nice. They are sorry that I do not have a place to stay in Vail anymore.

JOAN WHITTENBERG

My first trip to Vail was in 1967, and I still look forward to each return and am never "ready" to leave the beauty of the mountains.

"Down Valley" meant ranches, and there was very little development outside of Vail proper. We carried our frozen turkey on the plane, as there was not a super market. We skied all day and never locked our doors. We didn't complain about the wait in lift lines as it gave us a rest between runs. I could go on and on forever.

My first real introduction to the "people" of Vail was at the Bishops' Christmas Party. Arthur Bishop kept me by his side, and, as he greeted his guests, introduced me to everyone who entered. I'm sure that all who lived in Vail as well as many second homeowners, like us, attended that party. It was packed with friendly, welcoming, caring, and fun-loving people. I have enjoyed these friends for the years since. For me, they are the real deal.

My hope is that all who follow will appreciate being here as much as I have.

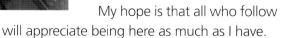

JoAnn Carhart Levy

I was the epitome of a Vail ski bum. Originally from a little town outside Rochester, New York, I grew up skiing in Vermont, upstate New York, and St. Adele, Quebec. I came west and graduated from the University of Colorado. Prior to my arriving in Vail, I literally had no work experience.

I started skiing in Vail in 1967. On the first weekend, I rented a room at The Holiday Inn. We could barely scrape up the money for a lift ticket, but someone in the group had their dad's American Express card to use, so 25 of us stayed in the same hotel room, and someone even slept in the bathtub.

I loved Vail and continued to visit on long weekends. I stayed often with my friend, Suzanne Wilson. I met Davis Webb (Marka Moser's brother) and his uncle, Bud Palmer, at Patrol Headquarters and spent many powder-filled weekends in the bunkroom at Bud's All Seasons condo. The best part was skiing with Bud and his private instructor. I introduced Davis to my best friend, Betsy; they married and now reside in Homer, Alaska. I worked weekends for Paul Johnston at the Nu Gnu but could never really figure out how I was hired. I could not even get past the bouncers at the Casino with my fake ID, yet I served drinks at my job and was under 21. Paul finally fired me

because I spent most of my time dancing with the customers. It simply gave me time to ski.

On graduating from college in 1969, I headed up to Vail to live. My first job was doing display windows at Pepi Sports. Located in the center of town, I thought that this was ideal for skiing. I made $2 an hour. By this time, I had convinced my dad to purchase a condo in Sandstone to help me with housing. If I timed it correctly, I could be at the bottom of Red Sandstone Road to hitch a ride to town with punctual Joe Staufer. The following ski season I was promoted to buyer/manager, working for Pepi and Sheika Gramshammer. My fifty-cent raises slowly mounted. We worked long hours, often 12-13 hours a day, as we always seemed to need more personnel. Business was humming in the early days. I went on buying trips to Europe and New York with Sheika. There was always a lengthy explanation for Vail's location. Everyone in Europe had heard of Aspen, but that did not always help us locate the lines we were trying to import. I finally figured out that if I said I worked for Pepi Gramshammer, it opened doors. Everyone in Europe knew Pepi.

I had many great gals working on our little team at Pepi's, many who still reside in Vail - Susie Tjossem, Monica Reynolds, Barbie Christopher, Terri Allender, Chris Walker,

Sharon Stenson, Betsy McCann, Diane Hughes, Chance Earle, Traudl Lafferty, Karin Barker, and Gigi Leroy – and many more wonderful individuals. I shared many fine moments with Gayle Holderer, who remains a true friend. I met my husband, Ed Levy, while skiing on Chair 1. Father White married us at the Vail Chapel. Neither of us ever could have imagined living anyplace else after living here and making so many wonderful friends and enjoying the sports that the Vail valley has to offer.

It was a great lifestyle for anyone wanting to experience the outdoors yet still obtain a job and not have to live in New York City. We were a tight ski bum group and had arrived with no money and no ambitions other than to break even financially and ski. We made minimum wage. These were the days when you knew every person walking down Bridge Street including a great number of visitors. We traveled

over the pass to Leadville when we needed groceries Vail did not offer. Many earlier pioneers had previous job experience and came solely to set up a restaurant or business. We arrived to have fun and that we did; however, many of us remained and made Vail home.

The world has changed, as has Vail. We have managed to keep our small village and our family values. It has always been sad to see friends move on. The down valley explosion simply has meant that many of us have moved a few miles west, but we have not lost our friendships. It is not as convenient, yet we make it work. Vail will always be a small village to me.

105

JOANNE MORGAN

I was born in the autumn of my 24th year…" to paraphrase John Denver.

I left eastern Pennsylvania on Monday, November 9, 1970, on a solo drive to Colorado in my brand-new red Mustang. No one told me it would be a terrible car in the snow. Fortunately, I didn't run into snow until the section from Summit County to Vail, and I had chains put on in Frisco. What a wuss.

On Friday, November 13 (a lucky day for me), I drove into the parking lot at Vail East Lodgings, and my new life began. I knew this valley was where I was meant to be, and since that day, I have never felt otherwise. My college roommate, Barbara Wall, convinced me to move here with her. She left after six months, but I'm still here.

The following day, she and I began our jobs as "Gorsuch Girls," and I met Maria Minick, Meredith Ogilby, and Marty (Getz) Cogswell who are still in my life – except for Marty who has passed away. The Gorsuch gang was a great group of young people, and Dave, Renie and her sister, Judy, were terrific bosses. Before moving here, I worked in the advertising field as an illustrator and designer. Renie allowed me to do a few fashion illustrations for ads in the Vail Trail, and I appreciated being able to continue to do that work.

The weekends at Gorsuch were special. A pot of Russian Tea was always simmering. Shoppers loved it because the store smelled like a spice shop. We Gorsuch Girls wore Roffe, under-the-boob jumpsuits that were more impressive on some than others.

The employees on "Main One" loved a vigorous game of charades, and the game became widely known among locals as an après-ski event of sorts during the week. Many nights after work Kathy (Hulbert) Penske, Barbara, and I and others would go to the Ore House for salad bar and a baked potato with all the good stuff. The Ore House was like a huge family gathering most nights.

I met Roger Tilkemeier on my first day of work. He and his family had a home here but lived in Denver and came up on the weekends. During our first conversation he told me his wife, Jeanne, was a good tennis player. She and I ended up playing together for 20 years, and I bet in all that time I took three sets off her.

On Christmas Eve, Renie rounded up all the Catholics (and anyone else) who were at work and we all went to Mass with her. Being my first Christmas away from my family I appreciated that little bit of home. I was very impressed with Renie's dedication to her three sons. It did not matter with whom she was talking, if one of the boys needed her, he became her focus.

Barbara's and my phone number was one digit different from the Continental Trailways bus station's number. We got calls at every hour of the day. Back then, you only had to dial the last four digits to call anyone; in East Vail, everyone was on party lines. There was no television, but we could get Denver's KOA and a Salt Lake City radio station that broadcast mysteries at night. Great entertainment.

In June, I started working at the Red Lion for the big bucks – fifty cents an hour and all the tips I could make. The first day, one of the waitresses, Sandy Pietz (the first Miss Vail) told me I'd make better tips if I shortened my skirt. So I did, and she was right. Owners Marge and Larry Burdick were wonderful, and I think Marge was one of the "finest" people I have ever known.

Erika McCall, Dale, and Trevor were my neighbors at Vail East Lodgings. One day, the neighborhood hooligan had taken my house key from under the mat so I had to break in. Erika held the ladder while I climbed up to the second floor. She was amazed at the red bloomers that I wore under my short Red Lion uniform. We still laugh about that episode.

After Barbara left, my friend from Gorsuch, Kathy Hulbert, moved in. She is from Salt Lake City and opened my eyes to cycling, hiking, and all things western. Kathy worked at The Clock Tower and was dating Roger Penske, whom she ended up marrying.

Erik Steinberg became a good friend. Through him I met Paul Jankauskas who had recently become a racer for the Hart Ski Team with Billy Kidd and Hank Kashiwa on the Pro Tour. All I knew about him was that he used to win most of the Vail Town Races and worked at the Gondola Ski Shop. The first time I ever saw him was at the Pro Race in Vail. Paul and I later married.

One winter, there was an article in *TIME* Magazine about Vail, and it talked about restaurant employees not necessarily reporting all of their tips. That January, the IRS came to town and we were all expected to be "interviewed." I remember hearing that Jean Naumann had gone into her interview and plopped down a tape recorder in the middle of the table. I guess that surprised the interviewer. Fortunately, I quit a week before the interviews began and started working with my good friend, Erika, at The Printery at Vail – Vail's first print shop.

Paul and I lived in Chuck and Meredith Ogilby's little cabin on Gore Creek for 16 years. It was like a big family with the Ogilby children, Kayo and Molly, growing up during those years, and many dogs and cats shared between us.

I lived in an apartment in Dr. Steinberg's house for a while and got to be good friends with Flo. Her sister, Lill, came for a visit during that winter and called her Florie. I loved that and called her Florie from that time on. After work, I'd go upstairs and sit in the kitchen with her while she made their dinner – she always had a glass of wine and a bit of Swiss cheese to nibble on. To this day, I think of her cooking routine every time I make a real dinner.

Living in "this world" has made it possible for me to make wonderful friends sharing common interests. I took ballet class from Denise Briner, and she opened up a world that I left behind when I was a teenager. Through that involvement I met Sybill Navas, Jamie Allison, Annie Lauterbach, Henry Hill, and dozens more wonderful people.

I taught children's ballet at CMC on my way to becoming "Miss Joanne, ballet teacher." During that time, I met Lyn Morgan, now my husband of 21 years. He is a black belt in Shotokan Karate, and the classes he taught followed mine in the same studio at CMC.

I have to say that working at the Vail Trail was the best job I've ever had. I originally teamed up with Mitzi "Mouse" Johnson who ran her advertising agency out of the Trail. I later took over her business.

I have come to realize that those people with whom you share your youth will always have a very special place in your life. We grew up together along with the Town of Vail.

Elaine speaking: Without Joanne's eye, this would be a different book.

JUDY GOLD

I was a child of the '60s born and raised in Massachusetts, attended The Walnut Hill School, and graduated from a small liberal arts college in Boston. I was 21 when I arrived in Vail, so my only work experience was summer jobs at a gourmet grocery store and restaurant on Cape Cod.

After graduation, I took a road trip across the US, zigzagging the country in a camper van with my prep-school roommate. We were "flower children," or so we thought and were headed ultimately to San Francisco. We stopped to spend a few days visiting a cousin of mine in Boulder who convinced us to head into the mountains to see Vail and Mesa Verde before leaving the State.

Arriving in Vail, I became infatuated with the idea of being a ski bum for a season. I interviewed for a job at the Red Lion, was hired, then left with my friend to complete our tour of the US. After checking out the scene in San Francisco, she went home to be married, and I came back to Vail. I skied, waitressed, made wonderful friends, and fell in love. But I left at season's end and went back home. The following November I landed a job with Brooke Franzgen, Doris Bailey, and later Dale McCall at the Vail Resort Association, sitting in the circular information booth in the Golden Peak House, wearing a head set, while operating what had to be one of the last PBX phone boards (think: Lily Tomlin's Laugh-in "operator" sketch) that linked callers with lodges in Vail where they booked their Saturday-Saturday stay. From there, I went to the Talisman Lodge, and eventually to Ski School booking private lessons at Mid Vail.

Marriage and family came along, and I stayed home for 10 years after our son Joe and daughter Martha were born.

It was my husband Fred who lured me back after that first season, telling me what we all know, "Winter is why we come, but summer in Vail is why we stay." There was never any question of leaving after that. Vail was our home.

In the early years, it was the crew from the Red Lion, "red beers" at Donovan's between shifts, and girls at the VRA. You knew everyone then, regardless of age or station. Freddie Felton (owner of "The Hand Maid's Shop" in the Casino building) was famous for his parties, inviting everyone in town, regardless of age, job or social standing in the community. Before we had children, our co-workers and ski buddies comprised our social life. When the kids came along, it was the couples in LaMaze class and families in the original Vail Babysitting Co-Op, who became lifelong friends. We raised our children together, celebrated birthdays and holidays together.

Skiing has been at the heart of my "sporting life" since the beginning. I would never call myself an athlete, but participating in outdoor activities has been a huge part of life in Vail. Downhill skiing, cross-country skiing, hiking, biking, walking, and swimming. I'm happiest when outdoors, and if the activity affords some

aerobic benefit, all the better.

Never one to spend the night in bars or out "on the town," we preferred family gatherings, summer nights eating out under the stars on our deck along Gore Creek, impromptu dinners with friends, nights at the movies, or a concert.

JUDY MINGER

Moving to Vail in 1968 was a mutual decision. My husband was offered the position as assistant to the town manager, Blake Lynch. We were living in Boulder, Terry was working for the City of Boulder, and I was teaching for the Boulder Valley School District. Terry was more enthusiastic about the Vail move than I. Visiting the town, I saw the excellent skiing, but I was aware of the many limitations of a new town with what I perceived as a narrow focus. Terry saw possibilities, and I had to agree that Vail was a special place and worth the move.

I loved teaching and wanted to continue my profession. The Vail Elementary School was located above the Vail Clinic. It was one large room partitioned into combined grade levels with first/second, third/fourth, and fifth/sixth in separate locations. Dwight Lee was the Head Master and the fifth and sixth grade teacher. The kindergarten class was in the Vail Chapel. When I saw the school, I remember thinking it would be a one-room schoolhouse experience. Luckily, there was a job opening, and I was hired as the third/fourth grade teacher.

Teaching the students in this small resort community was an exceptional experience. The classes were small. There were only 16 students in my third /fourth combination. The students were wonderful, and they exhibited the same optimistic energy that brought their parents to this place. They were bright and enthusiastic about learning and worked well with each other.

In many ways, we were like a big family and treated each other with respect and caring. Because of the number of students and their potentials, it was a joy to go to work.

During my first year, I made many requests for more materials from the Eagle Valley District Office. A representative from the district continued to tell me that the school wouldn't continue to grow. I persisted and stated that most of these families were here to stay, and we needed more supplies. Because of the district's distance and attitude, we turned to other resources. I still had a library connection with Boulder, and they allowed me to bring in 100 books every month. We continued, just like the town, to search for ways to fill our needs and make an exceptional educational experience for our students.

We never had a snow day and always went outside for recess. The students were prepared for the weather and loved the snow. The atmosphere in the school was welcoming and challenging. Staff worked well together and enjoyed researching possibilities and procedures to enrich the educational experience. We took advantage of the many talented people in the valley and scheduled them as speakers and presenters. I loved watching these students learn, interact, and appreciate their environment.

There were many aspects to Vail that could never happen anywhere else. The early residents had a can-do optimistic energy that was contagious. Not to say all changes were easy. Terry had become town manager, and we had a listed phone number so between personal

encounters on the street, at restaurants, and by phone we had an up-to-date account of the opinions of the residents and visitors. There was a wide range of feedback on issues. The growth of the town and its popularity were amazing, and everyone was in a quickened pace to keep up with the demands that were happening to this very special and fragile valley.

Our social life was busy. Between keeping in touch with locals and entertaining anyone you ever met that just happened to come to Vail was at times exhausting. But, mostly it was great fun.

The steady stream of famous and talented visitors infused an excitement and interest. Going to great restaurants and bars, visiting with locals, and walking along the streets at night brought an enchantment that made you realize how lucky you were to be in this place at this time. There was magic in the thin, crisp air and a camaraderie that connected the community. Vail continued to grow, and I think most of the early residents grew through challenges and changes that made each of us stronger and better for those experiences. I am grateful for the time that I spent in Vail and will always have a love for this spectacular place, its exceptional early locals, and my beautiful young students.

KARIN SCHEIDEGGER

I was born in Germany. When I was nine years old, I came to New York with my family and lived there for 16 years. I graduated from Long Island City High School and worked as an executive secretary for a publishing firm in Manhattan until I moved to Vail in early 1969.

Benno Scheidegger and I skied Vail in 1965 and fell in love with the town and mountain. I thought this was a good place to raise a family and saw the potential of great business opportunity, knowing this charming town would continue to grow. We came back in the summer of 1965 and purchased land in West Vail, when everyone said, "all the way out there." I live in my latest home development project in West Vail on land that I purchased then. I was involved in developing homes and condos in West Vail, was a partner with Benno in a plumbing and heating company, worked as a Realtor, and manage my own rentals.

Michael Smith, my boyfriend of many years, and I enjoy getting together with friends and family. I love skiing Vail Mountain and hiking the many trails in the valley and biking.

Like most in the early years, we came to Vail for the skiing, but it is the summers that keep us here. Also, the closeness of the community has always been appealing. When my son, Benno, broke his neck, the community was very supportive. You still see today how people rally around someone in need. I am so lucky to have my son Benno, his wife Kristi, and my two grandkids live so close by in West Vail in the house we built. Benno was born in Glenwood Springs since there was only a small clinic in Vail. Although I still enjoy the winters and skiing, they do seem somewhat long now. It is great to have all the services and facilities that we did not have when I arrived, but it has increased the traffic. I still enjoy living in a small town and being out of the hustle and bustle of a big city like New York, as well as being able to provide a comfortable living.

Karola McMillan

Born and raised in Germany, Karola was homesick for the mountains where she had spent her later childhood years in Bavaria. Her husband Bob had been to Aspen, Colorado on a business trip and decided to take his family on vacation in 1966 so that his wife could see the mountains and consider moving to Aspen. They flew to Denver and while en route to Aspen were "snowed in" at Vail in early June.

Karola had two daughters. Regina had just finished kindergarten, and Ingrid was still in pre-school when they first saw Vail. The family met Pepi and Sheika Grammshammer (who later became good friends) and stayed in their hotel. Vail was a ghost town during the off-season, and the weather was miserable with sleet and snow. Bob and Karola opened their hotel shutters, saw the mountain, a bulldozer pushing mud around unpaved roads and fell in love with Vail. Right then, they planned their move to Vail. They moved the following year in 1967.

At that time, there were only 25 children in the whole town. Regina went to school in the one-room schoolhouse above the ambulances in the town clinic. The grades were combined, and her earliest schoolmates were Brant Seibert, Julie Kindel, Fawn Pulis, Mike Brown, Nicki Poliac, and Johnny Buxman. Little did Regina know she and Johnny would marry, and Regina would deliver their babies in the same building where they attended third grade together. Ingrid went to kindergarten in the basement of the church, and Jeff Gorsuch, Tamra Nottingham, and Piney Pulis were classmates. Karola's children spoke German as their first language, but like many families in early Vail, they were bilingual.

The mountain was everyone's playground, and the pedestrian town was a wonderful place to raise children. The locals were composed of Europeans, die-hard skiers young and old, and many overqualified people working any job possible. In the mid '60s, there were few positions available, and Bob's first jobs were as clerk at the Holiday Inn, house painting, and a partnership in the construction business. Being in construction, Bob saw the opportunity to provide paint and other materials for the community. He started his paint business in a garage in Minturn and delivered paint in his Jeep to building sites in Vail. Their business grew, and he and Karola founded McMillan Decorating and Supply in EagleVail. Karola and Bob also owned and ran the family-style restaurant The Silver Buckle in West Vail.

Living and raising kids in Vail in the '60s was quite interesting. Traveling over Loveland

Pass was the only way to get to Denver. With no television, playing board games and family time were the nighttime entertainment. Skiing, sledding, hiking, biking, tennis, horseback riding, cross-country skiing, and camping were all things that Karola loved. She often took her friends "mushrooming" on Vail Pass after a big rain and picked mushrooms for cooking. She would often find Vail chefs out there doing the same thing.

Karola loved being a part of the "Superchicken" ski group and was a member of the group from its inception. Skiing with her girlfriends often ended at Pepi's for wine, cheese, and laughter. Many of the girls from this group would get together for moonlight

cross-country trips over Shrine Pass.

Karola died too young at age 45. She is laid to rest near the Eagle River in the Minturn cemetery. Her European upbringing fit naturally in early Vail. Her spirit and love lives on in her children and grandchildren.

—INGRID MCMILLAN-ERNST

KATHY VIELE

My mom was born and raised in North Haven, Connecticut. She used to tell me she "summered" in the town of Old Saybrook.

She went to Becker College in Worcester, Massachusetts, and met my father there. He went to WPI, which was also in Worcester. Prior to moving to Vail, she worked for Northeast Airlines as a flight attendant.

My father begged her to move out here to get married. Dad moved to Vail in 1969, and Mom joined him in 1970. They were married in the Vail Chapel in between hunting seasons. Mom's first job was at the ticket counter of the ski school office at

Golden Peak. She worked there in various capacities. She was a full-time mom from that time on and was also involved in the work of several non-profit organizations.

She loved the outdoors, her flowers, and her friends. Dad promised frequent beach trips to cure spring fever, and she loved the idea. Cross-country skiing, tennis, swimming, backpacking, hiking and traveling to kids' ski races were her favorite things to do. I know that she hiked up to Booth Falls every day that that she was pregnant with me. We were a family of five – husband Jim; and three kids - David, Jenny, and Emily.

Her closest friends were Chris Wright, Daphne Slevin, Diana Donovan, and Carol Collins. I don't know much about her early social lfe in Vail, other than her being witness to several events at Donovan's that became crazy stories. She didn't expect to stay long in Vail. She had visited many times prior to moving and thought of it as the Wild West. In time, she found it to be a wonderful place to raise a family and a great place to retire.

— EMILY

KAY DUKESHERER

I'm a Michigan native and received my Master's degree from MSU. My first visit to Vail was in 1963, the year I married John. He wanted me to learn to ski on our honeymoon. We liked it so much that we came to Vail to live. We stayed one year in a travel trailer across from what is now a gas station. After that, we purchased two condominiums and came here every year in winter.

I worked as a waitress and in reservations at The Lodge at Vail. Later on, I worked at the Casino and at the Vail Village Inn. The sports I've enjoyed are tennis, golf, and skiing (both on water and on snow). We went to the movies in Minturn.

Vail wasn't even open every day in 1963.

There were three lodges and a core group of people. There was the Rucksack, La Cave, and Blanche Hauserman's shop. I remember riding up the ski lift with Elaine White. We weren't very strong skiers then. The guys packed the slopes with their skis for free tickets. The whole area in front of the river was parking. The Night Latch (now the Mountain Haus) was considered far away from the slopes. There was Chair 1, the gondola, and three chairs up top – and that was the whole mountain.

The clinic was behind the Red Lion. The gas station was on the main corner, and the Frontage Road was the main highway.

Where did the time go? Forty-eight years.

Kay Pitcher

We came here in 1970. I'm from Iowa, originally, and graduated from the University of Iowa. I taught elementary school and also worked as a Braniff flight attendant. Before making the move to Vail we lived in Houston, Texas.

We'd skied in Vail and thought it was pretty nice. My husband Tom was a Delta airline pilot, so we could live almost anywhere. We decided to spend one season in Vail. We never left.

We often thought about leaving, but when faced with other options, nothing compared to living in the Colorado mountains.

My social life was not that interesting. On the other hand, I love the outdoors--hiking, skiing, biking, snowshoeing--anything to be surrounded by nature's beauty.

When we arrived in Vail, my family was my husband Tom and two children, Tommy & Stephanie. Tommy was killed in a skiing accident in Steamboat Springs. Stephanie became an airline pilot like her father.

We didn't come for just Vail as much as living in the mountains. Vail gave us more than I expected.

Life in Vail is more impersonal now—there's not much community feeling left. But nature never disappoints. What I love is the scenery, the mountains, the Wedgewood blue skies, the rainbows, and the alpenglow. It is all a thrill to experience every day.

Kit Abraham

Until I was 22 years old I attended Catholic women's schools in St. Paul, Minnesota, graduating from the College of St. Catherine. Though it was unheard of at the time, I did not attend the graduation ceremony to pick up my BS degree from the Home Economics department, because I was already on a boat to Europe. I worked at International Ranger Camps in Switzerland teaching waterskiing on Lake Geneva for the summer of 1962.

It was there that I met another staff member, Horst Abraham, from Vienna, Austria. By August, I knew that I needed to hang around Europe rather than return to the States as planned. I interviewed with the US Army in Germany and was hired to work as a Service Club girl on an army base where 10th Special Forces/Green Berets were trained in Bavaria.

I did not snow ski at the time, but the mountain town I was sent to work in was also a small ski area, and I was eager to learn. On my days off, I would go to Kitzbuehl and then St. Anton, where Horst was teaching skiing, and he taught me to ski. We were married in the spring of 1965 in my hometown of Mahtomedi, Minnesota and moved to Aspen, Colorado.

Neophyte skier that I was, I approached living in a ski resort the same way I stepped up to any activity, as if I knew what I was doing and would learn what I needed to know when I did it.

After the Aspen ski lifts closed in the spring, we would regularly migrate to Vail to ski and get ready for certification. As a result, we knew the mountain and the core village but had little knowledge of the rest of the Vail valley. When Horst was hired to work for Vail Associates, we were offered the last vacant lot available to supervisors: Lot 11 in Sandstone Subdivision. We had no idea where Sandstone was located, but we agreed, sight unseen, to buy the lot.

Horst's ski school office was at Gold Peak on the second floor of the little wood building called the Race Shack. We lived across the street; the Town of Vail tennis courts were between home and work. We both played a lot of tennis on those courts; Ellie Manzi was my doubles partner most of the time.

I skied with the original Super Class. We met our ski instructor at the bottom of the gondola at 12:30 pm two afternoons a week and skied until the mountain closed. I remember flying along trying to keep up with Carl Dietz, Inga Prime, Gerry White, and Mauri Nottingham, among others, as we barreled down the moguls on Look Ma or did repeated rotations on Prima-Pronto-Log Shoot. The days Anne Marie Mueller was our instructor we knew we were in for a beating.

As a family, our playgrounds, summer and winter, were Vail Pass, Vail Mountain, and Piney Lake. We skied and hiked on the mountain, using the snow-covered Piney Road to walk or skinny ski in the winter. All summer long, we camped, hiked, and sailed our little sailboat around Piney Lake. Frequent cross-country ski trips to Red Cliff started on Vail Pass, and after 11 miles skiing through the hushed and snowy mountains, ended with Mexican food and grande margaritas at Reno's restaurant.

Many of our Christmas trees were secured on the Pass after a thorough slog in hip-deep snow to find the perfect specimen. This was always a family outing, often with a band of families heading into the forest together and then having a pot luck dinner at someone's home afterwards. One year, when Don and Shirley Welch couldn't join us for the tree cutting, we offered to use their Forest Service permit and cut one for them. When they arrived at our house for dinner, we couldn't wait to show them their Christmas tree. Everyone gathered around as we proudly held up the tree for inspection. It was the saddest, scraggliest pine tree we could find. They were stunned and silent. We didn't crack a smile. They thanked us, took it, and turned away. Only then did we pull out the tree we had carefully selected according to their specifications and receive genuine thanks.

The accomplices who have sustained me for almost four decades are those adventuresome, fun and sturdy women who comprise my hiking group – The Happy Hikers. We were a cohesive band that met early every Tuesday and hiked all day – and sometimes into the night – through rain, shine, or snow. On mountain trails all over Colorado, I experienced the wonders of the high country with friends who offered a unique blend of friendship and support; sharing their lives and their hearts with me and from whom I have learned the most about myself. Any gathering of today brings out the stories of yesterday: Celine on the mountainside dressed in black, wearing her golf shoes, and carrying an open umbrella – Vi who mothered us all and is famous for telling

a television interviewer that the most important item to pack in one's rucksack is a lunch – the roof snow avalanche that took Alice too early – Wendy's long legs leading the way until she came to a cliff – Marlene first to the top – Sheika far ahead going the wrong way, darling – Mary Jo who goes her own way – Lucette who drove up early from Denver to join us – Barbara who is always up for a hike –the Joans whose tales while walking made the climb easier, the miles shorter – Nancy who can always be counted on - Ann Margaret and her mother, Babs, who braved the coldest alpine lakes for a refreshing swim – me, who walked on air to cross the creek and flee a bear - and Flo who saw the humor in it all.

Horst and I divide our time now between Florida and Colorado. My son, Lexi, always calls as soon as we return to Vail each summer to check on our arrival. I always say the same thing to him, "I feel more like myself when I am in Colorado."

117

KK Cherry

My personal story begins when I first visited Vail with a former boyfriend in 1964, standing in the middle of a dirt road enjoying a brief conversation with Pete Seibert about his ambitious dream of creating a Vail that was the world's #1 ski resort. I believed him. Then in 1966, a friend set up six interviews for me, three in Vail and three in Aspen. I made it to only the first one. After a fortuitous chat with a charming and delightful Nancy Kindel, she phoned her husband to come meet me. I was hired! So, the saga began when I became "nanny" to five stair-step storybook children (ages 5,4,3,2, and 1 year). The first evening, dinner was served in their cathedral-ceilinged

"used-barn-wood-clad home, next door to the Christiania Lodge, which they built and owned. When I said I would eat in the kitchen, Ted Kindel turned to me and questioned dryly, "What the hell's the matter…do you think you are too good for us?" That was it! From then on, I was considered "family."

Ted Kindel was Vail's first mayor; he and Nancy, entertained lavishly and often…at least two cocktail parties per week, one with Christiania Lodge guests, and another for Vail's founders, including friends. My assignment was to answer the huge, hand-carved front door and take coats from the guests (attired in splendid mountain elegance) before being called into the festive party with, "And now you must meet our 'Mary Poppins'."

Summer arrived when Penny Lewis phoned me (her husband Chuck was Vail's marketing director and went on to found Copper Mountain) and asked if I would accompany their family on a drive to Mazatlan, Mexico for a few weeks. "With pleasure!" was my answer. Since she encouraged me to date while in Mexico, one evening I introduced my friend to them, "This is Manuel, he is a bullfighter."

On my return, I moved into Vail's Row Houses and found two jobs. During the day, I was apprentice to Brita Sjooman and learned to weave with raw flax, weeds and yarns naturally dyed with colors extrapolated from mountain wildflowers. Evenings, I acted as heroine in Vail's melodrama, and junior racing coach, George Rau, played the perfect hero.

While no early Vail jobs provided enough funds for distant travel, many guests had an international flair and brought the world to us. Besides, for me, there were the "ego trips."

Lelo Staub, of Switzerland, had recently married Vail's first ski school director Roger Staub. Vail's early promotional film director Roger Brown and his friend Barry Corbet (recently returned from America's first Everest Expedition) were working on a film featuring Lelo and Roger, based on Homer's "The Odyssey." It showed Roger skiing smoothly through perfect powder until he spotted Lelo, provocatively placed upon a rock, much like one of "The Odyssey's" sirens. Roger looked…then crashed and burned. Since Lelo was out of town and Roger Brown needed a substitute for some footage, he called to ask if I could fill in… he wanted me to take a drag from a cigarette, then blow a puff of smoke up into thin air. Apparently pleased with the performance, Roger Brown invited me to appear in each of his future films. Modeling then paid $50 plus a self-congratulatory "ego-trip". Another flattering opportunity came with French ski racer Jean Claude Killy. Warren Miller was the director and closed down Bridge Street with lights and cameras, then instructed Jean Claude to, "Walk slowly…exchange glances with KK… then open the double glass doors into Gorsuch." Cameras rolled, Jean Claude walked, then handed me his sunglasses…"CUT!" "GLANCES," enunciated Warren …"not GLASSES!"

Working with children was a passion, one where I had had a great deal of experience. So, with a dream combined with confidence, I became certified by the State of Colorado and opened Vail Day Camp. Enrollment filled quickly with the likes of all three of Marty Fritzlen's (Head) children, Johnny Buxman, and

Denise Hofler. Camp was a two-week session, daily from 9-5pm, with a graduation overnight up on Shrine Pass and a final puppet show for parents, "A Small World." Sessions cost $50. The greatest reward came from little Denise, the final day, "After I have learned from you, KK, I feel like every inch of mountain I step on is precious, I almost do not want to put my footprint upon it."

Capable and always sought-after Doris Bailey was Vail's convention manager. She asked that I be recreational director and take children of convention clients on mountain outings. Hours again were 9 -5 including lunch, cost was $5. Once, with an assorted age group, we were on the mountain cooking hot dogs and s'mores over a bonfire when it started to snow heavily. One bold seven-year-old stepped forth to beg, "Lady, I'll give you your five bucks back if you let me go home."

Winters found me employed as one of the "Golden Girls of Gorsuch." Acting in sales or display or modeling, we were believed to be wholesome, All-American ambassadors, tastefully attired in uniforms of bright red stretch ski jumpsuits, crisp, fresh white blouses, finished with a neck scarf of patriotic red, white and blue and paying proud tribute to our owners, former members of our US Olympic Ski Team. While some things change dramatically, other things never do. During those early days, before computers, sales were rung up on an antique brass cash register that delivered a stomach punch each time it opened, while a basic rule that still holds true today…no employee leaves the Gorsuch store without strict attention to straightening, immaculate effort at tidying up, every floor vacuumed, all fresh preparations for the next day. Such an esprit de corps we all shared. I smile to this day when I recall sweet, flushed-faced, Sara Garton, in Jean Claude Killy's dressing room when second-skin stretch pants were de rigueur. Sara was doing all she could to keep a straight face until finally she achieved success in zipping Jean Claude Killy into his tight blue ski pants.

Looking back at early Vail, I believe what I remember most were the inextricable bonds of friendship. We came to really know people… those who blurred the bounds of mere "friendship" because they were soul mates, kindred spirits, people who were here because they coveted mountain living and that rich and wonderful world outdoors beyond the confines of four walls. They had pioneer spirit and unbounded enthusiasm to explore a new, fresh frontier. The walk of life they came from mattered little. While some scrubbed floors to live here, some ran countries…but the single most vital fact that held us together was a sense of camaraderie, a strong sense of standing on common ground. We all adored Vail and wanted our response to it to be contagious.

ABOUT OTHER WOMEN OF VAIL:

In those early Vail days, there were many role models, quintessential women of early Vail. Certainly Nancy, "with the smiling eyes" Kindel, whose mere presence could captivate and transform an entire room, known for her contagious energy and enthusiasm for Vail… Bunny Langmaid, legendary and much like her to-be granddaughter, Kim, founder of "Walking Mountains"…beautiful and enchanting Blanche Hausermann (now Christy Hill) whose commanding sense of charm launched a multitude of early Vail loves - including husband Dick - and certainly a lady whose personal pioneer spirit contributed immensely to Vail's early mountain beginnings…Flo Steinberg, former nurse and spirited wife of our Dr. Steinberg…and someone whose moxie emulated a sense of women's liberation long before anyone ever heard the term…Ella Knox, whose passion for plants ignited within me a lifelong interest in edible native plants of the Rocky Mountains…Renie Gorsuch, whose unbound enthusiasm and fierce loyalty to the family and her own personal extraordinary work ethic, set an example that, while employed by her, taught me what I was made of…Penny Tweedy, a stately, strong lady for whom I used to babysit as she wrote for Smith College's magazine and an eloquent woman who followed her heart to witness the winnings of her race horses, "Riva Ridge" and Triple Crown winner "Secretariat"…sensational Sheika Gramshammer, whose welcome warmth and friendliness promises guests and locals alike, "Where there is Sheika, there is a party!"… Thelma Brittan, authentic as an old shoe, yet sophisticated and full of clear-eyed vision… ever so elegant, Elaine (White) Kelton, whose first cabin in East Vail had a windowsill that always held a wineglass full of wildflowers, and who thoughtfully handed me her entire box of maternity clothes when my former husband and I decided to start a family…resourceful and clever, Camille Bishop, who entertained nearly every evening, creating memorable meals from nearly nothing (since Minturn's market had little more than dried beans and potatoes, Vail's small deli carried escargots and artichoke hearts but few basics, and Leadville was a scenic but very long drive)…Cathy Douglas, a warm and wise woman whose stamina allowed her to still ski race well into her eighties…Barbara Parker, a one woman worker-bee with an incredible ability to persevere in part of Vail's early beginnings, included the Post Office, located then, to what is now part of Gorsuch, and whose avid interest in wild mushrooms influenced me to study them, then go off into our mountains in search of these elusive creatures, every season…dedicated and devoted Betty Seibert, who with legendary Vail founder Pete, had three children whom she was determined to see well educated - thus, helped begin the Vail Mountain School… Marge Burdick, a lady of limitless grace and generosity whose charismatic warmth embraced you with every encounter, whether it be over a Sunday's Planter's Punch at her Red Lion restaurant, or simply sharing the splendor of watching the setting sun slip behind the mountain, she "walked in beauty," through to

the end. These are a handful of early Vail women whose examples left an indelible impression upon me…legends in their own time, rich with innate insight into possibilities and potential in Vail…all passionate, exuding quality, which was the foundation on which Vail itself was built, women I celebrated then and that I celebrate today.

Laurie McBride

Johnny and Laurie Mack McBride arrived in Vail the evening of January 6,1964. It was very snowy when we tried to find Rod Slifer, who had been entrusted with the key to the cabin Johnny had built by himself in Bighorn. He had bought the land from Jay Utter in 1963 when he was working for Owens-Corning Fiberglass, and he'd built his cabin, after resigning from being a salesman. Unable to locate Rod, we ended up sleeping on the floor of Bill and Gretta Whiteford's condo, my welcome to Vail as a newlywed.

I grew up in Pasadena, California, went to the Ethel Walker School in Connecticut, and then to Stanford, a family tradition starting with my grandmother, Class of 1896. After college, I worked on the Strang Ranch in Carbondale while Johnny was building that cabin in Vail. Then I went to New York City to work as a teaching assistant. Johnny finally arrived and saved me from the Big Apple. We married after he nonchalantly presented me with a 9-foot-tall camel; Johnny dressed as Lawrence of Arabia, at the bridal dinner. We returned the camel to Jungleland Inc. in Hollywood and flew to Denver to start our new life in a resort that was not yet on the map.

How I loved our cabin in the woods and my dog, Angus, a runt German shepherd that loved to jump in the air chasing butterflies. Johnny arranged for me to work with Joan Carnie in her day care center while he taught skiing. I had grown up playing lots of tennis, so I went into Johnny's skiing class that consisted mostly of Fitzhugh and Eileen Scott's friends. We called the Scotts "Ti" and "Unc." After one particularly heavy snowfall, I almost decapitated an older gentleman with my pole while falling and was asked not to return.

By this time, I was pregnant, skiing alone with Angus the dog, who sat on the chairlift next to me. I knew I was improving when I could ski faster than Angus could run and alone, I was not a liability to anyone. We were settling into our cabin on a very snowy blowing night. Suddenly, we were kidnapped with Angus, put in the back of John Donovan's truck, and driven freezing to the Red Lion Inn, where we had to buy drinks for everyone. This was apparently Donovan's Revelry Special, and now we were officially initiated into Vail.

Summer of '64, John and George Shaw formed a partnership and built Eileen Kaiser's house and a few other construction jobs. Later, I became Johnny's secretary while he was trying to obtain a loan to build the Clock Tower Building. Three months later, thinking the loan-interest notification was a bill, I blithely paid it off in full with next to nothing in our account. I was fired immediately [to my delight} while Johnny had to renegotiate the loan.

One starry night, we went up the mountain to help Bill Whiteford build his ice bar that VA was opposed to. We thought we were so clever. We were young and invigorated by making our own rules. Johnny and I ran a movie house in the Vail Village Inn cafeteria, renting 16-mm movies and showing them for $1 on weekends. Everyone was trying any kind of new business to make a few bucks.

John McBride Jr {Johno} was born December

18,1964, the same day as Pepi's opening. He was born in Pasadena, California, because there was no hospital in Vail. Summer of '65, Johnny built the Clock Tower Building, and then that Christmas the whole McBride clan arrived for Christmas. I love to cook, so I did the whole dinner and served it up in our cabin on a Ping-Pong table. My mother had sent a huge paper cloth and napkins for the event. We

were 18 total. A perfect day, plenty of snow, and a lovely sleigh ride was enjoyed by all.

It was a very small community, a population of about 50. There was a feeling of excitement in the air as we were on uncharted territory, pioneers of a new ski era. The Scotts were great friends. We put on a 4th of July party with everyone, all ages, serving a 1-2-3 rum punch. There was a treasure hunt, golf competition, and rubber rafting to town. Amazingly, we all survived. What fond memories that party brings back. Ellie Caulkins and George were great pals. Ellie and I had our first-born boys at exactly the same time. We thought we were originals. Our daughter Kate was born June 30, 1966. I remember Zane Hoyt's son being the best babysitter ever. Johnny was building the post office on the land next to the Clock Tower at that time.

We received an offer on our cabin that we could not refuse, so we sold it, planning on moving into the post office apartment building. "Ti" and "Unc" Scott let us stay in their

house on Mill Creek Circle until the apartment was completed. Bill Janss came by for lunch in August and offered Johnny a job developing the commercial core of a new town and ski area called Snowmass next to Aspen that he was planning. Unsure of our future, Johnny accepted the offer, as it was too good to pass up. We sadly packed up and moved to Aspen in September of 1966 with Johno and Kate, Angus the dog, and Alice the cat.

What a busy two years and so many wonderful friends - Heather and Rod Slifer, Gerry and Elaine White who lived up the road from us, Pepi and Sheika, Scotts, Whitefords, Slevins, Schuberts, Kendalls, Gorsuch, and Johnsons, Roger Brown, all the shopkeepers, Ella Knox, Connie Meade, and many more. All I can say is, THANKYOU THANKYOU for the memory trip we had together and all the fun adventures we shared, the mistakes, the naughtiness, and the great feeling of camaraderie. It changed and redirected our lives.

123

LILLIAN MILLER ROSS

I lived in Vail from 1965 to 1968 and worked as Bob Parker's assistant in the Vail Associates marketing department in Vail Village. I loved Vail in those early years. Everybody knew everybody. Vail gave me my happiest years.

Elaine speaking: Lillian Ross was an "original," and she worked with us all. Most notable were her roles with the Vail Players and in the melodramas written by Gregory Beresford Skeffington a.k.a. John Dobson, Mayor of Vail.

The Vail Players were formed by Vail's mayor from 1968-77, Gregory Beresford Skeffington aka John Dobson in order to promote cultural diversity, keep locals in the bars, and give Vail's three summer tourists something to do. These melodramas showcased enormous local talents that otherwise would have won Oscars in Hollywood. The troupe included Lillian Ross the frustrated spinster, George Ward the bad guy, Merv Lapin the handsome hero, L. Tracy the hussy, Wendy Bartel the naive heroine, Rod Shelsta the foil, Joan Garton the breasts, and Brooke Franzgen the dilettante. Skeffington was assisted by his beautiful wife and concert pianist, Cissy, in bringing a new dimension to the affairs.

The melodramas continued for 10 years until the rights were purchased by Steven Spielberg leaving the cast destitute.

— MERV LAPIN

LINDA FAAS

While I had skied in Vail earlier, I moved there in the summer of 1970 to work at La Cave. It was quite an adventure working with Markus Gatter, Freddie Obadia, and Karl Wegman, as well as spending time visiting with La Cave owner Joan Cramerus.

My two roommates, Linda Gange (Adkins) and Sue Caldwell (Tennant), and I enjoyed our summer jobs so much that we all resigned our teaching jobs in Denver to stay in Vail. All of us lived there several years. Besides La Cave, I worked at Los Amigos, Pistachio's, and Guido's Pizza.

We moved away but have returned to Vail to ski and spend time in the summer enjoying the mountains that brought all of us to that beautiful spot.

I played only a small part in Vail, but it certainly played a big part in my life.

LINDA GUNDELL JONES

The call of skiing and living in the mountains is what pulled me to seek my new job teaching in the Eagle Valley. I was offered a position at Battle Mountain Jr. Sr. High School in Maloit Park. My dad, Herbert Gundell, was an officer in the 10th Mountain ski division at Camp Hale, and my mother met him at a WSO dance at Camp Hale. They married before my dad was shipped out; he had been a ski instructor and climber at Camp Hale.

I moved to Vail and offered the first boys' Home Economics class there and enjoyed it immensely. I also was asked to coach the girls' ski team. In 1969, girls raced in GS, Slalom and cross-country; boys raced in the same events and also had to participate in ski jumping. We built a ski jump near the football field at school, practiced there, and then went over to Leadville to get a better experience. I was the pep club and sophomore class sponsor. The zinc mine was still running in Gilman, and teachers lived in Gilman and in teacher housing in Maloit Park. They were a close group of young people, and we had many great experiences in the '60s.

Then I met Steve Jones, and we married. Vail is celebrating 50 years in 2012, and we are celebrating 40 years of marriage. We spent a year in New Mexico, taking our first son, and then returned to the Eagle Valley. Steve worked for Adam's Rib Ranch, and I substituted at the new Battle Mountain High School, primarily for Ed Swinford who taught business classes.

Another passion was participating on the Eagle County Fair Board. I was a 4-Her all of my growing up life and feel 4-H for my children and me was a wonderful learning experience.

When I was single, I went to Donovan's and other local nightspots. I worked part-time as a waitress and La Cave as a hostess. In my married life, one event Steve and I hosted every year for 10 years was a lamb roast that Chris Jouflas and his staff used to help us put on in the Greek tradition. President Jerry and Betty Ford used to visit us for this event, and we had a long list of who's who that would participate and come to our Brush Creek home south of the town of Eagle.

Skiing, rodeoing, and riding horses are the main activities we participate in.

I had no expectations of what Vail might be like, but what I found among the locals was a place I could belong and call my home. One of my roommates when I first moved to Vail was Carol Fitzsimmons. There were four of us living in the grey and white condominiums, and we decided to do a Thanksgiving Potluck for all of us who had jobs and could not go home for Thanksgiving. Carol and I put that party on for years, and we all looked forward to it.

I am now part of the history of Vail and Eagle Valley, and it feels a little different, but I love living in this valley. We built my dream log cabin and love the home and its location. It is hard to honor all the changes in Vail itself, but we know so many people and always feel good when we see them and renew friendships.

LOIS BERNSTEIN

I taught elementary school in Denver, Colorado from 1963-1966 after earning a Bachelor of Education from Southern Illinois University. I headed to Europe and worked as a Tour Director for the Armed Forces Recreation Services in Garmisch, Germany from 1966-1968.

After working in recreation services for three years, I knew my passion for the outdoors and sports. Because I'd lived in Denver, the mountains were an obvious choice for me. In the fall of 1968, someone suggested I come to Vail.

I was employed by the Vail Resort Association as first a reservationist and then as a convention coordinator. I worked for Doris Bailey, Brooke Franzgen, and later Dale McCall.

I met my husband, Stan Bernstein, in November of 1968, and we were married in July 1969. Our wedding took place on the Mid

Vail deck with the reception at the old Gold Peak House. Our daughters soon began arriving: Meggen in 1970, then Carrie, and Amy. We built the fourth house in the Vail das Schone area on Davos Trail and still own it.

The friends we made back in the late 1960s are among our favorite people.

Stanley and I still love to ski. Our daughters were all born in Vail and have a special attachment to it as a result. We spend the holidays in our home in Vail. When I came to Vail, I just hoped for a continuation of my lifestyle in Garmisch, Germany. With time, I got married, had children and got involved with their activities. It's a special place, and we enjoy our times now as much as the first winter we were there.

Lorraine Higbie

Peter and Betty Seibert introduced me to Vail Mountain on a camping trip. We spent a lot of time camping in the valley that summer. We spent time on Gore Creek with Fitz and Eileen Scott, fishing for our dinner and listening to the traffic on Highway 6. We worried that the noise would be a deterent to Vail's development.

Our early skiing was not recreational; it was showing prospective investors the beauty of the mountain. There were no groomed trails, and the uphill transportation by snow cat was very unreliable.

Gretta Parks and I started the Gondola Boutique, a unique store that sold après-ski clothing and gifts. It was steps from the original gondola. We ran a beauty parlor as well; our hairdressers were young Austrians who would drive up from Denver, work for a half-day and ski the other half. At the time, there were only two other stores in town: Vail Blanche owned by Blanche Hauserman and The Rucksack owned by Ottie Kuehn. Larry Burdick's Red Lion Inn was close by on Bridge Street, where it remains today, and the kitchen would send over our lunches when we became too busy to leave the shop.

Raising a family of five children in Denver and commuting to Vail became impractical, so eventually I sold my share of the business to Gretta. Vail became a weekend vacation home for our family and for the friends we had introduced to the mountain.

127

Loyette Goodell

What I remember of the dust bowl and the depression was that my mother developed rheumatoid arthritis and it led us to Vail. For her health, my folks heard about the springs in Glenwood Springs. So, the summer I was six we piled into our old Model T Ford and headed west, driving over Independence Pass. It kept getting greener and greener. I remember the snowcapped peaks, wildflowers, and aspen trees. It was beautiful with creeks gushing down the side of the hill. We came to a spring of cold, clear water. "This is heaven," I thought. We ended up in Glenwood Springs to spend the glorious days of summer, and it would eventually lead me to Vail.

Dad bought a place west of Glenwood with a hot springs on it where he could farm, and that's where I grew up. I was learning to ski in Glenwood Springs, but I was a lousy skier. In Aspen, I got a job at the Jerome Hotel as a waitress and met my husband ski bumming in Aspen in 1950. After marrying, we were in Denver and read about an accounting job in Vail. My first job was herding teenagers in The Lodge at Vail during spring break. The Lodge established a canteen in the cafeteria, and it gave the kids a place to stay out of trouble.

Our son, Bill, was Vail's first high school student. I was immediately morphed into the clerical/secretarial/bookkeeping thing. It was a lonely summer in our office in The Lodge. It was like a tomb and our biggest excitement was to go and get a hamburger. We were working long hours, Hauserman was building his building, and we moved into it in the fall. We started putting together a real organization. The biggest difficulty was finding people to staff clerical positions. I shuffled as secretary for Pete and Dick Boar; this expanded my knowledge. Dick helped ride herd on Peter; somebody had to ride herd on him. Peter was wonderful; I loved him. He would go off and do his trips; we had to account for his expenses, so I had to go through his pockets for receipts. We had a payroll clerk who housed with ski patrol and got into the habit of joining their ramblings at night. John often had to go get him, give him coffee, and get him to do payroll.

People came because of the skiing, but office jobs didn't let you ski much. The Mountain Man Mystique, I called it. Guys that worked on the mountain were like gods, could set their hours, and had a great deal of freedom. Mountain guys got free passes for themselves and their families; other employees had to buy them. I've got to tell you that those first four years, those of us who had the responsibility to keep the place going financially had to be there seven days a week. We ended up doing just about everything imaginable to keep it together. We also helped The Lodge keep their clerical staff trained and working. The opportunity was there, and I'm the kind of person who will jump in and learn how to do it. One summer, they signed up a couple tiny groups. We had a cook, no bartenders or maids, so we pitched in. I waited tables. We needed to get that revenue, year after year.

We lived in an apartment in the Rucksack. Ottie and Susie Kuehn had put this little apartment together behind the drugstore, and we lived there for six months; then, in the lower part of the Tweedy house, and then we bought land in West Vail. We had a house finally in 1965. No P.O. No bank. For the bank issue, we had to find somebody who was trustworthy, send them by car to Eagle, and hope the roads were okay. Once, she got to the Gashouse in Edwards, something went wrong with the car, she put the stash behind the car seat, locked it, went in, and called the office to send someone down. Banking was a challenge at first. Claire Elliott was the policeman. He came in one day and said he needed a badge. He showed us this catalog with badges, "Police Chief." To buy the badge, you had to buy 100 of them, which we did. He was funny; he'd come in and say,

"I heard voices in The Lodge." He came in some mornings and asked, "Got anything to report?" Don Allman was also concerned about security; he was head of the ski patrol. We had a little kiosk for ticket sales, run by Rixie Flewelling. The ticket office sat out where Seibert Circle is now, and Don felt it posed a security risk. I could see it from my window; Don said that we needed to put in an alarm system. Sellers could hit a button with their shoe that would set off a buzzer under my desk, and I could look to see what was happening; I was supposed to call the top of the mountain and give them a code number, and they would know that a robbery was taking place at the ticket office. They could get the sheriff by radio. During one spring break, there were lots of people, and the buzzer went off. I was breathless, my hand shook as I dialed, and gave the code number. "We have a robbery in progress," I said. The reply, "What am I supposed to do?" "I think you're supposed to call the sheriff." Meanwhile, John walked outside and over to the ticket office, went inside, and said, "What are you guys doing?" Nothing had happened. The system did not quite work!

We became a close-knit group – Daphne, Betty - we got together for meals; that was our social life. We met at the Red Lion, The Lodge, people's houses; it was pretty casual. We were solving problems each day together. The year of the Johnson and Goldwater election, we wanted to see the returns. Slevins, Staufers, and we went to Leadville to spend the night and watch because they had TV. I remember backless benches at the movie theater in Minturn. Somebody had a projector, so we brought in foreign films the second summer. Blanche and Bunny had great things in their store, but you couldn't buy underwear up here. We went to Gaynor Miller's Night Latch to do laundry and dragged stuff back in baskets, no dryer. We had to be flexible to get things done. We were never sick, fortunately. Son Bill worked on lifts, a cable got caught around his thumb, and he needed to be taken to Denver.

I recall the night the boy was lost in 1963. Fortunately, it was spring and not a very cold night. He made a nest for himself under a spruce tree and slept till morning. It was a beautiful night; they skied yelling for him with no reply. The women managed the phones and made sandwiches and hot chocolate - Daphne, Barbara Parker, Betty Seibert, and the clerical staff.

One day, a young skier came and didn't have enough money for a ticket; he asked to barter a bottle of peach brandy, John said sure, and gave him a ticket, then wrote up the ticket for the day. There was always the human factor. I remember one story: Betty was in the office one day, and one of the partners came in with his wife. The wife talked about travelling always with her special pillow and necessities. Betty replied, "I always travel with my own bottle of Scotch." Betty put on great roast beef dinners and fixed a pitcher of martinis for one of my birthdays; it was really special. Beaver Dam Road didn't get plowed much, so to go home John and Bill stood on the car's back bumper. I would drive, gun it like hell, and go whipping up the hill. One story: Betty had to get into the trunk of the car one time so they could get over a pass; I don't know if that's true; supposedly, they used her as weight.

Ann Taylor and Blanche would put together these really unusual ski outfits and parade back and forth in front of our office. One time, Ann wore a Greek tutu she'd made herself; she was a clothing designer. There was Midnight Lumber and Supply. We wanted to put a fire hood in our living room and needed bricks and mentioned it to Art Kelton. One day soon after, this pile of used bricks showed up at our house, I don't know where he got them.

We could see the Gore Range from our office. Around 3:30 in December or January the sky would start to turn pink, and Peter would come out of his office and say it was "fringe benefit" time. Everyone had to crowd around the window to see it. At that time of day in December, I often think of Peter's fringe benefit. I was imprinted by this thing that Vail is.

LYNNE LANGMAID

The year was 1969. My husband at the time (Charlie Langmaid), daughter Kim, and I had just settled into a house in Marblehead, Massachusetts. No sooner had we done that than we received an opportunity for him to be involved in Vail Ski Rentals (started by his father, Joe, and Dick Hauserman). Without giving it a second thought, and even though I was pregnant at the time, we made the decision to move. We packed our bags, sold the house in Marblehead, and headed to our new life in Vail. We rented an apartment in the old Tweedy house on Mill Creek Circle. It could not have been a better location.

Our second child, Elissa, was born in Denver in early December. Vail did not have a hospital then nor was there an I-70, so my arrival in Denver before the baby's due date was a must. There seemed to be many other little ones born that year, making it easy to trade babysitting with other mothers, and this enabled us to enjoy the skiing. Although I loved living in Marblehead, it was a nice change to have the ski slopes and hiking trails in our backyard.

The next venture was building a house on Beaver Dam Road. Once settled in, it was like living in the woods with huge spruce trees, our own little pond, and a small stream. It was such a lovely location. In amongst the trees and pond, there was room for a small vegetable garden, which was a must for me. Although gardening at altitude was a challenge, it was most rewarding. To further my passion for gardening, we installed a small greenhouse that faced south just off the living room. I took the idea from my mother-in-law Bunny, who lived down the street.

My first employment in Vail was at Arthur Bishop and Co., then located in Crossroads but soon to relocate to the Mill Creek Court Building. It was a fun job in property management and real estate. After many years working there, I moved on to sales at the Squash Blossom, owned by John and Patti Cogswell. It was such an interesting and rewarding job. I had many wonderful customers and contacts, and my most fun sale was to the Aga Khan's wife. Recalling those educational trips to New Mexico to buy the Squash Blossom jewelry brings back such good memories.

131

MARCIA REED

Interestingly enough, I'm a fourth generation Coloradan from Colorado Springs. Unlike most of the early people to Vail, I did not grow up skiing. For medical reasons, I was packed off to ballet class at the age of four, continued ballet all of my life, and studied music seriously. It was during college that I both met my husband and learned to ski. On graduating from Colorado College armed with a degree in history, I began teaching and skiing. Bill and I skied Vail many times when it opened in 1962. It quickly became our favorite place to ski.

It was in ballet class that I heard that they were looking for ski instructors at a new area that the ski museum now calls a "ghost area," Holiday Hills. We went to yet another "ghost area" on Pikes Peak, taught skiing, and became certified. Erich Windisch was one of our examiners. We owned a part interest in the area, which led to our meeting Vail Ski School Director Jerry Muth at a ski school directors' conference. He invited us to come to Vail and try out. Both Jerry and Erich were examining and hired us to teach weekends. We began traveling from the Springs every weekend. Those were wonderful years spent teaching

skiing and at nights enjoying ski movies at The Slope or drinks around the big fireplace downstairs at the Clock Tower.

An important part of our story is that trip every weekend. Traveling from the Springs up Ute Pass and through South Park where there always seemed to be a sideways blizzard and over Hoosier Pass, still a dirt road at the time, through tiny Breckenridge and then through exactly where Dillon Reservoir is now and over Vail Pass, was often an adventure in itself. One time, I drove over Hoosier Pass and arrived in Fairplay to find that the road had been closed but no signs were up. Why, back then even the weekend people had to be seriously dedicated to the sport and to Vail to make that drive every weekend. We always stayed at the Avon Country Store, which housed a motel, grocery store, and the Avon Post Office. Eventually, we bought a big trailer and put it in a Mobile Home Park located where the Avon Center is now. We began buying and selling property until we could afford a home here.

Meanwhile, Bill was transferred to Boulder and I got a job teaching history there. I must say that if skiing and teaching skiing became

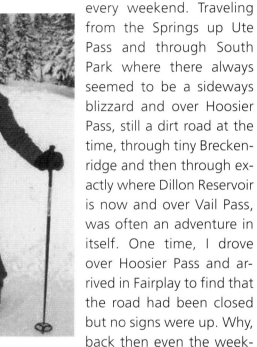

our passion, for me an even greater passion has always been history, so I couldn't give that up. Bill eventually started teaching skiing full-time, but I continued to teach part-time. I loved almost every minute of it. Like many others, I remember wearing the yellow parkas the women wore then. I also remem-ber that the women taught the little kids, and the men taught the adults.

Elaine speaking: Marcia and many others' stories were the core of Vail. I'm delighted she jumped in with her memories.

MARCIA SAGE

We moved from Denver into a condo-minium at Sandstone 70 in 1968 with our three-year-old son, a German shepherd, and a turtle. David's New Jersey family and my Wyoming relatives lovingly and politely thought we might be losing our minds to leave the security of a banking position, new home, and growing metropolis for the wilds of the Rocky Mountains and a place of which they had never heard..."Vail, where?" "You'll be back," some of our city friends told us while others sadly said, "I wish we had the nerve to do what you're doing." We found the valley already peopled by entrepreneurial Europeans, Vail Associates staff, energetic transplants from all over the US and adventurous ski-bum types - willing to take a chance on the success of the area or who just wanted to be there.

Sandstone 70 was on the western outskirts of town and provided housing for an eclectic population. The Gartons lived down the row and would sit on their back deck with beers and rifles shooting at an old barn across the creek on the empty hillside. I reminded them that kids were playing in the area. "Oh, yes," they said, and the firing stopped. They were great outdoorsmen and hunters. They would kill a deer, dress it out, and hang it on their back deck to age. One fall the neighborhood dogs attacked a carcass and pulled it down, scattering bones and meat everywhere.

Late another night, there was a huge ruckus down the way at bachelor-at-the-time Steve Boyd's condo. His very recently evicted (earlier that night) ex-roommate had returned to find his belongings removed from their shared abode and "placed" out on the lawn. He challenged Steve loudly several times and banged on the door. The door opened, a short fight ensued, ended with a loud smack. The man's girlfriend raced from their parked car, helped her man off the ground and back to their car, and they sped away. Another neighbor had shared custody of his young daughter. He

133

would get her to sleep some nights and head for a bar in town, relying on Vail's safety and help from his neighbors if there were problems. Occasionally, she would awaken crying, and we would rescue her. He was actually not a bad man, I think, just inexperienced and a bit clueless. When he noticed my new garden out front he came over to enlist my advice, telling me his potted marijuana plants were looking puny. I went inside, removed the label from an oven cleaner can, brought it out, and told him to give each plant a good spritz.

Bill and Rouene Brown lived across the dirt street separating our two rows of buildings. In the summer, Rouene would come home from work on her lunch hour, quickly don a bathing suit and take her lunch, a cold drink, and a good book outside for a fast sunbath in her small deck lounger. Many days, little Dave Jr, who was about four at the time, would take advantage of a good situation, squeeze in next to her, and engage in earnest conversation until Rouene went back to work.

David's brother, Dudley Holmes, came to live with us while establishing himself as an excavation contractor. He dug foundations and pipelines for many of Vail's early builders and created a long and successful career. There were some bumps along the way, however. Early on, he borrowed our small Jeep to go up Red Sandstone Road and fell trees for firewood. He returned that evening with the cloth top of the Jeep caved in, shredded, and completely ruined. More trouble with trees came later when he was dynamiting boulders out of Evi Nott's new lot in preparation for her planned home. That particular explosive process was somewhat new to Dud, got away from him a little, he did some pretty good rock shrapnel damage, and blew the leaves off many of her nice aspens. We encouraged him to drive his backhoe in Vail's popular 4th of July parade with a big sign naming his company and displaying the motto, "Your Sewage is my Bread and Butter." He declined. Dudley was involved with accountant, George Crowder, and many others in one of Vail's best attended bar fights at the VVI, where many of the town's working people gathered at day's end. He also gained a reputation as a good pool player after taking on and showing up all comers one year at the Slifer and Co. end-of-year party at Reno's Cafe in Red Cliff. Designated drivers were highly prized for the winding way back to Vail.

So many stories, so little time.

MARCIE MERRELL OLSON

I came to Vail in 1969 planning to ski every day, find a job that would allow me to do that, and make enough money to pay rent, eat, and have fun. My first job was working for Bud and Gretta Parks at the Gondola Boutique, later known as the Gondola Ski Shop. I planned to be here one ski season then get on with my life elsewhere, but I never left the Vail Valley. The reason I didn't leave was because I was run into while skiing the last day of the season and suffered a spiral leg fracture. I wound up with a full-length leg cast and on crutches for five months and knew I would never find a job anywhere other than where I had been working at the Gondola Ski Shop. I couldn't even pack up my belongings to move as I lived in East Vail at the "Gingerbread House," which had a spiral staircase that wound up two flights to my apartment. I stayed that first summer and then knew I would be here a long time. I was hooked on the lifestyle and the people that made living here so exciting – every day was a new adventure.

I loved skiing, summer camping trips, jeeping, hiking and exploring the areas right out our back door, and the people I have worked with. They are among my closest friends. I had many jobs and sometimes four at a time to make ends meet. Retail, merchandise buying at the Ski Trade shows, working for Vail Jeep Guides, selling popcorn at the movie theater, golf course reservationist, and babysitting for the Whites and the Staufers.

I married Tim Olson, and we have two sons, Teig and Turi. One huge memory that stands out was becoming the first married Ms. Vail. It was lots of fun representing and being able to promote Vail as a year-round resort. Vail was first known only as a winter ski area, and not many knew how great the summers could be.

I now have a lifetime ski pass and time to ski, something I never would have figured could happen when I moved here in 1969. I look back, and there is nothing I would change. I feel fortunate to have led an exciting and fulfilling life. Memories of my first days in Vail will always be a big part of why I am here today.

MARGE BURDICK

Marge Burdick was born southwest of Ft. Worth, Texas in 1919. She was an only child and part of a very loving home. When Marge was growing up, there were plenty of challenges and few resources. From the Ft. Worth area, she moved with her family to San Antonio. Her mother died of leukemia when Marge was 13. Her father passed away from heart disease four years later, so at 17, Marge had no immediate family. She headed to college at Southern Methodist University in Dallas, after being voted, to no surprise of anyone who knew Marge at any age, "The Most Beautiful Girl of Breckenridge, Texas." She wasn't able to complete her college education when the funds received after her parents' deaths ran out. As her son, Bill Walsh, says, "She always had a series of Plan Bs."

Marge met a dashing fighter pilot, Donald Bennett, and married him in 1939. Their only child, Donald Junior, was born in 1943. In 1944, she received the telegram no young wife wants to receive: her husband had been shot down flying back from England. She met Bill Walsh shortly after the war. They married and moved back to Bill's hometown, Kalamazoo, Michigan, where he had a wholesale grocery store. They had three children together - Susan, Bill, and Tad. Walsh was prominent in Kalamazoo, but Marge felt like a fish out of water. She had no one to turn to other than his friends. They divorced in 1960, and Marge was on her own, this time with four children.

Susan Lynch, her daughter, reminisces, "Marge was always ahead of her time. She understood healthy food. We never had dessert, and she would slide things by us. She'd say, 'Here, honey, I'm going to make you a banana split.' Then she'd split a banana in two and fill it with a mound of cottage cheese."

At that point, Marge had it put in her head that she would lose whomever she loved. She hadn't yet become a part of Vail. Marge met Larry Burdick in Kalamazoo in the summer of 1962 where they were fixed up at a party. The romance was quick, and the children were happy to have Larry in their lives; he was quite the opposite of their father. Bill Walsh, Jr., recalls an evening when they were watching slide shows that Larry had brought of the beginnings of Vail, and his sister whispered to him, "Bill, I think things might just turn around for us."

Turn around, they did. Larry, it would seem, was a walking party. He asked her to move to Vail, and though she was unsure of the mountains (and more cold), she was very excited to go to a new place with a happy guy. "It was an adventure," said Marge. "I was always up for a new adventure."

Larry had already invested in Vail and was building the Red Lion restaurant. He had to put something on the land, not just invest in real estate. That was the rule: if you buy, you build. He decided to open a stube or a bar in the style of Austria, where he had just visited. Colorado liquor laws, however, said that if you served booze, you had to serve food. So, he decided to open a restaurant. "Larry had the idea of having a bar, and discovered that to have a liquor license, food must be served. So, I found myself in the restaurant business," Marge said. Larry had three boys of his own. He had learned about Vail from his cousin, Gretta Parks, who was married to Bill Whiteford, an original Vail founder. Larry and Gretta grew up on the same street, and their fathers were twins. He left for Vail, then came back with stories of the beautiful, unspoiled Vail valley, and the excitement of being part of the new venture. He brought Marge to Vail to encourage her to move there.

In the business, Marge was a great help. She'd always enjoyed dining out, and Marge knew what she wanted. She hired people from University of Denver's hospitality department, generally new graduates. In the early days, the restaurant made almost no money at all. Fortunately, losing money was not an issue because Larry came to town with a nest egg, so they didn't feel under a strain. The Red Lion never closed, not even in off-season. The ski patrol took over the downstairs, called the Lion's Den. Folks would be out drinking beer when someone would come injured off the hill, and the joke would be that they should just give them a drink. "I loved it from the first moment," said Marge. They moved into the apartments above. Marge had a lot of input into the menu. She wanted to serve Mexican food and Texas-style barbecue, still on the menu today. "I didn't know anything about the business," she said, "but at those times, you learned by trial and error."

In her early 40s, Marge was one of the "moms" in town, older and more experienced. "Oh, we all helped raise everyone," she said. "We pitched in and helped with everyone else's children." Marge took Sheika Gramshammer under her wing and went to Aspen for Sheika and Pepi's wedding. The two women became very close, and Sheika referred to her as "Tante Marge." Vail was nothing but green hills and plans and possibilities for her. "Marge and Larry were like Judy Garland and Mickey Rooney," says her daughter. "It was, 'Let's build a city.' She wasn't a winter person, but once she got there, the spirit of Vail was in her heart."

Marge didn't have trepidation about much, but she was one of the only people to arrive in Vail at that time who didn't know how to ski, while Larry had skied for many years. She was surprised that skiing filled such a big place in people's lives in Colorado. After all, what's a Texas girl doing on top of a mountain? "We had so much fun in those early days," she reminisced. "I was one of the few who didn't know anything about skiing. So, Pepi took me under his wing and taught me how. It was such a sweet, wonderful thing to do. I remember him following behind me and whacking my legs with his ski pole. He'd keep shouting, 'Steady locks, steady locks.' The more he said it, the more nervous I got. I had no idea what he was trying to tell me. At the bottom, I finally asked him what he meant. He said, 'Marge, don't be serious. Stay relaxed.'"

"She didn't love skiing as much as us," says Susan. "She liked après ski better." Marge was a social leader and loved people, having a good time, and getting to know everyone as a friend. Marge shared some mountain memories, "We would meet in Mid Vail, which wasn't much of anything. We'd bring up picnic food on the gondola and have fantastic lunches, drinking wine, eating cheese, visiting. Eventually we'd all ski down or download on the gondola depending on how much we'd had to drink." Vail was the first time she had friends that she made on her own. She'd been so busy struggling to raise four children, she hadn't had time to make friends or be part of a community. Both Susan and Bill remember Larry and Marge driving all the way to Steamboat Springs every weekend where the kids went to school. At the time, they took it for granted, though now they realize that was a hardship, but for Marge, it was always about family. The drive was nothing to her; she wanted to be around her children as often as she could.

"I'd come home from school, and Mom had these tea parties where she'd put out tea and sandwiches. The tea would always have rum served beside it," Susan recalls. "I was enchanted."

Marge's two great loves were her faith and the arts, particularly music. She was raised in a very religious family and wasn't allowed to dance. Marge had "happy feet" and loved to dance, and she wanted to love God and be a good Christian. If you could be a good Christian and dance, too, that was a good thing. The Catholic Church, St. Patrick's, was located in Minturn. Early on, partially due to Marge, services were held in Vail at the Casino Building. It was one of the few buildings large enough to hold religious services, and the bar wouldn't be cleared out until three in the morning. The first mass was held at six am. "Often, we'd be cleaning up the bar right before the service," said Marge. "More than once we kicked out people who had slept on the bar." For her, there was no incongruence in having the bar double as a church. God, she believed, looked out for everyone and was certainly up for fun, too. Although her faith was the most important thing to her, she always had a sense of humor. It was no surprise, though, when the Interfaith Chapel became a reality, Marge was first in line to volunteer.

— CWP

MARGIE GALLINA HANSEN

I was working toward an MBA in finance until I saw "the ad" for a job in Vail. I had grown up in the Denver suburbs, first attending the University of Oregon, then transferring to the University of Denver, for my MSBA in Economics.

I had skied as a teenager and, while attending DU, I worked and skied three days a week in Winter Park. We heard about a new ski resort called Vail, and everyone wondered if they would make it. In January of 1967, I saw Charlie Gersbach's tiny ad for an assistant at Manor Vail, drove up to check it out, got the job, quit school, and loaded all my earthly belongs in my VW Beetle. I never looked back.

I worked as Charlie's assistant selling condos, then became the youngest female bank officer in Colorado. I was the first woman real estate broker in the valley; co-owned a general contracting business with my husband, Vic Gallina; a retail business at trade shows and conventions; and also a bookkeeping business for small companies.

At 23, my Vail expectations were mostly tied to anticipating skiing experiences. As time went on, I found it wonderful and exciting to be part of a new town that was growing fast and attracting smart, energetic people with common interests. We were true pioneers in the beginning, and the environment allowed us to start with nothing, work hard, and end up having successful lives.

My social life has always been about outdoor activities and the people who have the same interests as I do. My sporting life is centered around my love of horses. I've owned, ridden, and trained horses since owning my first one at age six. Nothing makes me happier than riding the mountain trails of western Colorado. My second love has been skiing and the sense of freedom I get from it. I've also enjoyed a lot of backcountry backpacking and bird hunting with my husband, Vic, and friends over the years.

I always accompanied Vic on annual bird hunting trips to Canada. The cast of characters included such names as Donovan, Testwuide, various Gartons, Benway, Westbye,

139

and Dixon. Being the only woman, it was really an experience. Once they got over the fact that I wasn't there to cook for them, everything was fine. In 1970, Vic & I moved to Lake Creek south of Edwards, which most of my friends thought was off the face of the earth. Colorado is my home, and I've always loved the mountains and ski resorts. Vail is a special place, but when Vic died suddenly, I initially wanted to leave the memories. However, after two attempts at leaving, I realized this is where I belong. It's the place I love and where I fit.

MARIA ERB

After several ski vacations, my husband Erwin and I moved to Vail in 1968 from New York City. We had skied Vail in March of 1967 at the time the international races took place. We loved skiing and moved to Vail for health reasons. After a few weeks, we purchased a Chamonix Chalet condominium. I still own and live in it.

We had with us a radio alarm clock, a record player, and lots of records. There was no radio or TV in Vail at that time. We worked for Vail Associates at The Lodge at Vail that first winter and made a lot of new friends. Happily, some old friends arrived from New York and also settled here. In summer, we hiked and went on picnics.

Minturn had a small grocery store and Gamble's,

which provided some necessities. I remember going shopping in Denver and driving over Loveland Pass and along Highway 6. There was no worry about traffic back then. We always met neighbors or friends at the lift line. Springtime meant mud season, and I recall lots of construction going on everywhere during those early years. There were new hotels and homes – plus, construction of the Interfaith Chapel and the clinic.

In January 1970, we celebrated my husband's 50th birthday at the new Lancelot Restaurant and danced to the Bavarian Trio. I worked at Gorsuch for many years until we opened the Fountain Café and Restaurant, where we enjoyed serving the locals and having guests from all over the states and lots of foreign countries.

140

MARIA MINICK

I'm a Colorado Girl and grew up in Golden. I worked in the "basket room" and as a swim teaching assistant at the city's municipal pool from age 14. At 16, I taught swimming and was a lifeguard there for eight summers before coming to Vail as a college graduate and young newlywed in May 1968. That early work turned into a bit of a career here in Vail.

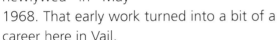

David and I were hoping to have some summer and winter fun in Vail before returning to grad school. In February of 1968, before coming to Vail in May, I wrote a letter to Vail Associates inquiring if there were many children in Vail and if there was a pool that might need a lifeguard and where I could conduct a swimming lesson program. Lillian Ross, of VA at that time, answered my letter and told me that there were some children and to write to The Lodge at Vail as they had the only pool large enough to need a lifeguard and hold swimming lessons. I immediately wrote to The Lodge but was very discouraged not to receive a reply.

When we arrived, I went to The Lodge and inquired at the front desk about a lifeguard position and whether they might permit a swimming lesson program at their pool. I was told, "Yes, but someone has already been hired." As luck would have it, Hermann Staufer (then assistant manager of The Lodge) overheard the conversation, came out from a nearby office, and asked my name. When I told him, he said, "You're the person we hired." Nobody had told me. That was funny and a huge relief; I had a job.

I thought it would be interesting for people to know that we had Red Cross swimming lessons early on in Vail. My swim program was affiliated with the American Red Cross to make their nationwide standards available here in Vail so that local and guests' kids could obtain their Red Cross certificate "at the next level."

Sandy Troxell had been the first to teach a handful of kids swimming lessons the previous summer, but she was leaving Vail. We taught a few classes together before she left. I finished the lessons for the summer and continued conducting my ever-growing Red Cross Swimming Lesson Program for the next 32 years. Of course, there were the Vail and Minturn kids, but families came from as far as Red Cliff and Gilman (people still lived in Gilman then), Eagle, Gypsum, McCoy, and beyond to bring their kids to swimming les-

141

sons. Later, the Ogilby/Garton Vail Intermountain Pool was the first "permanent" location for us (until its foundation started
sliding down the hill into Gore Creek, and the
pool was officially closed). Once again, we relied on the kindness of other Lodges' pools
and, finally, Bobby Warner and Jeannie and
Brian Hauff, allowed me to use the private
Homestead Court Club pool in Edwards.
Adult classes were fun, too, and Warren Pulis
was my first adult student in Vail.

Besides teaching swimming, I worked at
The Lodge's Bear Trap Bar in the late '60s as
a waitress for John Dobson's famous and
wonderfully funny Melodramas; next at Bud
and Gretta Parks' Gondola Ski Shop, followed by a job at Gorsuch. I loved winters,
summers, springs, and falls, outdoor life,
hard but satisfying work, and the good
friends I made. The Vail area became
"home," a place to raise a family and do
meaningful work. My kids, Sarah and Keith,
were both born in Glenwood Springs. There
were no maternity facilities in Vail at the time,

so they are not quite "native."

Back then, I was 23 and only wanted a fun,
yearlong adventure. Still here 44 years later.
Now, in spite of the loss of the wonderful
Wild West, rough-around-the-edges, small-
town-early-Vail where cowboys tied their
horses outside Donovan's Copper Bar, or
rode right in, where everyone worked hard
creating this new town and knew everyone
else, we now have what some might say is
"The Best of Both Worlds." There is still the
wild and rural beauty that surrounds us here,
and a variety of good schools and easy access
to amenities.

MARIE-CLAIRE MORITZ

Speaking from the heart…

Our original Vail restaurant, St. Moritz,
was very personal. Our next restaurant,
La Tour, was very popular for many years. I
was very proud of Walter and wrote that
book (Walter Anton Moritz) about him. My
story is what I'm telling you now. Because I
saw Walter work so hard, I didn't want him

to work for somebody else. Whatever he did,
he always did well. We were very popular,
but we were not well trained moneywise.
When you don't have any money, you don't
know what money is. Those were the best
times. We had everything we needed. My
cabin on Matterhorn was more than I ever
dreamed; it was like an old farm - I had two
chinchillas, one dog, one cat, birds, and three

kids. I always felt so blessed. I had everything – I took a vacation every year. For 35 years, we went to Europe every year. I liked to do it for him. He had that nostalgia for his country.

Coming from an orphanage, I called this place Camelot. Even the bad things were wonderful. You know, to me, every single thing was a bonus. People ask, what about the culture? Well, we all traded books. If I didn't have a book, I just asked somebody for one. Mrs. Knox was down the road, and she always wanted to convert me to Christian Science. We did not have TV. Sacha did not watch TV until he was eight. I had some records from Elvis Presley and the Beatles, and that's what my kids went to sleep with. I can't remember one thing that was bad. Even having to go to Denver to have the baby, Walter took twine, towels, and a big knife; he put this all in the back seat of the car. And he said, "If that kid comes, I know what to do." He was so pioneer. Misha came so fast at General Rose Hospital.

My drinking caused very difficult times when it caught up with me. My alcoholism went rampant very fast. It was a party time. Everybody comes on vacation. I sold the vino; that's how I made my money. Drinking well doesn't mean you don't abuse it - the minute I found that crutch I used it for every-

thing I didn't want to deal with. You know, Walter was not a good communicator; so when I was mad at him I drank. If I was tired, I drank. If I was sad, I drank. If I was happy, I drank. You don't take it because you are thirsty. I went to the Nu Gnu and drank. I still got up the next morning. You still had to perform. It's a very progressive disease.

At Christmas, we always put a glass of wine and a cigarette for Santa. Once, our son Misha said, "In America, it's milk and cookies, do you get it?" Lelo Staub, Roger's wife, was a big pillar of that time. Fran Moretti, Edie, Sheika, Bunny Langmaid, and Marge, Barbara Parker, and Betty Seibert were more like mother figures to me. They were so protective. "You've got True Grit," Blanche Hill came to the restaurant and said that to me – she saw me pregnant, kids, Walter and me arguing. She saw all that and said that to me, "And by the way, cut your hair. Come by tomorrow and I'll give you a sweater." They were motherly, and that was a very different group of women. They sheltered me. I always felt good when they came. I was the young wild one. They knew I liked a good joke, and a good evening.

We had a dream, a vision. We were all together to start. Vail was getting a name. The first few years: did it matter who you were or what you were? No, it just happened that some of us were funny talkers. I learned to ski at Meadow Mountain with Fran Moretti. She was puffing a cigarette on the chairlift. The pioneer ladies were tough. We're tough - Anne Marie Mueller, Ursula Fricke, Judy Gold, Barbara Shubert, Virginia Pyke, Rita Wasmeier, Daphne Slevin (she had La Cave), Anne Staufer. We all blended together. Renie Gorsuch. Sally Johnston looked like a preppie, same hairdo, little plaid shirt and skirt. I met Barbara Larese in Australia, and her Blue Cow Restaurant name came from a restaurant in Australia. Nu Gnu – Hanlons. The Vail Trail came to ask my opinion on what we should do at LionsHead, "This place over there, what would you do with it? "Flood it, we could have Vail by the sea," I told them. "We could have a gondola right on the water."

The best times were every time; the best years of my life were here. I never felt subordinate as a woman. I felt on the same level. My restaurant was mine. Sheika's was Sheika's. We were bosses. Marge at the Red Lion was very subtle. Sheika and I were loud and visible. I'm colorful. The women were very strong, and they were the spirit of the village. The men were the business. We were young, so we made mistakes. There were wild stories. I was still a little girl. I was more

of a little girl because I never had a home; you can't grow up if you haven't had a home. The early years of your life help you grow up. Without enough hugs you don't grow properly. Vail was my learning ground; my learning ground was really that village. I had no expectations. We just lived.

We loaned our clothes, we ate well, we drank well, we partied, and we got pregnant. We had baptisms. And suddenly this highway came in. When I came, there was not even paving, and I could not even use my pram for my kids. We were all tough. I went to Betty Ford: I wrote the steps. I never felt lonely in my strength.

Freddie Felton was a marvelous dancer. Paul Johnston looked like a guru in the old days, and he was so kind. Liz and Luc Meyer of The Left Bank came in 1970. When we sold La Tour, Luc said, "Walter was my only competition." It was the best compliment. We called our place the Right Bank. People telephoned us and asked if this was the Left Bank, I replied, "No, we're the right bank." Famous people came in the restaurant - Kennedy, Shriver. I worked in the evening and needed babysitters. Jean-Claude was born three weeks before opening the restaurant, and I brought him to work in a laundry basket. Our restaurant was a local hangout. Claus and Edie, Shuberts, Elaine White,

Sheika, Diane Lazier – and they all lived in town. Virginia Pyke was my best friend; she worked for me for 27 years. She was a schoolteacher, and her sons were like my boys. Virginia became somebody I relied on; I couldn't do it all myself. It was hard to get a babysitter at that time. I was not smart; there were many things I could have done. I needed time with Walter, but we didn't have time. Home had to be clean and nice and organized. There were two seatings at dinner in the restaurant; I had to look decent at night. I'm impulsive. I think I did jolly well.

I was a pioneer at heart. I wanted to start new, and I always had an agenda. I think it was okay for him. I wanted to have kids in a small town; teeny little house; I never dreamed really. I'm 21 years sober now in 2007. Sheika helped me; she has a big heart, and because of her I got help at Betty Ford. The core of women in Vail worked with each other. Elaine gave me clothes and a dog named Fellow that she couldn't keep because she was building the Rams-Horn, but he ran off.

FROM FRANCE TO VAIL

Marie-Claire Vigne was born in Montreux, in an orphanage 13 km outside of Paris near St Mandée. and the Bois de Vincennes. She moved at age 18 to Brighton, England and met Walter. Go West, young woman, she likes to say. She was an au pair and hated it. She went to school to learn English, "The English lady helped me to get a job in a hotel as a chambermaid and receptionist at night. Walter came to that hotel. I didn't fall for Walter; I was going with a Greek. Walter

brought me cookies and food every night. My mother would have liked him; she came to the orphanage once or twice a year. She was Belgian, and she said, 'Marry someone who is good to you.' One day, Walter said, 'What are you doing?' I said, 'Nothing.' He said, 'I'm going to America.' And I told him, 'I'd like to, too.' He invited me to Austria for a weekend, and I stayed nine months. His father was a pastry chef, that's how Walter learned. His father's bakery was taken three times: by Germans, Russians, and English. I told myself, 'This is it. I'm going to marry him.' I had an agenda: I wanted kids, but I was not that romantic. Romance was for a quickie and forbidden. In the '60s you could not move in together. I married him when we got to Chicago. Our common ground was English. Go West, young man. It's full of cowboys and Indians, and Al Capone in Chicago. Everything in America is big, like the Grand Canyon. We wanted to leave everything behind because of the war. It was March 15, 1964. I got a VIP job and became this French photographer at age 22. I told them that I specialized in portraits; I lied. I moved in with Walter and met Barbara Shubert in Chicago. Barbara came to Vail first, to this little place in the Rockies. Walter came to work at Manor Vail, and I knew I would love to raise my kid in this little place. I moved here in May '67 when Sasha was six months old. We had $30, my little wedding suit, a toothbrush, and another kid in my belly. Hermann Staufer came and picked us up in Georgetown in a huge storm. We opened the St. Moritz that same year."

MARIJKE BROFOS

In 1964, Dick Hauserman called us in Snowville, New Hampshire, where we worked at the nearby Carroll Reed Shop in North Conway. He invited us to Vail to interview for Vail Blanche. My husband, Francis, son Erik (then five) and our dog, Talley, drove to Vail in our Plymouth station wagon (a real experience over Loveland Pass). Dick put us up in the Plaza on Bridge Street, we had the interview, and were hired by Blanche Hauserman and Bunny Langmaid, who owned the sport shop. We immediately drove back to Snowville, packed the car, and returned to Vail.

Our first home was in the Skaal House. In 1971, Vail developer Bob Lazier asked me to be the general manager of the newly built Willows condominiums in Vail Village. Working there for 25 years, it became a home away from home.

Vail became my home and still is, although I keep moving west...to Wildridge to be exact. My love for the mountains, the summers with the gorgeous flowers, and, of course, many friends have kept me here.

The early days are not to be forgotten, with such places as Nu Gnu; the Deli; and the Casino, with its entertainment - Dick Gibson jazz parties, movies, and church services (Thank God!). We did not have a liquor store at the time, so we "borrowed" the priest's wine for our private little parties and replaced it before Sunday services after we had gone to Harry Hoffman's liquor store down in Denver.

The "little" town was great. I recall such things as Susan Moretti tying up her horse in front of Vail Blanche; keeping a large, prominently displayed birthday calendar of the then very few locals at the Kaleidoscope store so we knew where the next party would be; The Slope with its plush on-floor seating—and I mean on-floor—where we could watch ski and ski-related movies.

There was Barbara Parker teaching us about picking mushrooms and learning how to bake bread at Nancy Kindel's house, and Jean Naumann teaching our kids at the Vail Fire Department building, the Seibert's house, the Vail Bank in Crossroads, and a modular in Minturn. We called our makeshift school the Vail Country Day School; today, it has evolved into the Vail Mountain School.

I also recall we had no mail delivery in the

early days. Mail pick-up was at the Minturn post office, and packages were picked up at the railroad station. The nearest bank was in Eagle, a long way to go for cash or make deposits. My favorite things to do were tennis (especially those great Lord Gore Club tournaments), camping, hiking, and fishing.

My son, Erik, has been a Vail ski instructor for 37 years. His daughter, Whitney, was born in Vail, is a ski and snowboard instructor, and attends college in Boulder. My family life is strong and happy. I hope they never leave.

There was nothing here when I arrived. We were the 13th to get a telephone, and TV didn't come until 1967. And now, here I am retired, living in Wildridge, with its beautiful mountain views. The sun shines forever here, and I can look down on Avon's Fourth of July fireworks, and even low flying helicopters, in the valley below. I also enjoy the wildlife—bears, raccoons, foxes, and deer. And the birds serenade us.

Vail is far from where I was born in Wassenaar in the Netherlands on the opening day of Amsterdam's 1928 Summer Olympics. I attended Dutch schools, and my family also traveled extensively throughout Europe before and after World War II. The war years were tough. I was 11 when the Nazis invaded. During their early occupation of Holland, they moved into our home; we had to find other accommodations several times. As the battle went on, there was little to eat (tulip bulbs and sugar beets became commonplace). There was little water or clothing; electricity and gas for heat and cooking also became scarce.

At the end of the war, we finally moved back to our house—minus our goats that I milked daily. I suspect we gradually had to eat them (although my mother never confirmed it). Yet all the family was alive—my mother, two sisters, and I in Holland, and my two brothers and others who had been fighting the Nazis from outside and inside the country. I was 17 and was sent to study at the Sorbonne University in Paris and served as an au pair at a "castle" in Montfort l'Amaury near Paris. It was quite an experience. In total, I spent about two years in France before returning to Holland. During this time, I met my future husband, a Norwegian-American. In 1953, we married and sailed to New York where I became an American citizen upon arrival. We lived first in Washington DC; then Greenwich, Connecticut; after that in Snowville, New Hampshire; and finally Vail.

147

Marilyn Fleischer

I grew up in Portland, Oregon. I lost my parents when I was young and skied at Mt. Hood and Sun Valley as an escape. I started college in Portland and went to Alaska for a year and worked at City Hall in Anchorage, instructing skiing weekends at Alyeska to make money to get to Europe.

I was living in Europe using school as an excuse but traveling extensively, racing a Porsche on several tracks, and instructing skiing in Austria. I heard about Vail opening so I came back home to Oregon in the fall of '62 and wrote to Peter Seibert – the only name I had - asking him if I came to Vail, "May I have a job? I can do anything." He later told my husband, "The nerve of this kid writing a letter like that. I thought she probably could do anything." I got a letter back telling me to come, so I drove straight through to Vail with my letter from Pete and arrived December 17, 1962. I went to work in front desk/reservations at the Vail Village Inn. Many interesting people checked in. There were funny and not-so-funny times at work. I was also bookkeeper for Vail Fire Protection District, Vail Water and Sanitation District, and Alpine Landscaping. After Roger

Staub took over ski school, I instructed skiing part-time, doing the books at night and working 72 hours a week.

The main thing that kept me here was the love of the mountain in summer and winter and the many friendships. In the fall of 1966, I got married in Vail, our reception being the first function of the Lord Gore Club at Manor Vail. My husband had a law firm in Richmond, Virginia, and wasn't going to move to Vail for me, so I moved there. Right away, we started plans for a business in Vail. In 1969, with a small group of partners, we built the Kiandra Lodge, now the Sonnenalp, and later bought the Talisman Lodge.

Having a social life in the early years was fun but difficult, working so many hours a week. I remember coming out of my bookkeeping office in the middle of the intersection of Bridge Street and Gore Creek Drive where Gorsuch, the liquor store, Gasthof Gramshammer, and the Casino were located, and flipping a coin to see if I went up to my apartment above the liquor store to try to rock myself to sleep to the music of "Hang on, Sloopy" or "Sugar Shack" coming from the Casino across the street or go over and join them.

Sports have been in my life forever and are so important to me. I've been a runner and biker for years and enjoyed Vail tennis, golf, and skiing. Before coming to Vail, I don't know if I had expectations except that the thought of being a "pioneer" was exciting. I had heard it was a great mountain. It has been exciting to watch Vail grow and fulfill-

ing to contribute to its growth by building one lodge and taking over another. I must admit that, at first, I objected to some parts of the development, and part of me wanted it to remain the "early Vail" that I knew and loved. However, we know things will grow and change. There isn't another place I would rather come home to.

Marka Webb Moser

My introduction to Vail was with my uncle, Bud Palmer, a few days into the New Year of 1965. We bunked at Pepi's, where we met Rod Slifer and Sheika and Pepi Gramshammer. Bud was so enamored with the skiing and the beginnings of an alpine village in the Colorado Rockies that he bought one of the first condominiums in All Seasons. Since he lived in New York City at the time, his family could only travel to Vail during school holidays. If the condo wasn't rented – which rarely happened in those days – my two daughters, some friends, and

I could crash there most weekends. Living in Colorado Springs and then in Boulder, where I completed my teaching degree, we packed our ski gear in my Volkswagen Bug, traveled the two-lane winding roads over Loveland and Vail Passes (no interstate) and quickly became hooked on Vail as "weekend locals."

The exceptional skiing, with so few people on the slopes, meant a fresh powder dump lasted days. I had been skiing since the late '40s at Ski Cooper, Winter Park, Arapahoe, Pikes Peak, Climax, and Aspen. Vail's slopes, with the back bowls, certainly trumped my earlier ski experiences. Besides, it was such a safe place for my daughters, Mary Catherine and Barbara, to learn to ski. A Poma lift at Mid Vail allowed them to practice their turns without mom's constant attention. I could then enjoy more challenging slopes accessed by Chairs 3 and 4, checking in with them after each run. One afternoon as I took off for some final turns, the lift broke down. It took a couple of hours to repair, and by the time I skied into Mid Vail, it was dark. In those days, there was no need to worry about unattended four- and six-year-old girls. They were in good hands, drinking hot chocolate and eating sandwiches with a ski patrolman they knew.

My daughters loved "working" with George Knox at his Mug Shop on Bridge Street, which had a handy back hall connection to Donovan's Copper Bar. My friends and I could join in the raucous, weekend après ski at the bar, while George looked after the kids. With no radio, TV, or movie theater in Vail, the bars (Red Lion, Lodge at Vail, Pepi's, the Casino, Nu Gnu and the Vail Village Inn) were the gathering spots for everyone from shop owners and ski execs to ski school instructors and patrol, lift operators and trail packers. For a day of foot packing the slopes, you could earn a free lift ticket.

After graduating with teaching credentials, I searched for a way to move to Vail, but there were no openings in area schools. When I met Kris Moser, he was interviewing for a job with the Colorado Division of Wildlife. After we married in 1969, he signed on as a Wildlife Officer in the Minturn area.

We moved permanently in 1970 to one of the first condominiums in the valley developed and constructed by locals. Dave and Rob Garton sold us our first home in Buffehr Creek West Condominiums, with Steve Boyd and Carl Nelson (Closer Than Most Construction) building the project. Sons Michael and Matthew were born there.

The outdoors served as our playground. My family and I all look back at this time as some of the happiest of our lives. We played games, hiked, backpacked, camped, picnicked, inner-tubed down Gore Creek, skied and skated together and in tandem with other families. On Sunday afternoons in the fall, you could find avid football fans seeking a radio signal from Denver to listen to the game. The top of Davos became an accessible and popular hangout. We danced with the Bavailians, skied and coached with Buddy Werner League, and skated and played hockey on the outdoor rinks. Add to that the non-profit organizations that began with this group of pioneers and remain today: Buddy Werner League, The Eagle Valley Rummage Sale, Ski Club Vail, Skating Club of Vail, and Vail Junior Hockey Club.

The memories, the stories, the friendships continue to enrich our lives. What a magical time it was to be living in this fledgling resort. We all experienced firsthand that pioneering spirit – everyone pulling together to survive. There were dirt streets in town, no grocery or clothing stores, television or radio. We lacked many amenities that we had taken for granted where we lived before. But we had the basics and each other. We helped build homes, raise kids, start businesses and we worked as one, big family, while skiing, and partying together. Those friendships are treasures that have endured. I'm still in contact with many women who have moved away, but still come to visit, like Jane Langmaid Smith (we crashed a few times in Bunny and Joe Langmaid's home), Betty Stiles Stoner, Dorothy Orlosky, Pam Garton, Shirley Ward, Kasey Stanish, Barbara Parker, and June Simonton. I mourn those pioneers who have departed too soon - Marge Burdick, Celine Krueger, Judy Nelson, Betsy Robinson, Judy Nicholls, Patty Steinle Grubb, Imogene Doll, and Cindy Brennan.

I value the friendships that have survived. They are a treasure trove of support, hilarious stories, memories, and love. We fought fiercely to save our water, wilderness areas and to build a hospital, a church, schools and a community in which to raise our families. Our children grew up with wings to launch out on their own but with solid Vail roots. Many have returned after living and working in other places. It's been said that Vail's an easy place to leave, but it's a hard place to stay away from. Vail has changed, but that pioneer spirit lives deep in our hearts.

MARLENE BECK MCCAFFERTY

In December of 1962, my husband Donald and I had to check out this new ski area called Vail. We had been transferred from Salt Lake to the Denver/Golden area in 1960. I had grown up in Seattle, was a skier after the war, and ended up on the U of W Women's Intercollegiate Ski Team for four years. I graduated with a BA in Business Administration and took to the friendly skies with United Airlines based in Salt Lake City, and I skied Alta.

When we moved to Denver, we came to Vail often and bought a small place in West Vail in 1966. Many friends and neighbors from Applewood Mesa in Golden did the same. Don was a principal in Daleboot, a magnesium ski boot. He also worked with amputees from Fitzsimmon Hospital in

Denver, supplying the elastomer padding for their prostheses.

Vail was a wonderful and fun place to spend weekends and holidays with daughters, Shauna and Kelley, then three and five years old. Both girls were in Buddy Werner, and I helped coach. I remember one Christmas after leaving the Casino one night, they had to prepare for Mass that morning. The drunks who had spilled out of the bar decided they had to climb the Christmas tree in the middle of Gore Creek Drive and Bridge Street. Well, they and the tree fell down. It seems as though there were many of these episodes in those early years. Things were much different then, from gravel parking lots to the melodrama at the Outback behind the Vail Village Inn. I loved having the Conoco on the corner at the main Vail entrance.

For work, I did it all - retail sales, property management, and real estate. Skiing kept me here, as well as summers climbing 36 of the 14,000-ft. peaks, the 14ers. There were great picnics on the mountain with the other early residents. On snowy days, lunch at the Cookshack was a real treat.

My social life has been intertwined with volunteering for many local non-profits. It is a very important part of my life. Vail was a tight-knit and caring community with lots to offer. In the early years after the lifts closed in spring, we shut our doors until July 4th. There were no full-time, year-round jobs to be had back then…but we always made it through. I moved permanently to Vail, and am still here because I haven't been able to find anyplace better.

Martha Fritzlen Head

On February 3, 1964, my husband Jack Fritzlen and I arrived in Vail for the first time. We had decided to spend a few nights in this "new resort" on our way to Aspen for a ski vacation. We were staying at the Christiania, owned at that time by Nancy and Ted Kindel. It was Sheika and Pepi Gramshammer's wedding day, the first day I met Paul Testwuide, and my ski instructor, Dick Pownall. It was during this first visit that Jack and I decided we wanted to live here. We returned for another visit in March of 1967 with our three children: Lynn, Guerin, & Marla. In 1968, we bought a condominium at Riva Ridge South and officially made the move from Kansas City, Missouri to Vail. That was the start of our life in this glorious area. Vail had a very different feel to it in those days. There was a lot of testosterone and a huge amount of energy in evidence. This combination gave way to Vail's becoming a great town of the West. It had excitement, danger, and fun. For us, we found life to be just what we wanted.

The village was charming with its small stores where the proprietors gave their hearts and souls to their success. Pepi's and Gorsuch's were favorite places to shop. Many men who worked in Vail would have lunch on Pepi's porch. It was a gift to me that the children could walk by and see their fathers there each day. There were Bill Whiteford and John Donovan's bars. We even had our church services at Whiteford's bar at times. We used The Lodge at Vail as our theater, and Jim Slevin was the "do-it-all" man there. He acted and produced, and you never saw a better play in your life. At the time, we did not have a grocery store in Vail but drove to Minturn. I remember each trip to Denver coming home with a case of toilet paper, a case of coffee, and two cases of whiskey.

There were not a lot of options for services in town but you knew exactly who to go to for whatever you needed to have done. There were two photographers, one delicatessen, Barbara Parker was our postmistress, and Father Stone was our parish priest (who sometimes performed services at Whiteford's bar). There was a wonderful man

John Feagin

named Roberto who tended some sheep up on the mountain. He would bring them right down through town to graze and they brought with them a plethora of flies and a lot of noise. He would ride his horse into Vail and park it at either Whiteford's or Donovan's bar to have a nightcap. However, it was said that if it were raining that evening he would bring his horse right into the bar with him so that it would stay dry.

Our children went to school in Vail when they were younger. I would drop them off at school and go out skiing, sometimes even with my hair still damp. My favorite skiing route was Prima, Pronto, Log Chute, High Line, and Blue Ox. Those runs are where I learned to ski, and this was one of the highlights of my life. Once our children grew older they transferred to Kent Denver Country Day School for high school. At first, they would get rides to and from Denver with Kris Steinberg, Dr. Tom Steinberg's daughter, because she had a car. This was before I-70 had been built, thus they had to drive over Loveland Pass to get there.

The whole community was extremely welcoming and friendly. In particular, Camille Bishop was one of the kindest to me and made me proud to be part of Vail and her circle of friends. I loved her very much. The social gatherings around town brought us so

153

much joy. We gathered for hikes and wild picnics in the mountains with lots of laughter. We would have breakfast on Corral Creek and pick the chanterelle mushrooms that surrounded us there. Nancy Kindel once hosted a toga party where we all came dressed as if we were in the Roman courts. One of the guests was Bob Parker, who was a huge influence in the skiing world and coined the term "Ski Country USA." He was the hit of the night because he would not let us look under his skirt.

Upon coming to Vail, my husband Jack built a factory for his company, CMI Inc., where they made sophisticated law enforcement equipment. This first factory was in Minturn on Pine Street next door to the house of Bill Burnett, the famous plumber. With CMI, Jack developed several of his inventions including the first hand-held radar gun and breath test device for alcohol in the blood. Jack passed away at age 47. I ran the business and then sold it to a company on the New York Stock Exchange. A few years later, I married Howard Head and was once more in a state of love that gave fulfillment to my life. We lived in Vail part-time. Those eight years were an experience out of a glorious dream. His invention of the metal ski and the oversized tennis racquet changed the recreational world. Howard passed away, and I made the decision to make Vail my primary residence. I married John A. Feagin, MD Col. (ret), and our interests together and love grow with the years. We have many miles to go together before we rest.

I have traveled the world, experienced great things, and met extraordinary people, but through it all I have been blessed to call Vail my home. There is not enough time to tell of all the wonderful times I have had or mention all of the remarkable people who have shaped Vail. I want to thank Dr. Jack Eck for his lifesaving gifts and also George Gillett for the joy he gave us when he bought Vail Associates.

154

Mary Jo Allen

I came to Vail because I had always wanted to "ski bum" for a season. Vail was the first stop, and I never left. I was raised in Detroit, Michigan and spent 11 years in Santa Monica, California, working as a secretary and as a student at UCLA. In Vail, I worked as Mitch Hoyt's secretary at VA while LionsHead Gondola was being planned and built.

Bridge Club, parties, volunteering, Dickens Carolers, Mickey's at The Lodge were some of my social outlets. There has been lots of skiing, of course, and I loved skating behind the interfaith chapel. I made lifelong friends hiking with the Happy Hikers. I've climbed many 14ers and enjoyed family camping trips and travels, kayaking, and tennis. We loved going to the Leather Jug in Snowmass to hear this wonderful folk singer named John Denver.

My two sons Douglas and Duncan went to Red Sandstone Elementary, Minturn Middle School, and Battle Mountain High School. Our lives centered on their school sports and activities. There were no expectations except perhaps actually getting here. Trying to drive here over Loveland Pass in a raging snowstorm in January 1969 was a challenge I won't forget.

I married Bruce Allen on July 20, 1969 in the Vail Chapel, which was under construction. Cissy Dobson told us we were the second couple to be married in the Chapel, the first couple was just passing through Vail. So, I guess that makes us the first Vail couple to be married there. The windows were not in yet, and birds were flying in and out during the ceremony (one of my favorite memories). Cissy played her son's electric keyboard for us. Don Simonton had broken his leg, and we had to get the pastor from Leadville to unite us. The church used one of our wedding photos with people who attended the ceremony standing in the background for their first brochure.

MARY SUSAN McLAUGHLIN

The spring of 1970 saw our family move to Vail. After law school in Boulder and law clerking in St. Louis, his brother Chuck, who owned the Alaskan Shop, persuaded my husband Doug to come to Vail. There were very few lawyers in the entire county at the time. We were off to the Rockies having no idea about housing prospects or office space, but here we came like many others.

Will Miller, who worked at Byron Brown's real estate company, helped us find a place to live. Benno Scheidegger had just finished the final unit in Alpine Chalets, and we bought it. The short time that we lived there was happy, fun, and entertaining. There was no radio or television, the Wall Street Journal always arrived three days late in the mail, so we got to know our neighbors. We talked, we laughed, and how we partied.

The "golden arches" did not exist yet in Vail. We would come back from Colorado Springs with a large bag of Big Macs and pre-measured sauce separately in a jar. The Big Macs lived in the freezer until we put them in the microwave and added the sauce.

Bob Lazier had office space available in his Arcade Building with a balcony facing the mountain and The Lodge swimming pool.

Doug spent a considerable amount of time there in the summer. There was the Copper Bar downstairs, which later got TV. I was the secretary for our law office, and our younger daughter, Kristen, was my helper because she was not old enough for school. Marka, our older daughter, went to kindergarten in the basement of the Interfaith Chapel.

Doug and a friend decided that Vail needed an eyeglass shop, and Sport Optics was born. I was volunteered to manage it; but first, my co-worker Jane York and I went to Colorado Springs for training. We opened in a 100-square-foot space next to the Silversmiths of Vail. Jane owned the Cheese Shop in the Arcade, so when she was not slicing cheese or making sandwiches, she manned the shop. I would pull away from the typewriter, run down the back stairs, and do my time. Acetone and warm salt were our "quick fix." Any real problems had to be sent to Denver. We always hoped skiers who wore glasses remembered to bring more than one pair to Vail. The shop lasted a couple of years. Jane met Dick Hart, who became Doug's partner after about a year of practicing. They married, and Dick went on to be a judge for Eagle County. Doug hired a secretary, and I put my efforts into building a house.

We bought a lot on Vail Valley Drive from Gerry and Barbara Hoyt. With the architectural knowledge of Dick Bailey and Mitch Hoyt's construction crew, our "Hummingbird House" was built. The location was perfect for an early morning 9 holes. You didn't need a tee time in advance to go out and play.

The whole community volunteered for one project or another. Doug was a volunteer fireman, and they were in charge of 4th of July fireworks. Volunteering to help with the Eagle Valley Auction rewarded me with friendships that will last forever. I was proud to help the energetic women like Vi Brown in the task of sorting, labeling, and pricing articles, and then standing at registers all day during the auction and rummage sale, not to mention the follow-up work afterward.

The elementary school was above the then Clinic. They needed volunteers to help with tutoring in Math and English. We were also "recess" helpers. The young children who lived in Vail at that time could race down a ski hill, but they were not as good when it came to ball handling. We ran, jumped rope, and did calisthenics in the parking lot.

I came from southeast Missouri where the only hills are made by ants. I had never learned to ski, and when we moved to Vail, the closest I got to the slopes was to help hand out bibs for Buddy Werner skiing.

My winter sport was bowling, and Tuesday was Ladies' Day. Skiers, shop owners, workers, and homemakers all came to the bowling alley to laugh, gossip, and exercise. Christy Sports eventually replaced the Avon bowling alley.

Meredith Ogilby

I was 23 when I arrived in Vail. I had graduated from the University of Colorado in Boulder in English and German and was in graduate school in English. I had lived in Freiburg, Germany as a student for a year and a half. My new husband Chuck Ogilby and I had grown up together in Illinois. In Boulder, we renovated old Victorian houses and resold them.

Adventure and chance brought me to Vail. We were spending weekends at the Avon Country Store and Hotel and skiing in Vail. Then one weekend, we applied for jobs and stayed here.

Besides working at the Valhalla Lodge for Jim and Jan Cunningham, I was a continental breakfast girl for Nancy and Maury Nottingham at the Talisman, a Gorsuch "Girl" with Joanne, Maria, Beth, Lucie, Anneliese, Mary Ann, etc. for many years. I taught swimming to the White girls at the Rams-Horn Lodge. I became a photographer in Vail and worked for Jeff Nicholls at Images Unlimited and at Susan Milhoan's "Cut it Out." I was a backcountry ski guide for Buck Elliott of Paragon Guides for probably six years.

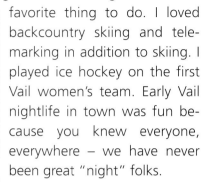

We loved it and bought our 1890's log cabin in Intermountain for $100 from the Gartons and renovated it with Tommy Sachs. We raised our kids in it, added on a log cabin from East Vail for more room for the kids, and still own it. Great memories. It never occurred to us that we would ever live elsewhere.

We made wonderful, lifetime friends in Vail and raised our children together. It seemed as if we were more or less the same age, all starting a family at the same time, and all loved the mountains and the small town atmosphere. Our children Kayo and Molly both live in Car-

bondale now, as do we.

Backpacking in the Gore Range became our favorite thing to do. I loved backcountry skiing and tele-marking in addition to skiing. I played ice hockey on the first Vail women's team. Early Vail nightlife in town was fun because you knew everyone, everywhere – we have never been great "night" folks.

We didn't have any expectations of life here, never thought of it. We just showed up for the adventure. Over time, Chuck and I both became involved in non-profits that related to Vail, the environment, and the community. We originated – especially Chuck – Eagle-Piney Water Protection Association, with Roger Brown, Tam Scott, Pam Garton – and the "Walk for Water." The first meeting was in our living room.

Even though Vail didn't stay the intimate community we originally found, it did remain a vibrant, close community that has always supported us.

Monika Brown

There are two stories for me - I come from Silesia, Germany. After the war, I ended up in Munich because Silesia was given up to the Russians. I am a girl who went through the war in a way that my friends up here haven't experienced it. I lived in the mountains, warplanes couldn't fly in, the diplomatic corps was evac-

uated into the mountains. The navy had U-boats that had sunk American boats; it was totally isolated, and the children were more or less alone with their mothers. We were the first to be evacuated at the war's end, my mother didn't want to leave because it was my brother's birthday, we missed the evacuation.

My mother took us and we climbed over the mountain. We had big sleds and a rucksack each; my aunt was to be on the other side; she picked us up there. From there we fled, and when we came to the border at Germany, troops were there, our car was taken, and we got a note – "Please present this Card when the war is over and you get your car back." We hitchhiked and were put on military trucks, where do you want to go? Car was covered with tarp and we sat on top of it. We could see the streets blocked off by brick walls. The bodies were piled there. When they stopped us and put us on next truck we learned we'd been sitting on dynamite. We arrived at our aunt's and uncle's, but we were under arrest by the Russians. (Mother had taken a birthday present for him; she put out a red-checkered blanket with goodies and a little car, fancy toy.) Two years after the war, my sister and I were by luck in a boarding school. We didn't have a home. The Americans had Leipzig, but we were on the other side.

There was a Christmas knock at the door, and my little brother shows up – he had gone to an American and asked could they drive him across the border. At 14 or 15, I was brought separately across the border so they wouldn't notice, told to take a later train and spend the night in a farmhouse. But no one was there, so I continued walking. It was getting dark, and two motorcycles came, I hid in a ditch, then I saw a young man, and he said, "Can I join you?" I found my way to the man who would take me to the family at 4 or 5 am. I wore an apron and scarf and rake. He told me, "Now you say, 'Good Morning.' We will go to the fields to work, then you run to the village, don't stop." And it worked.

Right after school, I went to Italy and worked there many years. I was one of the first girls allowed to have a passport because Germans had not been allowed to leave the country after the war. From there, I studied history in Italy, came back to Munich, and then visited New York. My mother had been working with the Americans on the "first apparent clan" program for children who didn't have families. Americans started it in the '50s. We didn't have a home anymore, so when she was invited to come to America, she asked me to join her, and that's how I got to the States.

Ernie Blake from Taos sent me a letter asking me to visit, and I packed my bags. He then sent me up to Vail to look at the competition. I went with Jerry Mullens in a VW. It was before 1965. We arrived in the village and there was no office, nothing. "I'm looking for Peter Seibert," I said to someone. "Just go up the mountain, there are no more than five people skiing." In Munich, I had been working as a model with Bogner and traveled with the clothing line.

159

Pepi Gramshammer, Dick Hauserman, and Joe Langmaid wanted to show me Vail. We skied the Back Bowls, which they opened only for us. "Why not just stay in the mountains and ski? You will love it," Dick said. I saw him at a big meeting and dinner party in Sun Valley when the importer of the Bogner line took me to meet him. I was a ski instructor there at the time, and he said to Dick, "Being a ski instructor is not for Moni, don't you have something for her?"

As it turned out, Blanche and Bunny Langmaid wanted help in their shop. I arrived and stayed at Joe and Bunny's; there were practically no houses then. "Would you like to come and stay here?" they asked. I thought: this looks nice. I went back home to Munich and made the decision to come; those first three to five years, I went back and forth between countries and ski resorts.

As for Blanche and Bunny, the ladies didn't want to work in the store anymore and were happy to have someone running it. When we went skiing, we put a sign at the door with a flag, "If you need something, wave the flag." How can you not like that? One of my first tasks was to call and order the jackets for ski patrol; they had forgotten. I would like to know why nobody is pulling Blanche in and giving her credit – she opened the door to everybody. When I left Taos, there was a lot of press. I talked to a reporter from SKI Magazine, and he said, "I want you to meet Blanche Hauserman; you will not believe her. She is amazing." She had a long braid down her back; she was the star. She opened the door for anybody and everybody. Knowing Dick the way I know him, he's the one behind the scenes.

I lived with Brita Sherman (weaving store) and Birgitta in the Skaal Haus in Dick's apartment; he closed off the downstairs and I had that to myself. When the pilot light went out, Dick would fix it. We had parties in my one little room; we had tea parties in my place. We had such a good time. I was working for Vail Blanche then; Joe Langmaid had his ski rental and tuning store downstairs. He and Bunny lived on Beaver Dam Road, and Roger Brown lived on Forest Road. They could look from their place into Roger's. I had met Roger in Taos, and we liked each other. There was nothing between the houses and town; it was one road, no trees, no houses, nothing. They saw everything – "You were late today" or "You were taking a sunbath yesterday!" It was fun. I had a good rapport with Joe and Bunny, and they opened their house to me.

Roger's dog would follow me to work and sit in front of the store. Whose dog is this? Nobody knew! He kept the secret of me dating Roger, even until we were married. We had our wedding in the house. It wasn't a big deal; we didn't announce it anywhere. The priest came with a cross and big candles, and you could

160

smell the dinner. Bob Parker came. We thought nobody knew, but the very next day, everybody congratulated us.

My furniture arrived but couldn't be delivered, so Dave Gorsuch sent the ski patrol to come and unload the crates from Munich - silver, pewter, rugs, and my beautiful antiques. They had the crowbar ready to open those crates. I closed my eyes and said, "Careful." Nicholas arrived in 1968. I probably was an overprotective mother, coming from a doctor's family. I worked until the baby came. Roger's boys, Gordy and Michael, also lived with us.

Eileen Kaiser was one of my best friends, and we started Rive Gauche gallery with beautiful antiques. Rive Gauche was next door to Daphne Slevin and Anne Staufer's Kaleidoscope. The best thing was when ex-Olympic skier Grace McKnight visited me in the gallery. She brought a silk flag to me; I called Sheika, and she bought it for $50. Eileen served tea and rum after skiing for the people from Denver. Freddie Obadia sat in the open door with a little desk and drinks and his Moroccan camel stories. Barbara and Hans Shubert opened Vail's first men's clothing store.

One winter, I was working at My Favorite Things for Sally & Paul O'Laughlin in Crossroads. It snowed like crazy, and we were totally snowed in. No pavements, no roads, and no cars driving around. I left the car in front of the store, and I forgot about it. The next morning, I looked out the window at home and said, "Roger, my car is stolen." "Give me the phone, I'm going to call the police," he said. The kids started crying, we went out to play, and I remembered, "Oh, I know I left the car in town." I went and told him and he said, "Okay, but I'm not calling the police; you do it." With such snowfall, Pete Burnett did the plowing, and our house was on a rocky ledge on a bend. Roger insisted it be hand shoveled.

There were perhaps five families in town, and you would go from house to house having dinners with the same people in a different house. I knew Pepi from the time he was the coach for the little Bogner boys back in Germany. I have images of a few silly things, like when Bob Parker's horse looked through the bedroom window of our house. There were early rules, too: you were not allowed to hang laundry out, and you couldn't have fences so people could ski through back yards. There was no struggle to make Vail my home.

NANCY LOOSE BURNHAM

Growing up in Kenilworth, Illinois, I graduated from high school and then SMU in June, 1964. I found a job in Chicago and worked there until November, 1965. After taking a ski trip to Aspen and Vail in the spring of 1965, and when both my roommates got married that fall, I decided to move to Vail to work and ski. My parents were horrified, but our next-door neighbor knew Dick Hauserman, which seemed to help, so I met with him when I came to town. Mr. Hauserman got me a job as a waitress at The Lodge at Vail (not exactly the type of position I was expecting), and thus received housing (over the Rucksack with five other girls, including Susie Potts Simoneau), a ski pass, and food. Note: a good meal at The Lodge cost $4.95 then, so a $1.50 tip for a table of two was good. There were three seatings: 5:30pm for families, 7pm for regular folks, and 8:30 for larger tables of drunken tourists; and then we served the Staufers and their friends. Hermann Staufer fired me in late January for not wearing pantyhose with my bread wrapper uniform. Gaynor Miller found me a job with the Vail Resort Association. I loved it there and stayed until the end of the ski season. Meanwhile, I had to move into the basement of Valhalla, where Susie was now working the front desk, having also been fired. The German and Austrian girls were much better waitresses than we were.

I stayed because I loved Vail and I'd met Tom Burnham, who had arrived in the fall of 1963. Though we left for the summer, we returned in September, and were married October 29, 1966, at a church in Minturn with our reception at the Red Lion. I worked nights that ski season on the front desk of Gasthof Gramshammer. I was even there when Pepi and Sheika's daughter was born, what a night! Tom ran a teenage hangout, Young Lions, in the basement of the Red Lion. Social life in Vail was always fun in those days because we knew everyone in town. We drank a lot late at night, but I met Tom early on and that was that for me, socially.

Ted Wegener was my ski instructor, and I graduated from stem christy to parallel with him. We had long skis with dangerous long thongs on the bindings and thought we were hot stuff. Tom was also an instructor and helped me learn to ski. We are still married 45 years later, and we both ski.

After skiing, late nights after work were spent at Donovan's Copper Bar and the Casino Vail dancing to Zorba the Greek. We had loads of friends and dinner parties in the basement of the Night Latch, where Gaynor and Tom lived. It was a really fun time. I had no expectations other than a good time, and I certainly had that.

Tom and I moved to Steamboat in the summer of 1967 and bought a ski lodge. We have two kids who both ski raced, so we often returned to Vail and watched it grow, grow, grow. My perspective has not changed much. I don't think we could have had a better time than to be present at the real beginnings of a ski area. No one can do that today. Of our old friends, some are still around, some split, but include Gaynor (and later Nancy Langmaid) Miller, John and Diana Donovan, Charlie and Ginny Crowley, Hemmie and Irene Westbye, Larry and Willie Benway, and many more. It was a wonderful time to be young. Nothing is more special than those early years in Vail.

NANCY FOWLER DENTON

I was born and raised in Boulder, Colorado, where I graduated from the University of Colorado. During the summer months while attending college in Boulder, I worked in the Vail Valley. I vacationed in Vail with my family every winter beginning in 1965 and began teaching for the Vail Ski School in 1969. I later moved to Vail permanently, and taught skiing as a Certified Instructor. Besides teaching skiing full time, I worked for the Vail Recreation Department during the summers as a receptionist at the Golden Peak Tennis Shop. The healthy lifestyle and the beauty of the Vail Valley kept me here. I married Craig Denton, and we had four children. It has been a wonderful place to raise children.

I came to Vail for the skiing but was born into a "golfing" family, as my father was the golf coach at CU for 30 years. I played golf growing up and have continued to enjoy it during non-snowy months. Because I had visited the Vail Valley with my family many times before moving here, I knew that Vail offered an active lifestyle that appealed to me. I can say that I have never been disappointed.

I have seen the Vail area grow from a small unassuming place, to a vibrant international arena. I feel as if I have virtually grown up alongside the growth of the valley, as if we've been lifelong friends. I call the Vail Valley 'home', now and forever.

163

NANCY KINDEL

When we saw the wonderful powder in the Back Bowls, we couldn't believe it, and we wanted to ski. That was February '63. We met with Rod Slifer, and he showed us the most beautiful lot in town - 30,000 sq. ft. at $1/sq. ft. They wanted us to start a boys' camp, but we didn't want that. We asked, "What does Vail need?" Lodging. "OK, we can do that." We sat at The Lodge at Vail and typed out our Prospectus. VA called us, "Sorry, someone else has the first right of refusal on this land." Ted said, "If you can't let me know by tomorrow, the deal is off." But they called us right back.

We came back in April and bumped into John McBride, whom we'd met skiing in Portillo, Chile. We met with architect Fritz Benedict in Aspen – he was not encouraging about finishing our building by Thanksgiving. He wanted us to build condos on the other side of Gore Creek. In walked Stein Erickson to The Lodge dining room; we'd skied at his first American ski experience, where he did the flip before people did them. Stein was having lunch with Fitzhugh Scott that day, and we met with him about our need to build. He told us, "By November, yes." He was so wonderful.

I found out there was no doctor, no nurse, no hospital, and no school. I was up till 5:30am crying, "We can't do this with these three little kids." This was not good. We didn't know what the future of Vail was going to be. Then, we just made up our minds we were going to move here. Later, when we went to parties – we always toasted Fitz – we wouldn't be here if it weren't for him. We were in by early November and fully booked for Thanksgiving, but there was no snow. We told them not to come, but one couple showed up from Dallas and helped us get it ready.

Those early days were incredible. We just

loved Vail. No one has really written the stories. We took horses way out. Our little girls loved it. We were renting rooms in the Christiania and decided to build our house. We rented a house from the Smiths on Gore Creek, and they adopted us. They were such great friends. Art taught Ted how to fly fish. They hauled in native trout off the deck, and we'd have them for breakfast. They were so good to us.

Father Stone, the Catholic priest, was sent to Minturn for disagreeing with the bishop in Denver. Everybody adored him. They loved Father Stone because he had television. Our phone service was The Lodge at Vail; it was very primitive. Rod and his wife came for dinner one evening, and our daughter Amy fell off the railing just when they arrived and split her chin. We took her to Gilman Clinic. I held her head; Ted held her feet. The doctor turned off his hearing aid. We got dinner on the table somehow.

School was in the bar at The Lodge with one teacher. We called it Vail Country Day, but later changed it to Vail Mountain School. I started the Rummage Sale and the Home Tour fundraisers. Betty Seibert really started the school in the bar. When they moved school to her house, a goat met the kids at the door. Once, John McBride asked if we would babysit the goat, which chewed the chains on our cuckoo clock, and it cried all night long. When I asked if the goat was housebroken, he said, "Oh, that doesn't matter, it's just hard pellets." I had the goat for a week! The kids thought it was great. Our house had seven rooms including a loft for babysitters, balcony off the master bedroom, and a play area. Ted was the first mayor; he didn't have much choice. Ted was involved in everything. We fought to get a golf course. The Denver people wanted to keep Vail their private ski area.

We chose the name of Christiania for our lodge because of skiing – stem Christy, King Christian. We sold it the second year; Ted did not want to be an innkeeper. Hardest thing? Nothing – the only thing we thought about was, "Is Vail going to click?" I remember parking employee cars in front of The Lodge to make it look busy. We had use of facilities with Ted being on all the boards. Our property was in a prime location – they could never build in front of our house. We gave permission for the bike path and playground to be built.

Marge Burdick took private lessons from Pepi; she was not athletic. He kept saying, "Steady locks." She broke her ankle. "What were you telling me?" she asked him in the hospital. I was saying, "Marge, stay relaxed."

We who lived in Vail were equal. There was no discrimination. Joe Staufer had a party every Saturday night; the whole family/town went to Mid Vail. We'd come down, put the children to bed, and go to Rathskellar and party. We were best friends with everyone. The ski patrol ran the bad guys out of town. It was a great place. We had horses right in town and a pink jeep; we could ride our horses to the house and tie them up. The kids were never bored. We camped out and sometimes pitched a tent by the stream. That first year, I taught skiing to the Texas water skiers. They were big guys, and I introduced them to the Poma lift. I taught them how to get up and ended up lifting them up. I wasn't a ski instructor, but one woman always requested me, even when it took us all day to get down the mountain. Ted and I both taught classes on Golden Peak. Ted worked with Rod at Slifer & Company in real estate. A woman named Mrs. Knuckles was a basher; she skied with Ted in the Back Bowls, hit him, and he broke his ankle. The problems made it more exciting. It's not that kind of fun anymore.

Penny Lewis was going to have a baby. There was a doctor from the Mayo Clinic here who hadn't delivered a baby in seven years. He delivered the baby in a little room in the Red Lion. In 1965, the ski patrol drove the ambulance to Leadville and had a flat tire. We really needed a doctor, but the prospective doctors all wanted a clinic and a guaranteed salary, so I interviewed some doctors. One man was an MD and vet. I said, "That's perfect." Salary? No salary. Finally, John Murchison said, "Nancy, would you like me to take over?" Dr. Tom Steinberg was an industrial doctor in New Jersey. John brought him to Vail and had a party, and Vail had a doctor with an office in the Mill Creek Court Building. Tom made house calls; he did everything. He is a great citizen.

We made bank runs to Eagle before we got a bank and post office. Ted fought hard for the first golf course. Golfers had to shoot over a chairlift. Dick Hauserman decided to have a golf camp and housed them in Avon someplace.

We had to go to State Bridge to meet anyone arriving on the train. Everything was so primitive, including the roads. We drove fast and thought nothing of it, but it was a treacherous road. We went to the dentist in Denver; finally, he said, "Why don't I just come to your house and see the children?"

The whole life here was exciting and rewarding. You couldn't have a more fun life. We left because we liked powder. The back bowls were being roped off, and the powder was being skied off. We wanted to learn to play golf, so we moved.

Elaine speaking: Nancy Kindel died this past year, leaving a "Kindel Legacy" here in Vail.

NANCY LANGMAID LOTH

My first visit to Vail was the opening ski season in the spring of 1963. My aunt and uncle, Joe and Bunny Langmaid, original investors/pioneers invited me to visit during my spring break from college, and I jumped at the chance, though it was a little scary to think about taking my first airplane ride.

In 1965, at age 21, armed with a secretarial degree, it didn't take much arm-twisting for my cousin, Jane Langmaid Lancy, to talk me into moving from the East Coast to this mountain paradise. My parents sent me off from my hometown of Falmouth, Maine with encouragement and to "find a husband to take care of me." Upon arrival in the valley via Loveland Pass, pushing my way through the Seven Sisters (avalanche chutes that crossed the road), which had been cleared for nothing wider than my VW Beetle, my adventure began.

The job market was tight, it seemed, so I felt fortunate to land a position as a reservationist/front desk assistant at The Night Latch that offered reasonably priced accommodations in the Village and was home to the US Ski Team for a few weeks each winter. I worked with Tom Burnham, manager, and Diana Mounsey Donovan, also a reservationist. The owner Gaynor Miller oversaw operations mostly from the slopes where he was a fulltime ski instructor. He and I married in June 1967. That first winter, I lived with Jane, Betty Stiles Stoner, and Caroline (Pidge) Coventry in the only multi-family residential building outside the Village, about three miles west, on Buffehr Creek Road. There were a few homes nearby; however, it seemed far from the Village. We worked most days and tried to arrange our schedules so that we could squeeze in a few runs on the mountain.

The community was small, so age didn't seem to be a barrier. All ages mingled whether skiing or socializing. Many an afternoon was spent après skiing on the Red Lion deck, evenings dancing at Casino Vail, topped off with a stop at the Scopatone to watch the "running of the bulls" before heading to breakfast at Jeff's in Minturn. Other favorite spots were The Copper Bar, La Cave, and the St. Moritz Restaurant in the Wedel Inn. Vail was quite isolated with no radio or television, so we missed much of what was making news in the rest of the world. Skiing, of course, was paramount. Learning to ski the deep powder was an amazing sensation and unlike anything I had experienced on the slopes in Maine and New Hampshire. I had experiences in Vail that never would have been presented to me if I hadn't been living in such a unique area surrounded by people who loved adventure. We joked that as much as we loved living in Vail in the winter, summer was why we were here. It was the secret most visitors hadn't learned about yet, Vail's fantastic summers.

I'll never forget heading out early one morning to hike from the top of Chair 4 to China Bowl with the intention of ending up at the bottom of Chair 5, just a few quick turns before lunch. Gaynor Miller, my husband, was our guide. After making fresh tracks down China Bowl, we took the wrong drainage out and ended up sidestepping up what is now Teacup Bowl, several thousand vertical feet. With only one chocolate bar to sustain us and a brilliant sunny Colorado day to keep us warm, we were rescued by the ski patrol on the ridge overlooking Adios in Sun-up Bowl during their late afternoon sweep.

A number of my women friends, Dorothy Schneeberger, Jane Boldt, Liz Mudd, Gina Lepman, Susie Heymann, Pearl Newman Rieger, Marcia Vermillion, and Janet Boyd Tyler were regular visitors from across the country. Vail was their second home where they introduced their children to mountain activities, became involved in the community, and made lifelong friends. We skied, hiked, went camping, played golf and tennis, and picnicked winter and summer together building memories that we reminisce about to this day.

For several years, Marge and Larry Burdick arranged to have Dick and Maddie Gibson's "Jazz Party" held at Casino Vail. Performing were many of the greats of traditional jazz including members of the "World's Greatest Jazz Band" and favorites, Ralph Sutton, Peanuts Hucko, Bob Wilber, and Joe Venuti. Their improvisation was mesmerizing; it was a weekend I looked forward to all year. I recall Lelo Staub inviting a few of us women to come to her condominium at the Vorlaufer to learn to speak basic German. She would write out the lesson on her green, slate-covered dining room table, which looked like a chalkboard. We had lots of laughs but didn't grasp much of the language.

Holidays focused on vacationers in the valley, so celebrating Christmas, or other holidays, usually wasn't on the actual holiday. For a number of years, Heather and Rod Slifer invited many of us to celebrate Christmas on July 25th at their home on the Vail Golf Course when we had more time to enjoy the celebration. We  didn't have many everyday conveniences; I did not own a washer and dryer in those years. There was a small grocery store in Minturn, but we drove to Denver monthly to purchase groceries, easily a five-hour trip one way. The movie theater in Minturn showed a film once a week, which many of us looked forward to, and hoped we wouldn't get picked up for exceeding the speed limit on the winding road back to Vail. Living in the Village in 1967 meant walking to pretty much everything we wanted

to do. I looked forward to the social aspect of picking up the day's mail at Vail's first post office on Bridge Street. Everything was close, maybe too close, to the Night Latch. The night when The Covered Bridge Store was ablaze is still vivid in my memory.

In 1969, the Night Latch was torn down and replaced with the Mountain Haus. It was the first high rise in the village, the beginning of Vail's "urban renewal," which complements today's skyline. I married into a ready-made family; Gaynor had two daughters, Gretchen and Stephanie. Our daughter, Tanya, was an early surprise while we were taking a short golfing vacation in Scottsdale at the end of the 1970-71 ski season; and, Alison, arrived rather quickly the day after a bumpy jeep ride to Piney Lake. With the hospital on the other side of Loveland Pass in Denver, the five-hour drive was not too treacherous in mid-July. I moved in and out of the Valley three times. However, the pull was too great, and I always moved back. Vail is a very special place, and I will always call it home.

NANCY NOTTINGHAM

Born in Denver, I moved to California at age six. Dad had always paid taxes in Colorado, so I was eligible for in-state tuition, about $72 per semester in Boulder in1952. My friends thought I was coming out to the Indians, it took three days by train, then a bus to Boulder. In 1956, I met Mauri, who was from the Vail area, and we married after graduation. He then taught at CU until we came to Vail.

We built the Talisman Lodge in Vail in 1968 and could not have done anything we did without our 31 partners. We bought land on Forest Road in 1964, borrowing on life insurance, and used it to entertain prospective clients. It was to fulfill Mauri's dream of having a ski lodge; by coincidence, this wonderful ski area was located next to his parents. It was an adventure, being on the ground floor of the growth of Vail. We worked really hard and did things like picking up the rock for the fireplace along the highway outside Georgetown. We opened the Talisman with 26 rooms on Christmas Eve 1968.

I remember one evening when I was pregnant with our youngest, Shelley, and the phone rang. We had adopted a kitty from the Laziers because of mice in the mountains, the cat was bouncing from mattress to mattress, and I answered, "Good evening, Talisman Lodge!" It just seems so silly, remembering that.

It was the first year of the rummage sale, and that's where I met Vi Brown. She said, "You've got to come over to the story hour, so the kids can get together." Celine and Ben Krueger had just moved up. That's how I met most of that first group of friends, through Vi and Celine. We started playing bridge together, and we still get together for Christmas Bridge, but we don't play bridge. Our bridge group solved each other's problems, did babysitting, and shopped for each other. Most of us were up here because we'd gone out on a limb to be here, and we were going to do everything possible to make it work. I remember all of those early friends - Annetta Dixon, Willie Benway, Marka Moser, and Ann Holland from the telephone company. Vi and Celine developed into deep friendships. Vi was especially strong; she had been here three years at that point. She really got me through the early times in Vail.

I'm adventurous, and I think you need to be that; you need to be self-sufficient. I think we all had that streak. I don't know if it was self-confidence, but I knew, "You can do this." Helga Pulis and I had girls the same age, and that made all the difference. You had to be resourceful; basically, we had no money. I would shop in Leadville, then I'd buy milk and bread at The Rucksack before Village Market. At home, we had a birthday box, and the kids picked gifts for their friends from there. We lived in the Talisman until we sold it. In the meantime, we had added onto it. Chuck Ogilby and Fred Gold were our first night staff. My mother and sister moved up for a year and lived in Sandstone; Mauri's sister Claire moved up and did our continental breakfasts for us. There were two bedrooms on the lower floor and a swimming pool. The Tannery and Ichiban restaurant were in The Talisman. We had employees who were here to ski who lived in the laundry room and helped with our kids; I worked full time in the hotel. Having family around was a real resource. The first real Christmas was in1969.

Shelley was born in June '69. Mauri read all the books on how to deliver the baby, and we went to Denver a week before she was due. There was a Fireman's Convention in Vail, and it snowed in June. My doctor decided I'd better stay in Denver for the birth. I had Tamara, and Mauri had Kim. I was sure Kim was going to be hit by a drunk fireman, so I told the doctor he had to induce the baby, because I was so worried, "I have to go home."

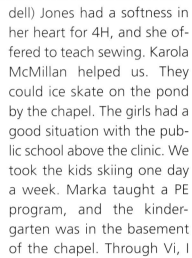

The morning after I came home, I woke up and one side of my face was paralyzed. It was the 4th of July weekend, and I called Tom Steinberg – "You've been under some stress, you have Bell's palsy." He gave me a shot of Vitamin A, and that was it. It took me a week to get back. I credit him for that.

We were entertaining our prospective partners and living on Forest Road when Sue Rychel knocked on the door with two kids in the car. She was looking for a place to live and had all her belongings in the car. Our main problems were being on call 24 hours a day, working the front desk, and hoping the maids showed up. The best Christmas present was in 1969. It had been a hard year, and guests hadn't used their bathtub on Christmas. It was the best present, because the next guests were due at 4pm.

The girls made good close friends and had a freedom in town that you can't have now. The Kindel girls lived nearby. When Marka Moser arrived, she and I decided we needed to do something club-wise for our girls; we debated between starting a Girl Scout troupe or 4H. Ella Knox taught knitting for us at 4H; she would invite the girls to her house and serve tea and teach them to knit. Linda (Gundell) Jones had a softness in her heart for 4H, and she offered to teach sewing. Karola McMillan helped us. They could ice skate on the pond by the chapel. The girls had a good situation with the public school above the clinic. We took the kids skiing one day a week. Marka taught a PE program, and the kindergarten was in the basement of the chapel. Through Vi, I got involved in teaching Sunday school. I also thought it was important to get to know down valley kids. Halloween was great. Gordon Brittan always wore this rubber Indian mask, and he'd come down the outside stairs and scare all the kids. Kindels had big decorations. It was all locals.

I do remember standing in the middle of the kitchen one time after I'd had Shelley and said, "I am so damned tired of being flexible." And I wasn't normally one to cuss. I don't remember being isolated as a woman in Vail, and I was very involved in the beginnings of the schools. Vi and Celine had boys that age. The girls and I talk about what it would have been like if we hadn't moved up here. They all felt very positive. They probably would not have been involved in sports elsewhere. Kim got involved in 4H government and went to DC twice. The girls came through public schools and got an excellent education; they worked very hard. It was a good place to raise the kids. Since there was no TV those first years, they did home plays. I don't think I ever felt trapped. You could get ahead here if you worked hard, and there were people supporting you to help you work hard. You could do it. After selling the Talisman, I managed children's programs for 31 years. In all, we have moved 27 times in our marriage.

NANCY REINECKE

Before coming to Vail I was a stay-at-home mom with two little boys. I did some secretarial work for my husband Jim while we lived in Cheyenne. We had heard many things about a new ski area and came to Vail for the 4th of July in 1963. During the visit, we met Rod Slifer, and he mentioned that they needed contractors and told us to go talk to Mr. Scott, an architect. Jim secured the

building contract, and we moved to Vail before the end of July to build the Caromba house on Forest Road. For me, it was a great experience to work with the three couples that owned the property and to have their friendship.

We built many homes and condos through the years, and I did the books and payroll, etc. for the company. The Covered Bridge project is still a fond memory. John and Cissy Dobson were a strong influence in our remaining in Vail. We built the Covered Bridge and the Covered Bridge Store. And then I learned to play bridge after moving to Vail, and our group numbered over 30. It was a great way to meet people.

I was unable to ski due to an accident just prior to moving to Vail, but I became active in Ski Club Vail and began timing ski races and eventually became the certified chief timer with the Rocky Mountain division of the US Ski Association.

We spent time with many friends entertaining in our home. I'd had no expectations of what my life would be like when we moved to Vail. I only knew that if it didn't work out, we would go back to Denver. It was a wonderful time in our lives, and we are grateful for the many friendships that we have from our years in Vail.

NEVIN NELSON

I worked as administrative assistant for Terry Minger, town manager of Vail, for a year and a half, then as an ASID interior designer. When I first arrived, I got to know everyone, and we were all on the same level. I'm originally from Ohio, transferred to CU for my studies and graduated in 1964 with a BA in interior design. I was a single mom with two kids, Doug and Brian. In 1966, I started an interior design business in Boulder.

Vail was a great place to raise kids, a good place to be an interior designer, and I liked the small-town atmosphere. I loved the people and had a ton of fun. I had never been to Vail and had no idea what to expect when I got here. I think a lot of us were pioneers, adventurers, and came to see what could happen. I didn't have much of a social life in Vail with two kids and a job that took over 50 hours a week. I did manage to go to Mickey's Lounge after work and listen to music. Mickey is still a good friend. Then I met Stig Bergman, a Finnish ski instructor, and went with him for five years before finally marrying him, a never-married bachelor.

I skied a lot, of course, ice skated, and took my kids to all of their sporting events. My kids and I were pretty close during those early years. They went back and forth to Boulder to see their dad, over that very scary Loveland Pass with a rear wheel drive car in the middle of white outs. It's a miracle we are still alive. They were involved in every sport, and I bought a big van and drove them around.

As time went by, there was more of a division between the very rich and the workers. The new arrivals to Vail weren't pioneers. I don't think there will ever be a better place to live than Vail in the early years. We had a blast, and Vail has the best groomed snow in the world, and is definitely the place to ski in the state of Colorado.

NONA WILKE

My path to Vail started in a central Wisconsin town, where I graduated from a small liberal arts college with a degree in Business Administration. It got me a job as an Assistant Buyer with a department store in Brooklyn, NY. While in New York I started skiing, and that made me think about Colorado. So, I moved to Denver and got a job at May D&F depart-

172

ment store. Some fellow apartment dwellers were friends with Vail's George Ward, who then became a friend of mine. George eventually moved to Vail, and some of us started making day trips to ski in Vail that led to my spending weekends, thanks to the hospitality of Carol Gillis, now Fitzsimmons, and Shirley Anderson, now Ward. It became more and more difficult for me to go back to Denver and my corporate job. In July of 1967, I packed my belongings in my new Corvair convertible and moved in with Shirley in "downtown" Vail. To be precise, downtown Vail meant the apartment above the liquor store.

I wanted the excitement of the ski bum lifestyle and good friends. I started as a waitress at The Lodge of Vail and a sales clerk for John & Cissy Dobson at the Covered Bridge Store. In a couple of years, I was waitressing at the Clock Tower for John Kaemmer and helping Ginny Crowley at the Gaslight gift shop. In time, she made me a partner. During the off-season, when I stayed in town, there was an interesting mix of part-time work, from meeting the buses, helping set up new restaurants, and fill-in waitressing at the few places that stayed open.

I stayed because of the good friends and lifestyle. I left because my then-husband, wanted to get an engineering degree, which got him a job with an engineering company contracted to build the Alaska pipeline. When our marriage ended, Alaska's economy was in another bust period so I moved back to Vail for the friends, climate, and job market. My second Vail life started out living with Shirley Ward in EagleVail and working for the Gorsuch store catalog.

Living in the apartment in Vail's center came with a built-in social life. Locals dropped off their dogs for safekeeping. Mornings could find various locals and canines sleeping in our living room. Of the several parties we put on, one was a black-tie event for the premier showing of Jerry Blackwell's melodrama film. The party was great, and the film was awful. One summer day, a very irritated Ernie Chavez, Vail's postmaster, showed up at the apartment, needing to deliver a registered letter to the Garton boys sent by Bill Whiteford. This was the sixth registered letter sent between the parties in two days, and Ernie was way over it. He was the only employee, and registered letters meant he had to close the post office to deliver them.

Minturn had a movie theater and Jeff's Café for late-night breakfast. Working several jobs and shifts allowed only enough time for skiing and some hiking in the summer. The Ruder brothers organized a few jeep trips, the most memorable being the one through Ashcroft, over Pearl Pass into Crested Butte with the night spent at Paul Johnston's Ore Bucket Lodge. There were nine assorted vehicles and around 20 people who made the trip.

173

For most worker bees, nightlife started after the dinner shift. It usually was drinking and dancing at The Casino (the Labastella), the Black Bear/Nu Gnu, or the Vail Village Inn. The Casino sponsored an Irish troupe that included The Irish Rovers for one summer, hosted Jazz Week, and occasionally a concert (always a chance to dress up). There were the summer melodramas in The Lodge at Vail, written and directed by John Dobson, and performed by some colorful thespians. Like many locals, I was single and arrived without any family. That made friends and co-workers very important. I was too immature to think very far ahead, so great skiing and a fun lifestyle were good in my book.

What made the early days memorable was the intensity caused by our isolation (no interstate highway, tunnel, TV, or radio reception), the emerging ski industry with few rules, and the social upheaval brought on by the baby boomers and the wonderful sense of adventure among both the investors and the workers, which has now been replaced by prestige. Time forces changes. Since my return, I've worked more, skied little, partied even less and have retired after working at Colorado Alpine Wildflower Farm.

THE OMI OF VAIL – "WALLY" KRAUSS

The real story is the back-story of Omi's life, the skills, and faith she brought to the young mountain community.

Clara Wally Wessling Krauss was born in 1897 in Germany. One of three daughters, she spent her childhood in Wahren, a suburb of Leipzig, Germany. She entered nursing school in 1918 at the prestigious order of Hamburg Schlump Red Cross Mother House, graduating in 1926. World War I demanded that student nurses participate in medical services as surgical assistants, care providers to wounded warriors, and give patient care at orphanages and pediatric sanato-

riums. Children were her favorites.

In 1927, she married a former patient, Otto Gustav Krauss, a decorated WWI veteran 25 years her senior. They had two sons, Horst and Siegfried, and she settled into the role of mother and homemaker until the outbreak of WWII when all women under age 45 were ordered back to work. She rejoined the Red Cross as a nurse.

WWII and the following Occupation changed everything. On February 27, 1945, Horst was killed in an air raid when our house took a direct hit. "Wally" helped 35 neighbors out of the burning inferno and directed them to safety through the phosphorus firestorm. On May 16, 1945 Otto died from injuries suffered in the February air raid, leaving her with a young son of 10 years and no home. In June 1948, she was officially recognized by the City of Leipzig and honored for her humanitarian service during WWII and the Occupation. Because of a dangerous political climate in spring of 1954, her son Siegfried, now 17, escaped to West Berlin and the free world where he pursued an international culinary career. Contact and communication between them was difficult and hazardous because of State Censorship.

Little Sheika

Assigned by the Red Cross to accompany returning sick POW patients home across national borders, she moved freely with special papers and traveled in a Red Cross uniform. These assignments provided two opportunities to visit her son. Siegfried's return to East Germany was not an option. He would have faced punishment and imprisonment for escaping. Their separation lasted 13 years.

In 1966, at age 70, she retired and learned of a slim possibility to leave what were oppressive conditions where she lived in East Germany, the first step in rejoining her son in the United States. The official permission statement declared that "because of her age she is no longer a threat to the State."

Siegfried's career path led him to the position of Executive Chef at The Red Lion Inn in Vail, Colorado. In April, 1967 "Chef" Sigi and Gunther and Cecile Hofler partnered to purchase a duplex on Beaver Dam Road, each moving into one unit. This was the breakthrough opportunity to share his home with his mother. In the fall of 1967, Omi arrived in Vail.

Language and lifestyle were not a barrier to a woman who loved people, and the community embraced her. In the early days, German, French, and English were spoken daily in Vail Village. Personally, she loved the freedoms of the US and was charmed by the peaceful mountain environment. In those days, Vail Village was small enough to walk everywhere. She loved the community spirit and energy of people who were young and happy, full of hope and enthusiasm. Everyone focused on creating a new resort town for a winter sport new to the American public - Skiing. The zany antics and mischievous camaraderie of the international transplants were a constant source of amusement. Above all, she drew a sense of personal connection and fulfillment looking after children. Omi's first experience came when she was quickly recruited by Sheika Gramshammer to look after her six-month-old daughter Kira.

One winter day there was an accident. While pulling the baby girl on a sled, out for a walk in the golf course area, a passing garbage truck lost control on the icy road and slid into the area where they were walking, pushing them and the sled off the road into the snow bank. Without hesitation, she threw herself across the baby protecting her from harm. Omi, however, suffered bruises, whiplash, and minor injuries. Other young mothers also engaged her in childcare and planning children's birthday parties. She was Omi Krauss for the Freemans, Browns, Hoflers, among others, becoming an adopted member of their families and often accompanying them and the children on vacation. Personal highlights were trips that included Maui, Hawaii, and Jackson Hole, Wyoming.

Her advanced age didn't permit her to ski, but Omi is remembered as sliding down the ski run on a serving tray in the 6th Hotel and Restaurant Race, an annual rite of season's end. Summer in Vail is magical. Omi had a green thumb. She created a showcase of blooming flowers during a short growing season. Travelers on Beaver Dam Road would take pictures of the riotous show of color. She maintained strong ties with friends in Vail after moving with Sigi to his Manitou Springs estate and restaurant. Although she lived elsewhere, they remained part of her daily life.

Omi's last trip to Germany was in 1983, planned for 10 weeks. She suffered a fall on a gravel walkway resulting in internal injuries. Surgery and medical care in hospital meant she would soon be able to travel, and then she suffered a series of strokes and died on September 25, 1983. She was laid to rest in the family plot in Germany. Memorial Services were at Vail Chapel with a reception celebrating her life at Gramshammers'. The ladies in Vail wore silly, vintage hats in honor of Omi Krauss. It was her kind of party.

— SON SIGI KRAUSS

PAM EHRENBERG

I came to Vail in 1968 to start my first job as a hair stylist at Lady Vail Salon, located in the Gold Peak building on Bridge Street. Edie Fricke had recently opened the salon, and I enjoyed working for her.

I was very fortunate to meet many of the incredible "women of Vail" who were clients at the Lady Vail Salon. One of my fondest memories working at Lady Vail was the opportunity to do Jackie Kennedy's hair.

I learned to ski after moving to Vail, and it soon became a favorite sport of mine. I worked for Edie until she sold her salon, so she could open Tea Room Alpenrose. I then worked in LionsHead at Salon 21. After that, I moved to Eagle when I got married and now have a son and a daughter. I am glad that I made the mountains my home.

PATTI DORF

Driving across Wyoming in early December could be risky. Driving a Volkswagen station wagon towing a trailer filled with frozen deer, antelope, and dozens of jars of canned vegetables added stupidity to the risk, resulting in what was called "full-blown idiocy " (at least one person would make that assertion). Add to this insane mix: a 27-year-old ski instructor, his 21-year-old wife, and their 2-week-old son. Now, imagine that this brain dead group (not the baby, he turned out to be quite bright) was heading to Vail to spend a winter. The husband had a contract to teach at the Vail Ski School (guaranteed pay: $13 big bucks a day); the young wife had a quiver of practical knowledge gained from growing up in a small community of farmers, hunters (well, mostly poachers), gardeners, and independent sorts who had to know how to do almost everything. She also had a sense of wellbeing that surely would have made Pollyanna look like a despondent melancholic right on the verge of suicide.

The weather was treacherous, a huge storm (the blizzard of 1969) rolled in, making it nearly impossible to get up some of the passes. Saner people would have turned back and taken the teaching job waiting in Bozeman, Montana. Saner people would have realized that $13 a day would be almost impossible to exist on. Saner voices did warn the young couple, but, like all young couples, they knew best. Like all pioneers, they focused on the good that would come their way, the life ahead. The opportunities! The glamour! The fun! The experience!

Like all parents of pioneers, their parents maligned the adventure. They scorned the plans of their offspring. It was as if they were going into the Congo with one canteen and a Boy Scout knife.

I am Patricia Dorf, and I was that young wife. This is the very abbreviated story of how "one winter" turned into a lifetime. Bob and I met teaching skiing in Red Lodge, Montana. After we married, Bob wanted to teach at a major area for one year before settling down in a "real job." Through our friend, Denny Hoeger, Bob was able to secure a job with the Vail Ski School. We had vacationed in Vail the previous spring, and he had made a reconnaissance trip during the fall to find us a place to live. So, what could go wrong? Well, actually, nothing. At least, that is how we saw our first winter in Vail.

Our home was a room rented from Tom Sachs. We were in a condo in East Vail, with beautiful two-story windows. Single-pane windows. On cold nights, we would sit in front of the fire, wrapped in our electric blanket with

177

our baby (Erik) and listen to records. The Fifth Dimension, The Beatles, The Mamas and Papas, Elvis, and Henry Mancini would play while we watched the fire burn. The Mancini album was a gift from Henry himself, a ski school client. Days were structured around the sun; I would wait until the sun was just about to hit our little part of the valley, bundle the baby up, and head out with him on the sled for our daily constitutional. Ever the optimist, I was undaunted by the incredible effort it took to get out the door for the brief time that the sun actually hit the valley floor.

Daily life was complicated by the fact that we had just one car. I would have to bundle the baby up and take Bob into work if I wanted to be mobile. Since we didn't have a washer and dryer and did have lots of dirty cloth diapers, I had to go to the Laundromat in Crossroads to do the wash. Two mornings a week I did laundry, went home, and returned at the end of the day to pick Bob up. We usually took that opportunity to go for a beer at Donovan's Copper Bar. Babies were a rarity in Vail and even more rare in Donovan's. Beers were three for $1.05, Bob would have two, I'd have one, and we would head home. Once established in Ski School, we started going out more, having dinner with Bob's clients at the Clock Tower Restaurant and the Red Lion with Erik sleeping in his infant seat under the table. Doggie bags would provide a few more dinners, and clients who rented condos with kitchens would leave us leftover food. Let me assure you, I had stuff we had never even heard of in Choteau, Montana. It took me very little time to become accustomed to Brie cheese, tins of caviar, and

smoked salmon. We have a very different kind of smoked fish in Montana; we never ate the raw stuff. Three weeks after our arrival, our first New Year's Eve, we were invited to the home of Bud and Daisy Palmer. Bob had attended Middlebury College in Vermont with Bud's nephew, Davis Webb (Marka Moser's brother). I was in heaven. Bud made me feel like the most important person in the world. He gave Erik a beautiful mobile that hung in our home for years.

Our store of wild game and veggies dwindled as the winter wore on; I needed to shop for groceries more frequently. I found a great butcher shop in Gilman and would continue on to Leadville for the rest of the shopping. The trek would involve most of the day, so I made sure to stock up on everything.

My first jobs were tied together. I worked at "Pooh Vale Nursery" (now Buzz's Boots and Boards) in exchange for child care on the days that I taught skiing. The only problem was that when I worked at the nursery I inevitably caught some germ, making it impossible for me to work at the nursery or at ski school. As soon as I would get well, Erik would come down with the germ. The only variation in the process was that occasionally Erik would get the bug first, I would stay home to care for him and then myself when I caught it. The passing of the bug finally took its toll, and I gave up on working. This gave me more time for free skiing, but I had lost my free childcare so I had to resort to either taking Erik to a woman who lived in an apartment in The Lodge Promenade (those ground floor street-side shops were apartments then), or I had to arrange for Bob to take Erik. The woman in The Lodge liked to leave the kids alone and go down to Pepi's for a drink, so that option soon was eliminated. Next plan: I would plan my ski time for Erik's nap time, take him to Bob (if his clients didn't mind), and Erik would nap in the backpack while Bob taught and I skied. Timing was important: Erik woke hungry, cranky, and unwilling to be in the backpack, so I had to stay fairly near Bob's group. It was a little like being a stalker but more fun and colder.

As we neared spring, it became evident that we needed more space; sharing a house with a bachelor wasn't the ideal setup. We contacted Will Miller and started looking at real estate, finally buying one of the new Chamonix Chalet condos. We paid a sum that my father assured us would purchase a large home on 10 acres in Montana if we would just come to our senses and return. Having proven that we had no sense several times in the previous six months, we plunged on with our plans to buy the condo. It turned out to be a great place for us because we finally had

neighbors like ourselves. You know, those rare few living in Vail at that time…parents. It is also likely the main reason that we ended up staying in the valley.

We loved our first winter in Vail, and after a brief visit to our families, returned to our little condo and never looked back. Our two grown children Erik and Heather live nearby and are raising their children here. Hopefully, our grandchildren will learn about the pioneers that made our town unique and will know that they come from a tiny mountain town where we knew every single resident and counted them as friends.

179

PATTY FENNELL

I am from a small town in Ohio where everyone knew everybody's parents and grandparents, so early Vail was like putting on my favorite old pajamas. It was a magical time for all of us. I had spent some time at Ohio State University with summers in Lake George, New York, and the winter preceding my arrival in Vail was in Stowe, Vermont.

One of my coworkers in Stowe was headed to Aspen in 1966, so I came out intending to winter there. When I got to her place of employment there were about 20 people, and I knew 18 of them from Vermont. I decided that was not much of a change and, having seen Vail on my way, I decided to go there instead. I arrived at the Village Inn and went to work in their bar and dining room. Merv Lapin was their night auditor and had a chalet in West

Vail, so I eventually moved there and went to work for The Lodge at Vail. Work at The Lodge was whatever position they needed filled - from running the switchboard (it was the old plug-in connections type) to cashiering or serving.

After a year or so, I started tending bar at Donovan's days and continued to do that for several years. I also tended bar in La Cave for Jim Slevin at night. In those days, Vail only had Ski Season (the week before Thanksgiving through the week after Easter) followed by Construction Season when most of the businesses closed. I found work for Don Meyers as a guide in the summers. He was located at the junction of Booth Creek and Gore Creek on the north side of the highway, a two-lane road at that time. I led day rides up Booth, Pitkin, and some of the drainages on that side of the road and five-to-seven-day pack trips on the back side of Holy Cross Mountain.

In the early days, Vail did not have TV or radio reception, so we found our own forms of entertainment by socializing with each other. We formed some very close bonds. Unless Bob Parker brought us up-to-date on the news of the world, we lived happily in our never-never land.

I stayed until the town grew beyond that small intimate feeling and then decided it was time to rejoin the "outside world" and moved to Grand Junction. Living in Vail was such a fine time, for which I am very grateful.

PENNY LEWIS

I remember as a child talking to the ranchers in this valley. We used to stay with ranch families in Eagle. The area that became known as Vail was not new to me. Pete Seibert and my husband Chuck met in Aspen in '60 or '61. Most of Chuck's accounting clients were there, and he had a reputation as a skier. Vail was a dream come true for Pete. This was a sheep pasture that would become a ski resort. Chuck had been working with Vail for several years; we even helped haul the plastic model around. They offered him the job as Executive VP and Treasurer. Whitefords and Sheika and Pepi were his clients. We were here for all the businesses opening, and I ran the cash register for those opening nights.

We drove over the pass on Memorial Day 1964, and the snow on the side of the road was 5 ft. high. I thought, "Oh, no, this can't be true. Does summer ever come?" The Tweedys offered us their basement apartment. We had two children, ages three and five, and I was a full-time mom. When we built our house on the golf course, that made two houses – Seiberts and ours. I can still tell you when the sun came up at what time of year–

before the trees. I felt it was a narrow valley. The minute I drove over Floyd Hill heading to Denver, I felt like someone had taken a rock off my chest. It was dark in the winter; the sun didn't hit our house till 10 past 10 in February, and it left at 2:45.

Everything was focused on Vail. We entertained endless rounds of travel agents. In the early days, it was Vail first - God, country, and everything else afterward. Everyone had one goal: to develop the ski area. There was a cooperation I haven't seen before or since, and I don't remember conflicts. Because the kids needed some kind of life of their own, I had to set rules. We stopped entertaining in our house, except for very close friends. Kids loved it here because they had total freedom, and everybody knew who they were and looked out for them. It was pretty primitive and remote, and I wasn't convinced about it. Our families were certain that Chuck had totally lost his mind and that no one could ever earn a living in the ski business. Other family members viewed it as something of a lark.

Anne Staufer, Daphne Slevin, and I would have gourmet dinners, and that was fun. Lelo Staub and I went to Denver at any excuse. She had left a wonderful cosmopolitan and international life to come here. She was the Jane Pauley of Swiss TV. It was fun to go into restaurants with Lelo because the maître d' would move people off a table for her.

The hardest thing was schools for the children and lack of services. At first, they home-schooled K through 8, using the Calvert system. We started our own school because the school district thought the Vail community was transient and would not send a bus up here. I taught Head Start one summer. We needed to bring kids who didn't speak English up to that level by kindergarten. We hired two teachers for the nine grades; it was very structured. The Director of Education for the State of Colorado gave us access to libraries, and we designed our own program. That first year, our house was finished Thanksgiving weekend. It had snowed three feet in five hours; the moving truck overturned in the driveway, and they were stuck here. The movers couldn't go home for Thanksgiving. Everybody in the village contributed something to the dinner and all went to the Vail Village Inn. You had the great hunters like Ted Kindel who delivered exotic meats; the chef fixed mountain lion, mountain sheep, mountain goat, elk, deer, and turkeys. When the snow came the first year, they didn't have the equipment to groom the slopes. Instead, they skied it out. As Bob Parker always said, "It doesn't matter what is said or done as long as you spell it correctly." If you had to prepare hors d'oeuvres for 150, you prepared hors d'oeuvres. If you had to listen to some travel agent from Wisconsin babble on, you did it. That was your job. If you had to ski or meet somebody for dinner, you did that. There were so few people here everyone had to jump in. Phones were an issue because every time they ran a phone line they had to dig it up. We lived with those guys in the trenches. Fire was my greatest terror. You really had no help if a fire started; VA had a little tanker truck. When there was a fire at Dowd Junction, Chuck went in and pulled John Donovan out; he was a volunteer fireman and had gotten caught. Peter's and our driveways got plowed first. Chuck called VA the benevolent dictatorship before Vail became a town. We left due to a corporate issue, went back to Denver, and ended up starting Copper Mountain Resort.

There was a robbery, and they yelled at the cops not to scare the visitors. Whitefords opened the Casino right after Pepi's. Bettan and I cleaned out ashtrays so they could have Mass there on Sundays. If you went to church, you went to the Catholic one, because it was the only one. I did a Christmas party for all the children of people who worked here, I made popcorn balls, and Father Stone played Santa Claus. I would rent the suit for him and keep it at the Casino. One time, Chuck asked me to ask Santa to go outside for a minute because there was someone who needed to see him.

They had caught a fellow on the mountain cutting down a Christmas tree and brought him down. Chuck decided the guy needed to talk to Santa and told him, "You can either pay a fine or make a contribution to Santa." The lumberjack made a very nice contribution to the Christmas party.

This was such a small community; there weren't more than 30 people here. Ski instructors lived in and cared for our kids at night. There were accidents before we had a clinic. Little Peter (Seibert) shot Guy Parker in the stomach with a pellet gun. The nurse was here that day and dug the pellets out. When my son hooked his sister with a fishing hook, Dr. Steinberg got his pliers and took the hook out. When John Murchison broke his leg in Aspen, they sent him to Texas. The doctor in Texas recommended he go back to the best orthopedic man who was in Aspen. The Aspen doctor said he would operate on one condition: if Murchison would finance a clinic in Vail. That's how the Vail Clinic first got funded, and they hired Dr. Steinberg. The early directors of Vail were huge supporters in every way you could think of. They were amazing, whatever you asked they would give, and whatever you needed they would do. I remember everyone standing in the middle of Bridge Street arguing whether they should pave it. The argument went: "If we pave it, we'll have

182

trucks and traffic on it." No one envisioned that Vail would become what it's become.

Women had a lot of influence – certainly Penny Tweedy did. The wives of the directors had influence, too. We were part of each other's lives. It was very rural. They brought sheep through town, and hunters camped in our front yard.

We had a Labrador that would float down Gore Creek into town and go to Chuck's office. Loyette Goodell, the secretary, fed her potato chips. Fishing was about the only summer activity, and I was in the store one day where they sold fishing licenses. A man was there and said he wanted his money back. The owner asked, "Why, wasn't the fishing good?" His reply, "It was excellent, but this big black dog came floating down through my fishing hole."

The ultra-glamorous and the rest of us lived side-by-side. For me personally, that was the hardest thing, here I was in my blue jeans with two little kids, and there were the glamorous women of Vail. Some of us were just mommies. And there were these beautifully coiffed and dressed women, and we were wiping the baby cereal off our shoulders. We had to laugh about it. In the summer, Betty Seibert and I would put our five kids in one gondola, and we would get in another and read the paper. On Father's Day we would do a picnic somewhere. My children were inseparable from the Seibert and Kindel kids. You had to enjoy the outdoors. My kids didn't know what TV was for years, and they didn't seem to miss it.

We had a nine-hole golf course at first. When my youngest was in preschool, I took the kids to school, played six holes out, went and made beds, and did the dishes. Then I would play four holes in, get in my car, and go pick her up. At night, I put dinner on and went out and pitched balls for a while. When Vail transitioned from a company-owned town, they went through the exercise three times before incorporating. The impetus was political – you could form special districts, things you couldn't do when VA was the "benevolent dictator." Although VA felt they had the best interest of the community at heart, there were some who chafed under that and wanted to be part of the decision-making.

When we went back to Denver, I missed the sense of community, belonging. I still miss that. We were a tight community in the mountains, and it was a very special time.

PHYLLIS FINLAY

On August 16, 1969, I drove into the Vail Valley with a U-Haul full of my earthly possessions, a Siamese cat with four kittens, and a Honda Trail 90 motorcycle. I was on a year's leave of absence from a teaching job in Helena, Montana. I had gotten a job teaching English, speech, and drama at Battle Mountain High School, a 7-12 grade school at the time. I taught all 8th grade and most 10th grade students English.

I chose to come here because I had just learned to ski, but the local area outside Helena had only rope tows. In Vail, there were ski lifts, plus they advertised that teachers skied for $6 a year. Imagine my chagrin to discover that in just one year the rate had gone up to $16.

With three years of experience, I started teaching here for $7200 per year. That was enough for rent, food, and gas ($.33 per gallon), plus I had enough to go out four nights a week into Vail, drinking and dancing. What fun to see the "Masked Man" movies at the Slope, go up to Garton's Saloon above Kentucky Fried Chicken, dance the night away at the Nu Gnu below the Clock Tower with tourists in their ski boots and a two-inch wad of lift tickets hanging on their jackets.

There was a movie theater in Minturn and one in Vail. The main problem was that Vail's Theater would get "Downhill Racer" with Robert Redford for two weeks at a time about every four to six weeks. A lot of our entertainment was to go to friends' houses for games and meals. We did enjoy $1 spaghetti night at the Blue Cow where the Tyrolian is located. Of course, Donovan's Copper Bar & Grill was a favorite with beers for $.35 or three for a $1.

As a teacher, I could only ski weekends and school holidays. We would get to the slopes early, park in the dirt lot where the main parking garage is now, walk up Bridge Street to get up the mountain, and try to ski every run. I found it could be done.

PIA RIVA McISAAC

Growing up at the foot of the Alps near the Dolomites meant skiing was always part of my life. I preferred it to studying. Racing followed quite naturally, and I made the Italian National Team and was 10 times Italian National Champion. I went to two World Championships and two Olympics (two 4ths in downhill and a Silver medal in 1962). I was also a ski instructor. After high school, I studied languages at the School of Interpreters, preparing me for international travel.

I heard of Vail from Pepi Gramshammer who had been my very first ski coach. He told me to come to the new resort to work and live because it was going to be the "place of the future." In March of 1964 while racing with the US Ski Team, I visited Vail and learned about the mountain, the Back Bowls, and skiing powder. I did get a job with the ski school (under Morris Shepard), but it was a few years before I made it to Vail to work as I had gotten married in California.

Pepi and Sheika invited me to a party where I met great locals: the Seiberts, Dick and Christie Hauserman, Bob Parker, Antonio Guadagni, and George and Ellie Caulkins. I knew the Gorsuches and Anneliese Meggle-Freeman from ski racing. It was fun from the very start.

When I arrived in 1964, Vail stole my heart. It was very small, quaint, and buried in snow. You could walk everywhere. The ski runs were magnificent, and the powder superb. There were no bumps anywhere, and I could ski untracked snow all day long. I had had a lot of curiosity about Vail. Even though I knew many mountain villages and ski resorts in Europe plus a few in the USA, I was curious to see how this one was going to turn out.

For me, Vail is the best mountain for teaching. It has fabulous snow, good organization, and wonderful people. I have great friends here. I come back every year to ski with the "Fast Ladies" (a group of Olympians from the '60s) and to enjoy Vail all over again.

Ski racing was my event, the faster the better. But I also liked rock climbing, hiking, and swimming. The mountains of Colorado were perfect for me.

Note: My last name is Riva. On my first day of skiing in Vail with other US ski racers, we were going back down to the Village, and they led me down a trail. When I saw the name, Riva Ridge, I was so pleased. "Ohhh," I thought, "I am really famous. Even in Vail, they know I won a Silver Medal." After I met Pete Seibert, I learned the story of the 10th Mountain Division in the war and the naming of Riva Ridge.

185

RENIE GORSUCH

I went to the Olympic ski racing tryouts and competed in the 1960 Winter Olympics. David Gorsuch and I traveled the world for skiing and fell in love. On June 15, 1960, I married him and finished my degree at the University of Denver. David and I spent four years in Crested Butte and then had the opportunity to buy Sporthaus Vail and make the big move to the Vail Valley. Were we excited!

Gorsuch Ltd. is and has been our focus. We opened the store with a small space in the Clock Tower building and used the first floor and lower level for equipment. We shared space with the US Post Office, Norge by George, and the Shuberts' Italian fashion store.

The love of Vail kept us here. It was like living on a frontier. We had to drive to Glenwood Springs for our groceries. Our social life was family oriented. The first invitation we received was to Elaine and Gerry White's home, and I remember going to Gretta Parks' for a beautiful summer dinner. There was little time or money to be social.

Our sporting life was skiing, skiing, and more skiing. For entertainment, I remember things like the Irish Rovers at Bill Whiteford's Casino and floating down Gore Creek on summer evenings. I have fond memories of driving up Vail

Mountain along Mill Creek for summer picnics with three very young boys.

Before coming to Vail, we were so excited that we were going to be in a community of positive people who believed anything was possible. I'm still excited to live in Vail. I've seen educational alternatives become available – David and I volunteered our time doing PE for the elementary school and JFK physical fitness for youth. I was the first female member of the Vail Hospital Board. It's great to see how far Vail has come. Yes, of course it has changed and evolved, and I have tried to evolve with it. I have embraced both the sport of skiing and the mountain lifestyle all my life.

ROUENE BROWN

For Christmas the year I was six, I got a little pair of skis. They were probably ordered from Sears & Roebuck, since that's where most of our stuff came from. They had a leather strap through a slot in the center of the ski through which one could put a foot clad in a shoe and rubber overshoe. We lived on a ranch so there were pristine snow-covered hills down which to slide. Trudge to the top, get the feet securely through the straps and slide down in as straight a line as possible, hoping the ever-present dog would not playfully attach its jaws to a mitten or some loose part of the snowsuit and cause a fall. This would be done over and over until hopefully, a nice, icy track was developed creating a speedier and speedier descent. There were no ski poles involved in this get-up, which was probably just as well as that would have been another target for the dog's jaws. We also had a couple pairs of very long hand-hewn wooden skis with the same kind of crude strap. Some of the adults (my dad, or an uncle or cousin) would occasionally come out and help develop some of the icy tracks and have a few falls and a little fun in the process.

Skiing was already being enjoyed elsewhere as a sport and competitively but not in that part of Wyoming and certainly not in my world. Although I continued to slide down the hills around the ranch until after high school, I never really skied until I was living and working in Denver in the '50s. I skied at Winter Park, Loveland, A-Basin, and Aspen, and then Vail opened. I came up to Vail whenever and however I could get there and as often as possible.

Although I didn't live in Vail until late 1969, I was involved in its infancy, as I started skiing there the first season it was open. At that time, I was working in Denver for United Air Lines at the City Ticket Office in the Brown Palace Hotel. Since airline employees were in a good position to promote ski areas, Bob Parker, Vail's first marketer, established a relationship with the airlines with special rates and enticements. "Airline Weeks " were a big time, with lodging, parties, lift tickets, parties, ski lessons, and more parties all made very attractive and affordable. There were a limited number of passes to exchange for a lift ticket, available to Denver employees if one was able to get one's name on the list in time, as they were a hot item and in demand. After all, a daily lift ticket went for $5. Elaine White probably arranged some of the above-referenced parties. According to my diary entries, in January '67, there was a "Paul Masson" party at The Lodge, and the very next night the "Old Crow" party at The Lodge. The next night, UAL gave a party at the Black Bear, next night a party at the Casino, and the last night of that Ski Week, a ski school party.

On one of the trips to Vail during the very early days (February 1963) we stayed at the Vail Village Inn; the night desk clerk was a guy we knew from Denver by the name of Charlie Gersbach. There was some kind of foul-up with our reservation, and one guy and we three ladies had to share a room, definitely had not been in the plan.

On another early trip after Pepi and Sheika had built the Gasthof Gramshammer, there was a similar foul-up with reservations, and they accommodated us in the basement in what must have been the furnace room.

I became acquainted with Jim Slevin during the time he was making a decision to move to Vail. He had come into the UAL ticket office one time with a hand full of pictures and the enthusiasm of a child with a new toy. These were all pictures of various scenes in and around what there was of Vail Village at that point. He announced that he was going to live there. Sure enough, by what was for me the start of the "summer Vail" experience in July of 1965, we enjoyed eating at his restaurant called La Cave in the basement of The Plaza Lodge.

By the winter of '66, Manor Vail had been built, so a friend and I stayed there for a week in February. There still wasn't much between Bridge St. and Manor Vail. I still have the confirmation letter from Manor Vail and the receipt for payment made on 2/27/66. The letter was typed and signed by Mrs. Irene Westbye, Reservations Secretary, and the room rate was $20, double occupancy. We just had a bedroom (this would have been the lock-off belonging to one of the suites). The three-bedroom deluxe suites (with three baths, kitchen, living room, stone fireplace, and balcony) went for the whopping sum of $65. Way out of our range.

As new places were built and opened for business, I stayed at, ate at, or partied at all of them. In February of 1967, I was at a party at The Golden Ski in The Lodge and, if my memory serves me correctly, it was the night of Rupert Oberlohr's arrival in Vail, and there was great jubilation among the rest of his family already living in town.

In July of 1966, there was a strike at United Air Lines; we weren't working, so what better to do than go to Vail? There was a pool at The Lodge, and Dick Hauserman was very generous with rooms at The Plaza Lodge. We had become well acquainted with him as he flew back and forth to Cleveland during those years and was frequently at our office. I believe that was the summer that Jim and Jan Cunningham built the Valhalla, so we checked their construction progress during that stay. I was driving a VW Bug, and when staying at The Plaza, could park on the hillside between The Lodge pool and The Plaza.

In late March of 1969, a friend, by some stroke of fate, invited me to join him and his wife for a weekend in Vail. They were to be guests of an army buddy of his and could I go along and be his blind date for a party? Well, could I ever! As it turned out, the old army buddy was Bill "Sarge" Brown. The trip from Denver to Vail that evening involved spending several hours trying to get over Loveland Pass in extreme weather conditions. When we finally did arrive, Bill had a wonderful dinner waiting. We went to the party the next evening after a fine day of skiing. It was a party given by Ski Club Vail, and I had my first meeting with Flo Steinberg, who impressed me when she recognized the fragrance I was wearing (Joy) and commented on it. I later learned she had a sort of obsession with perfume.

I could say that "the rest is history" but will elaborate just a little. Bill and I continued seeing each other frequently. Winter came to

Vail early that fall of 1969. In October there were a number of snowstorms that left a great base for the season, scheduled to start in mid-November well before Thanksgiving. At the end of a wonderful ski day on November 25, we had to be evacuated from Chair 6. I remember that specifically because about the same time the next day we met Don Simonton at the Vail Chapel where he performed our wedding ceremony. The new chapel was dedicated on November 28, 1969 by Rev. Don Simonton and Father Thomas Stone. The carpet had been laid earlier on our wedding day, and Don asked Hans Weibel, who was there vacuuming it to turn off the vacuum while he conducted our wed-

ding. Some years later, Don told me that when Hans saw who was being married, he said, "Vell, I be Gott-damned," and promptly left his vacuuming job to spread the word around town before we left the church.

We lived in a Sandstone '70 unit, and I worked for Rocky Mtn. Airways who provided daily service between Denver and Eagle. My ticket counter was at the back of the Manor Vail lobby. Although I was equipped to handle reservations and ticket changes for any and all of the airlines, it was difficult to get people to "come all that way from their lodges around Bridge Street to Manor Vail," which they considered to be out of the way.

SALLY HANLON

I was born in Boston and educated in Boston and Philadelphia; my chosen career as a young woman was education. My first teaching assignment was on Long Island, where I met Sally (Cox) Johnston; I taught first grade, and Sally was the music teacher. We eventually moved to Boston, where we would be closer to the New England ski areas and where we roomed together through graduate school. We discovered Sugarloaf, Maine, where I eventually met Bill Hanlon. Bill had a tiny car and a buddy named Billy, and they used to pick up Sally and me after school almost

every Friday, and drive us to Sugarloaf to ski.

After we got married, our mutual love of skiing, together with adventurous spirits, brought us to Crested Butte, Colorado. It was there that we became close friends with Paul Johnston and David and Renie (Cox) Gorsuch. I had met Renie, who was Sally's sister, many times before moving to Colorado, and our families grew closer as we shared in the Colorado adventure. After a couple of years, we realized the growing opportunities in Vail, and we struck out on a new chapter.

Paul learned that the Black Bear Bar in Vail

had suddenly closed and was available. Paul, Bill, and I opened a nightclub and named it the Nu Gnu. We were located in the Clock Tower building, underneath the Gorsuch store. Our families thought we were crazy as we finished our jobs in Crested Butte and worked frantically through the weekends in Vail to build out the club and to hire a chef and staff. Though we had envisioned owning a sophisticated, elegant supper club, we soon realized that we were in fact the owners of a popular and raucous rock-n-roll club. The club was busier than we'd have dared to imagine, going to standing room only almost immediately. It was a party spot, with live music and lots of characters. I will never get over the memory of seeing one of our regular customers with a stocky kitten on a leash, and realizing, as it brushed against me, that it was a very young lion.

When we were expecting our first child, Bill and I sold our interest in the Nu Gnu to Paul, and opened The Emporium, which is known today as Wild Bill's Emporium. I worked at the shop and tended to the kids, and when he wasn't at the store, Bill also worked at the Clock Tower Inn with our friend John Kaemmer. We all still remember the amazing desserts that Julie Kaemmer, John's wife, would bake and deliver to the restaurant.

Our shop sold flowers, candy, and antiques, along with a few gifts. I sold a lot of antiques, but mostly flowers and candy. The European families liked flowers; people came in all the time. We often went to get the flowers in our Volkswagen van (a long trip since the Interstate hadn't yet been built), or sometimes they came on the public bus delivered in front of our door, as Vail village was not pedestrian yet. If we didn't sell the flowers, I got to take them all home; some weeks, my house looked like a funeral parlor. Our freshest flowers came from the garden of Ella Knox, who used to bring them in often. Once someone bought a bouquet to be delivered with the message, "May I please come home?" Another standout was a rose with the message, "Tonight?"

As the mother of two small children, my interest in education was rekindled. There was a kindergarten under the Interfaith Chapel, and local teacher Allen Brown's mother lived with us every winter. I served on the committee that worked to build Red Sandstone Elementary School, and when the decision to open it was delayed, we became involved with Vail Mountain School, working to open its elementary school. At that time, the school was located in several trailers in Dowd Junction, and I think that there were 38 students the first year we were involved. Being a teacher at heart, I stayed heavily invested in education, and I am delighted that through the hard work and dedication of many parents, the school eventually grew to success. It seems somehow fitting that Sally Johnston (my first teaching friend and later the wife of our first business partner in Vail) and I would share duties on the board of directors of Vail Mountain School for a number of years.

It was fabulous raising children here; we're an outdoor family…small town life for kids; you could let children go outside, you could let them ski on their own, and you could let them ride the buses. We didn't have the organized activities that they have today. It was wonderful; the kids made snowmen and

snow forts, and ran through the creeks and beaver ponds in summer. No TV. Guys went to watch football with Father Stone because for a time, he had the only local TV. We moved to Forest Road and then bought an apartment at the Vorlaufer. We eventually bought another, combined the two, and are still there.

We went on to open Vail Village Travel Agency, then Vail Boot and Shoe and finally Bridge Street Antiques, which later became a souvenir shop called Graffiti. Together with Bill, I have remained active in the Vail community. I am happy to have started a family tradition that is being continued by our son Joe and daughter Meg, who live and work in Vail today with young children of their own.

SAMMYE MEADOWS

This is an opportunity for me to dredge up delightful memories. I graduated from Centre College of Kentucky with a degree in history, got married, and moved to Fort Collins, Colorado, in 1966. Though trained to be a high school teacher, I worked as a receptionist at the Hewlett-Packard voltmeter plant in Loveland to support my husband in graduate school. I also learned to ski, and it changed my life. Skiing and the mountains were awesome. I was often reprimanded at HP for not following the rules. Marriage was bad, and I ran away. While

searching Denver Post want ads for "secretary" jobs, I noticed in the line just above that section a "sales clerk" job at the Gondola Ski Shop in Vail: Contact store manager Dooper Hicks. I did, got hired, and arrived in Vail for the 1967-68 ski season.

Escape. As a proper Southern girl, I had a lot of guilt over leaving a marriage but also had developed a ravenous appetite for mountains, snow, skiing, and freedom. Freedom to breathe without judgment, freedom to ski, and freedom to create my own life. It was the boldest leap I ever made.

Since moving to Vail, I have leaped boldly at every opportunity, and life has been rich because of that first leap in 1967-68. I bet I'm not the only one to say this.

The first season, I worked as a sales clerk at the Gondola Ski Shop. I also did a little skiwear modeling for the shop and Hart Ski ads. Dated the Hart Ski Team. Skied as much as humanly possible. The next couple of seasons I worked as reservationist for Elaine and Gerry White at the Rams-Horn Lodge, met fascinating guests, and their three beautiful daughters (Courtney, Vanessa, Ashley), whom I will always adore.

A Vanessa story: at about age three, Vanessa ran barefoot, in bathing suit, dragging big towel past the reception desk, stopped, came back, and poked her little face around the corner to say to me, "Sam-I-Am, I love you," then ran on to the pool. Melts my heart to this day. I earned my buckle as a member of the Rams-Horn Demo Team by turning thou-

sands of slow dog noodles down the face of Prima. I left Vail for about a year, returned to work for the Town of Vail and later became executive assistant to the Town Manager, Town Attorney, and Town Council. I worked for the Town until leaving Vail again in 1978 to follow a Blueberry Gypsy to Alaska. In Alaska, I worked mostly for Kodiak Island Natives and hiked and kayaked throughout the Great Land, including an astounding month-long trip through the Arctic National Wildlife Refuge to the Beaufort Sea. After Alaska, I ran away from the Gypsy and worked on the film of Milagro Beanfield War. After the film, I went to work as personal assistant for the director, Robert Redford, at Sundance – this, too, had its roots in Vail. I later returned to Vail as the executive director of Betty Ford Alpine Gardens. I left to move to Montana and work on the Lewis and Clark Bicentennial as coordinator of the Circle of Tribal Advisors. I now write American Indian history. I am an Eastern Band Cherokee Nation descendant.

The people are the reason behind it all. Friendships for a lifetime, and those friends keep me coming back to visit. With the skiing, a mountain like no other, the Gore Range, and the people. I had more fun than any life ought to be allowed to have. Skiing, hiking, backpacking, climbing 14ers, getting high, laughing, carousing, writing poetry. I was part of Vail's considerable counter-culture, never destined for the Vail "society" that evolved. I loved loved loved to ski (and still do) – on the mountain and in the backcountry, downhill and cross country. And snowshoeing. I loved backpacking (and still do) – with girlfriends and boyfriends and general friends. Together we learned the Gore Range and New York Range like the insides of our hearts. We spent many nights at Piney, Pitkin, Booth, Deluge, Mystic Isle and other lakes, soaking up the (psychedelic) colors of wildflowers in the spring, hiking ridgetops and mountaintops in the summer, listening to elk bugle in the fall.

We were wildly blessed.

Hummm….you may not want to print too much about my delicious nightlife. Any place that had a good band also had me, especially the Nu Gnu. Donovan's Porch after skiing, even with no band. A member of the Alpine Gardens board once asked me if I was "wild" during my early years in Vail. "Yes," I replied. Since I escaped family life to move to Vail, I basically had none except for occasional visits from my parents and sisters. But I had F-Troop – as a Vail Ski Patrolman once labeled the group of friends that I skied, hiked, and enjoyed altered consciousness with. What's left of F-Troop, which is now decimated by many premature deaths, is still my family. I especially miss my best friend Mary Ellen Canniff.

The only thing I hoped to find upon moving to Vail was freedom, and I did. I knew it was a small alpine village designed to be pedestrian-oriented, and I knew it was already famous for incredible skiing. Beyond that, I had no expectations. My time in Vail prior to 1970 was just about the happiest I've ever enjoyed, and I've always been pretty happy.

Of course, Vail had to "grow up." It was destined for ski country success. In its early years, it was one of the most eclectic, eccentric, creative, and caste-free places in the country. Great, wild adventures happened routinely – like Ottie Kuehn's tower; the Bridge Street Shootout between Jean Claude Killy and Leo LaCroix; a certain boyfriend chasing a naked man out of his home and through the streets with a butcher knife; the hysterically funny melodramas penned by Gregory Beresford Skeffington and Belle Forest, snorkel skiing and the incomparable milk runs, great community conversation, and love of place. It seemed that all who lived in Vail then were accepted on equal footing, not measured by degree of wealth or family background. Those things were magic and had to fade some day. As time went on, I felt Vail becoming more like other places, less eccentric, less free. I grew up a bit, too. But every five years, at the Vail Pioneer Reunion, that early Vail re-emerges – like Brigadoon – out of the mists of time.

193

SANDY WIECHMANN TROXELL

I grew up in Wausau, Wisconsin and spent summers water skiing with the MinAqua Bat Water Ski Club. I graduated from the University of Wisconsin in 1964 with a degree in Education and completed a Master's Degree in Education at the University of Montana. I spent one year teaching 3rd grade in Denver before moving to Vail in January of 1966 to ski and live in the mountains.

My first job was working at The Lodge of Vail with Helga, Jinny, Suzy, and Erika as a waitress. I also worked for the Vail Resort Association in information and reservations, taught Red Cross Swimming Lessons, worked with Rod Slifer, knit "toe socks" for a local ski shop, and taught kindergarten and third grades in the Vail and Minturn elementary schools. One job was teaching kindergarten in the basement of the Vail Church where there was lots of room for fun activities. I loved skiing, the mountains, the snow, and the good friends. I left Vail in June of 1971 when I married fellow teacher Tom Troxell in the Vail Church, and we moved to Noorvik, Alaska, to teach in an Eskimo village above the Arctic Circle. Tom helped survey the LionsHead Gondola and coached the Battle Mountain High School basketball team.

Social life was great, and I made lots of good friends with whom I still keep in touch. I especially remember parties with the Vail Ski Patrol and Vail Ski Instructors. Good friends,

Carol Wendt and Jim Rein, came up from Denver for the weekend. At different times, my roommates were Lillian Miller, Cindy Lopez, Shirley Anderson, Meryl Goldschmidt, and Lee Caroselli.

I remember great skiing, hiking, and jeeping. Vail season ski passes were $25 for employees of Eagle County Schools. We partied most every night, and the next day we got up, skied, worked, and then did it again. Great fun. Please don't tell my former students or husband. Speaking of my husband, we have two children, Holly and Hobie, and four grandchildren.

SARA NEWSAM

I grew up in a small farming and ranching community in South Dakota and attended the University of South Dakota. I came to Denver to work at Martin Marietta and arrived in Vail in November of 1967. Friends told me about an interesting job opening. I met Dick Hauserman at The Red Carpet Room at Stapleton, and he offered me a job working with him at the Plaza and then at The Arnold Palmer Golf Academy.

The Golf Academy closed in 1968, and I worked for John Kaemmer for the winter at the Clock Tower. In July of 1969, I became Pete Seibert's secretary. The Vail Associates offices were on the 2nd floor of the Lazier Arcade Building. We moved to LionsHead in early 1970. I also worked with Dick Peterson when he became President of VA and Peter became Chairman, and I continued to work for Peter until he left Vail. Working for VA in those years proved to be exciting.

My social life for a very long time revolved

around my jobs and was fun and interesting. There were only a couple of places to go, so you could find anyone at the Copper Bar, the Casino, the Red Lion, or the Nu Gnu. It was so easy to get to Denver for Bronco games or to Boulder for CU games. My outdoor sports have revolved around skiing and golfing with friends and walking my dog in this beautiful environment.

One of my main reasons for coming to Vail, other than a really interesting job offer, was to learn to ski. I had skied prior to 1967 (snowplow turns only) and had broken my ankle at Aspen Highlands, so I thought that this would be a good opportunity to learn to ski. I learned to turn them both ways, but it sure took a long time. I expected to be here for a couple of years and then return to the city, but it didn't happen that way.

Vail has been a wonderful place to live. There have been endless numbers of interesting people that have come through this small town. Some have stayed and some have been here for a short period of time, some come back often, and they all remain friends. People newer to the valley have a difficult time envisioning what Vail was like in the very early years and it is fun to show them pictures, tell them about things that you could do then that you can't now, and tell them about the people that we have had an opportunity to meet because of the popularity of the place that we chose as home. I lived above the Ore House by Gore Creek, and our apartment was above the fireplace – so we heard many interesting tales, even though we tried not to listen. There is no better place to have "grown up" than Vail, and now I feel that if I ever leave I will grow old. The diversity and vitality that Vail offers today, the exposure to the outdoors, and the climate keep us young.

195

SHARON BELL

I was an Iowa farm girl and took a medical secretarial course at a junior college in Rochester, Minnesota. Before coming to Vail, I worked for two years for an orthopedic surgeon in Denver and made the decision to come to Vail and learn to ski. My first job was doing telephone work for Vail Associates, and I worked at the front desk when Pete Seibert, Chuck Lewis, and Bob Parker were there. I spent a short time working at the Casino for Bill and Bettan Whiteford. I moved on to Vail Secretarial Service, owned by Shirley Ward. I later took a job at the Vail Valley Medical Center in the front office when Drs. Tom Steinberg, Bill Bevan, and Bill Holm were the doctors there.

I loved the small-town atmosphere, and genuine fun-loving people. It was the lifestyle of the small community, outdoor sports, and work opportunities that kept me here. My social life was fairly quiet. I wasn't a bar-chasing type and had a mostly quiet nightlife. I did go to the Casino – it was a wild place with drinking, music, jazz, you name it.

Sports that I liked included hiking, skiing, fly fishing, and bicycling. I was married to an ex-ski patroller, Chan Welin, who was my partner in outdoor activities. I had absolutely no expectations of Vail but looked to the total adventure ahead of me.

The characters living in Vail amazed me. One, Rixie Flewelling, ran the ticket office for VA and, as I recall, read three to four books simultaneously. She could read while doing a variety of other activities (rumor, of course).

It was possible to arrive for work in those days and be the first vehicle in the dirt parking lot, now the main Vail parking structure, and that was around 8am.

Another rumor: Bill Whiteford (otherwise known as "William the Good"), owner of the Casino, would stomp into Pete Seibert's office, complaining loudly about the behavior of VA's ski patrollers. Seibert would then instruct the patrollers that under no circumstances were they to stop and drink at the Casino. Later the same afternoon, outside the Casino on Bridge Street, a smiling Whiteford would be seen with an arm draped casually over the patrollers' shoulders, welcoming them inside for some refreshments. The cycle would start all over again.

SHEIKA GRAMSHAMMER

I remember when I first came to Vail. It was Christmas Eve, 1963. I was in Aspen and was driving to Vail to spend Christmas. When I left Aspen, the weather was nice, and I had the top off the Jeep. I made a wrong turn in Newcastle and got lost. I made it to Vail very late, around 10:30, and it was very, very cold. The temperature was around -20 degrees that night. What I remember is that everyone stayed up for me and greeted me with open arms. That's what Vail is like. Open arms.

What attracted me first of all was Pepi. What attracted Pepi was the combination of my not wanting to go back to Austria and his having an opportunity to buy land in 1963. Then we could build something. With me being in fashion and Pepi in racing, the ideal thing was to build a shop. What we found out later was that you had to build within one year. They didn't want people sitting on the land and not building because they wanted to build a town. We submitted plans to Vail Associates, and they said we couldn't build a shop because Vail Blanche and Blanche Hauserman had the exclusive rights to retail for three years, so no other retail shop could come in. However, we just had to build something.

My father had hotels, so I thought we could build a little Gasthof, and then in three years we could build some shops. With no experience, we decided to open a hotel. We got married in May of 1964 and opened in December of 1964. I had no idea what it would be like in the business, and so I went to Barnes Business School in Denver for three months to learn about business. Every day was a new day. Then, it was more or less learning day by day.

Three years later, the opportunity came to open the shops. We immediately turned that into reality. We all needed to get our feet on the ground in town. Not just anybody could come in and open a restaurant. You had to prove the need of the neighborhood. It was very easy to learn because there wasn't competition. We all had one goal, and that was to build a town. While we were building Gramshammer, we had no idea about this thing, so I became the manager of the Plaza Building for Dick Hauserman and learned how to delegate the rooms, how to make up the rooms. I learned how to deal with maids. Then I went to the Red Lion because the owners were my friends (Larry and Marge

Burdick) and worked for them as a bartender. I modeled when I was in Aspen, and I was friends with the owner of the Red Onion and had worked as a cocktail waitress there. That's how I learned to manage a hotel and how to tend a bar.

Entering the business world of Vail, I had to learn fast. I loved people and had been into the social life in Vegas, Hollywood, and New York. I loved socializing. As Vail was so boring in the beginning, I came up with some ideas, like the picnics. The town needed a hospital and fundraising for that. I learned step by step from my friends who were experienced. I wasn't afraid to ask, "How do you do this?" and I wasn't afraid to say, "I'm sorry, I did something wrong." That's just part of growing up. The wonderful thing was at that time there was no greed, no competition, only a dream to make something. People came to Vail from all over the country to establish themselves and raise a family. They all had a dream to make something good of it. That's what it is still today because of the foundation; the way it was laid out was with strong, honest people.

I would not change anything in my life and certainly not the first five or 10 years in Vail. They were some of the most beautiful years. It started out with potlucks and dinners; no one wanted to eat alone, so we had potlucks, and we'd play games. We had no

197

television. Because of that, we had an intimacy and friendship among all of us. Some I liked more, some I liked less – but you talked to everybody. What was unique about this resort was that you had the richest of the rich - we called them millionaires then, but they are the billionaires of now: The Hunts, the Taylors, and we were all invited to their homes. There were no social differences.

It was wonderful being a young mother to Kira. Everybody helped with babysitting. I was for three years in business, so I needed to bring someone from Europe to watch the kids. We brought over Omi Krauss when Kira was just six weeks old. Omi had been a nurse, and then she started babysitting.

There were always challenging times. There were times when I wondered if what we were doing was right, especially when the competition started coming in. There was always somebody more experienced than you were. But if you had hard times, there was always someone to go to. There was never a time that I said I wanted to leave town. It was never that hard. Yes, I wanted to leave when I missed my old friends and the social life in New York City, the fun, the parties, and the things that were going on. I missed that, but I was the buyer for Pepi Sports, so I went to New York several times a year, and that was good. I never had a moment when I said about moving to Vail, "Why did I do that?"

I always laugh when I think of the experiences with the volunteer fire department. From the beginning of Vail, there were six or seven of them. You know, they were the jacks-of-all-trades and masters of none. Pepi

was also a firefighter, along with Larry Burdick, Donovan, Joe Langmaid, and Joe Staufer. They all had to do it, and watching them was so funny. We had one fire chief from Eagle who taught them. We had one police chief who was more professional, so he gave the orders. I remember the fire at the Covered Bridge store (Cissy and John Dobson's place). Pepi had a cold, and it was late at night. The telephone rang, and when it rang, there was a recording saying what was happening because it was connected to all the phones. The recording said, "There's a fire at the Covered Bridge." Pepi was hard asleep, so he said, "Oh, don't worry about it." Then he jumped up and shouted, "The Covered Bridge! That's just next-door. We share a wall with them." He got dressed immediately and helped evacuate everyone, hanging on to their jewelry and their furs. It was quite a fire. Bobby Jo Britton climbed up the ladder, slipped and fell down and broke his leg. We had to take care of the fire, the broken leg, and the guests.

When we opened in 1964, there was no Clock Tower Building. We lived in the room above the restaurant and hadn't unpacked all the stuff we had for the big opening on December 15th. We had some guy sitting in the bar with the bartender and a cook, and he wanted something to eat. I went into the kitchen, made sandwiches, then came back out and served him. He came back for dinner, and I brought out spaghetti for him, but the guy was gone. I asked the bartender what happened to his friend, and he said he didn't know, perhaps he went to the bathroom; for five or 10 minutes, he still didn't know where he was, and I thought it was strange. Then Cheryl, who married Bobby Joe Britton, said she saw someone walking out with Pepi's skis. She knew they were Pepi's because he had Look bindings. We went out and looked for the guy and got him. He'd taken our suitcases out of the rooms, and was robbing us while I was serving him dinner. The sheriff came, and I got in a fight with the man. I got so mad when I saw it was our stuff, I pummeled him. The sheriff said, "Stay away from Sheika, she's violent!" I looked across and saw suitcases, and they were our suitcases. While I was looking after his dinner, he was robbing us. And then, of course, we dragged him back as quickly as we could, and I got so mad when I thought of my suitcases, I took a ski pole and clobbered this guy with it. Everyone said, "Stay away from Sheika; she knows how to fight."

Picnics were fun because you never knew what was happening. Dinners were fun because something always went wrong. I took good care of the property – it was clean and beautiful. We had aspen trees in front of our deck, and they kept growing, and the roots were going underneath the porch and cracking the boards. I went to the Town of Vail and told them I wanted to chop the trees down, because they were ruining the awnings, and the roots were ruining the concrete floor. They told me I couldn't do it. Then someone from the head of the Town Council said, "Why don't you just tell them you're going to trim the tree?" I called them up and told them I would just trim the tree, and they said I could.

The town was happy and thought that trimming was a good idea. So, at 5 am one morning, I took out a chain saw and completely trimmed them. I left just the bottom branches. Well, it looked horrible. If I'd ever seen a lousy haircut, that was one. The Design Review Board was there by 11 am. I told them I had just given them a little haircut. The trees looked so bad, that they told me to go ahead and take them down.

Vail became what I never had before - a home. It's my home, the only home I ever had. It opened its arms to all of us, embraced us with such a force, and such love, that you cannot help but being happy and in love with this town. I still believe that if you are willing to work really hard and have a goal, even now, you can do something yourself. We proved it here, that we could build a town. We worked hard, and we are still working hard today. You cannot sit back and let someone else do your job. If you work on it, you can be successful and reach your goals.

In the early days, the woman was more respected than the man. They had much more power because it was the woman who had the ideas. The men were the businessmen coming from different cities or Europe. It was the woman who really was the power behind the man in town. "Honey, we can do this, let's do this, darling. Come on, Pepi, we can make this. We can make it." There's Christie Hill. When she and Dick Hauserman came here, she was a social girl from Boston. She didn't want to be idle and saw opportunity and quality in this town. She was the one with the idea for Vail Blanche and started that store. The women at that time were the foundation of Vail. Behind those men and the businesses were the women. We had the time and energy to say, "OK, come on, we can do something." And we did it. We proved it.

SHIRLEY WARD

My sister and brother-in-law Doris and Dick Bailey came on a ski trip to Vail in 1962. They walked up Bridge Street and saw Fitzhugh Scott's beautiful blue door; Mr. Scott was an architect, as was Dick. He telephoned Vail's first architect, who called him back, and asked, "How soon can you start?" My sister and her husband moved to Vail soon after that. Then I came to visit and never left.

Fitzhugh Scott owned the Vail Bridge Chalet, and it had the first toilet. I started to work for Vail Associates in '64-'65. I was a junior in college, but I'd stopped and ski bummed in Killington that winter and drove to Vail with a friend in June. She did not stick around; she didn't love skiing as much as I did. Summer was gorgeous. I lined things up for the upcoming winter. My first job was with VA, but I only worked part-time. Film-maker Roger Brown and Perry Willett also had work for me. I used to transcribe for Roger. Loyette Goodell was Pete Seibert's secretary. We were in the old Plaza Building - Pete and Chuck Lewis were upstairs with Al Bridges, and ski patrol. We only had 25 ski patrol and instructors, and they came in each day after the lifts closed to check out. It was the post office, too.

Oh, those early years. We all fell into a bar at night. What else do you do? There was no

TV; you had the Red Lion, La Cave, the Casino, Nu Gnu. Pepi's was just a bar and restaurant, not a lot of Rock 'n' Roll there. That first summer I worked at the Vail Resort Association; Doris was there at the beginning of VRA. Gaynor Miller wanted to start the Vail Valley Camp for Girls. So he put me in charge of it; it didn't go very far even though it was a perfect place for a girls' camp; it was wilderness here. We had the sheep drives go right through town and up the mountain, because it was the best grazing.

I lived with Doris for a period of time. Then I moved over the liquor store. I met George Ward at The Red Lion, where he bartended. We married, and I had four kids in three years. You didn't have anything, including your mother, at your disposal for a birth. The plan was to use a doctor in Denver for the first child. I was at Norge by George Laundromat, and my water broke in my car. I went to Dr. Steinberg down the street, and he said, "You won't make it to Denver." So I told him I'd go to Glenwood, and he replied, "But go now!" I was smoking and drinking through all of that.

My wedding was in 1967. Bridge Street was just being paved that day for the first time; it was a Tuesday in October, and the Red Lion was closed, so we had the reception there. Whoever was in town that day came to the wedding. It was Don Simonton's first wedding in Vail. We were married in the little white church in Minturn (now Holy Toledo consignment store). We sent George to Glenwood Springs to pick up the flowers. He ran into a sheep drive on the way back. Every-

body was already at the church. Cissy Dobson ran out of repertoire to play, and Don Simonton wore his white robe with cowboy boots sticking out. I wore my sister's full-blown wedding gown. I just sat with my father and lit up a cigarette. Larry Burdick's comment was "villainous to the end." George used to be the villain in the town melodramas. Finally, he showed up at least an hour late; people were still listening to the same music over and over. After the ceremony, the German girls kidnapped me according to an old German custom, and the groom had to look for the new bride. They took me to different places. After the reception, they handcuffed George to a bar stool at Donovan's. He was attached to a bar stool and had to go get the car key. They took me to Jeff's Café in Minturn for bumper pool with guys who frequented the place. I won a bumper pool game with some guy. Helga Rein will never forget that one. George appeared, and he retrieved me.

The tourists would ask, "Do you really live here?" Tourists became your best and life-long friends and came to live here, too. Everybody knew everybody else. People worked different hours; we had instructors who didn't stay up all night, but bartenders who did. Instructors worked all day long, and they could only stay up so long. You'd have early crowds, late crowds, and shifts. There was no gender bias. Most of the women in Vail were jock types, more aggressive, and independent. My sister carried the development torches; I avoided town politics. I was aware but never quite got into it. I probably played and drank a lot, but you were fairly safe, because your car was buried in snow. You didn't go many places; it snowed like crazy up here. You were "here," and the trip to Denver was long. People with businesses might have done it differently, but ski bums had no real need to go. If you needed a bra, for instance, you'd go to Frisco. You couldn't buy things like that here. Leadville was at higher altitude, so it was safer to take the two-lane to Frisco. I didn't have a car then, so I went with friends.

Stacey

I worked for Gunther Hofler at the Red Lion. He and his wife were second parents to me. Once I started there, I made a lot more money. VRA was booking conventions. I even remember corn and sheep conventions, and a firemen's convention. Whatever went on in Vail on a given day, everybody did it. I remember Christmas in July at Slifers' house and making nose warmers as a surprise gift. You had one street in town, with a cross street. We had a sense of adventure, and the core thing was a love of skiing. I don't think anybody who didn't love skiing came. Anne Staufer came with Josef, who loved skiing. It was all starting then. Men were looking for more mountains to tame. Women who came on their own were more rugged. And I think everyone liked everybody. I missed my friends when I left, but they are long-lasting friendships. I never thought I'd made a mistake coming to Vail. I miss it.

SHIRLEY WELCH

I arrived in Vail in 1968 with my husband Don Welch, who came to teach skiing. I had grown up in California and gone to college in Denver, where I met Don, who was from Pennsylvania. We found a half-duplex to rent, which was the first building constructed in East Vail. Bob Smith of Smith Goggles constructed the chalet-type structure. It was a two-bedroom, one-bath duplex and from the start, we had the second bed- room occupied by someone who needed to rent a room. Most of the time it was a ski instructor. We lived in that duplex for 10 years. I got a job at Vail Blanche, working for Marijke and Francis Brofos. I knew nothing about selling ski clothes and remember one customer coming in the store in the summer and asked for an athletic supporter. I handed him a wristband for tennis. What did I know? Another nightmare was fitting kids in lederhosen with suspenders that were measured in centimeters. It was a learning experience. We moved across the street, and I worked at Christy Sports. Just down the hall was Donovan's Copper Bar, and there I would land at the end of the day to find most of the ski instructors and patrol guys having a brew or two or three. Back home at the duplex, we did not have television for seven years.

For entertainment we went to the Minturn theater, complete with the cry room and usually a film that didn't finish before it melted and the screen went dark. My father sent us a Grundig high-power radio, and at nights we listened to Mystery Theater. Anyone who was in the duplex would sit on the kitchen floor and listen to the scary story. Before I-70 was built, when we had a big snowfall, we would take our Toyota Land-

cruiser and a towrope and go skijoring up Vail Pass, which by that time had been closed. One night, we had Brian Woodell on the rope as we headed up Highway 6 and made the left just below Carnies' house. There was a covered bridge over a creek up there. We had forgotten about that and took Brian over the bridge. Looking back, we saw sparks flying from his skis.

The most mischief we did was the night

Don and I brought the great billboard down. This was before I-70 was built and the road from Denver to Vail was pristine with no ads or billboards, until one day when a giant billboard appeared in the meadow just west of where Vail Mountain School is now. Armed with a chain saw, ax, and wearing cross-country skis, we skied down Highway 6, off the road, and through the field to that awful billboard. I was sure we would be busted and tried to hunker down while Don started the chain saw. It took a while to saw through those phone-pole-thick logs. Finally, I looked up to see the thing waving back and forth. I wasn't sure which way it was going to fall. With a crack, it wavered one more time and then went over with a thundering whoosh and geyser of snow tossed on us. We packed up our ax and chain saw, skied home, and decided we had accomplished a good thing that night.

We were not night owls because we both had to be at work early in the morning. Mostly, we played outdoors winter and summer and worked hard. So did our friends. One winter night, Brian called us at about 6PM. He and his roommate, Tom, who was on crutches with a hip-high cast on a broken

203

leg, had driven in Brian's Volkswagen to Leadville for groceries. On the way, they decided to stop at Cooper Hill and take a look. Once there, it appeared there was nothing between the parking lot and the Poma lift hill, and it looked inviting. Brian and Tom decided to see what would happen when they drove the VW up the Poma lift hill. So they did, only to find that it augured in to its axles. With Tom on crutches, Brian could not get the car unstuck. Obviously, this was before cell phones. Brian walked and Tom hobbled down to the warming hut. There, they broke a small window to get inside and use the phone. Brian called us. We arrived to find Brian and Tom munching on candy bars from the refreshment counter. We brought our trusty Landcruiser that had a winch, and we towed the VW off the hill. Brian had about $12.75 on him and left it at the warming hut with a note and his phone number in case that amount didn't cover the candy bars and broken window. He never heard from Cooper.

I bought a horse and kept him across the street in a pasture that seemed to be owned or managed by Mahaney's Stables. Mahaney never charged us for keeping the horse there. Later, we figured out that the state owned the land, and Mahaney simply kept his horses there, too. Don had a horse for a while that he bought from Sparky, the lift operator at the halfway house on Golden Peak. Don and I would have dinner after work in the summer, saddle the horses, and mosey down to the rodeo arena at the end of the golf course. That was where my horse showed me he could buck and tossed me nearly to the moon.

I learned to ski powder with Dougie Walker. He had clients who rented skis from the shop and always invited some of us to come along on powder days. For those who knew Dougie, he was as smooth as silk in powder. Sadly, Dougie died while working on the installation of the LionsHead gondola. I will never forget him drifting down a powder-packed slope up to his hips and me making two turns and crashing, doing two more and crashing, and so on. I taught skiing to kids for a few years, and we were pretty much on our own with our classes. I remember one day when the wind whipped up to more than 60 mph, and shut down most of the lifts. We weren't supposed to bring the kids inside, so I took my class on the shuttle bus, and we rode that around for the rest of the afternoon. You had to be creative. Those were the times.

SUE RYCHEL

I was an artist for Hallmark Cards after finishing college at the University of Grenoble in southern France before coming to Vail in 1968 with my son Kent and daughter Leigh. There were fewer than 100 full-time residents in Vail then. We fished, hiked, and camped in what is now Beaver Creek and Bachelor Gulch. I am an avid fisherman and have made my own fly rods and tied my own flies.

I was born in Rochester, New York, and lived in Kansas City before Boulder, Colorado. Attending school in France allowed me to ski in the Alps. Early Vail reminded me of that time in my life. I learned about a woman who lived in Vail (Isabel Schober) when I met her brother at the Kansas City Board of Trade. Isabel was married to an Austrian ski instructor, Manfred. I visited Vail and knocked on her door. She was very welcoming, "Come on in. I'm having a party tonight, and I hope you will come." I did and met Rod Slifer, Dave, Tim, and Rob Garton, Packy Walker, and Chuck McLaughlin. After three days in the tiny town, I drove home, quit my job, packed up, and brought the children to Vail. We arrived in August of 1968. I had no job, no place to live, only a few dollars, and a lot of determination.

I was soon a waitress at The Slope. I also worked at The Gondola Ski Shop, Gorsuch, The Clock Tower, Porter Industries, where I cleaned the church and bank at night. I cut men's hair, child sat in my home, and completed year-end taxes for people. I painted the hunter and birds on the door of The Alaskan Shop in the Lodge Promenade. What kept me here was manifold - my children, their friends, our church, the small town lifestyle, the mountains and aspen trees, and the beauty. There wasn't much of a social life ever, because I worked many jobs. I love to work, so it's not work to me.

At the beginning, I slept on the floor of a ski shop that no longer exists. We slept under the ski racks, bathed in the sink, and brushed our teeth there. I went door to door along Beaver Dam Road with my kids in tow and found a one-bedroom ski-in/ski-out apartment and rented it for $125 a month. Once, running at top speed, I ran into Robert Redford and knocked the wind out of him. I was looking the other way and had no idea who it was.

In addition to my real estate career, one of my claims to fame was selling Elvis a black diamond pinky ring when he visited Vail.

Summer Holm

The Holm Family made a trip to Vail in 1969 for a ski vacation. Dr. Bill Holm answered an ad in a medical journal, and a meeting was conducted at the Red Lion with Dr. Steinberg. Thus started a lifelong love of skiing for the family of four - Dr. Bill, Summer, Bill Jr., and Winter. Courtney was born after our arrival. We put her on her first pair of skis as soon as she could walk. We always knew where she was because of the bells on her hat. Soon, the littlest one kept up with all of us.

Everyday events were special in those early days. Families came together to ski and skate at the outside rinks. Food and drink were always served at each other's houses. Our entertainment was watching the movies of family and friends skiing that day, which got everyone to laughing and having a great time. After moving to Vail, we had more friends and family than we had ever known before. We had great times skiing, hiking, and biking.

When we went skiing for the day, the chalkboards by the lift shack would always have a message for "Dr. Holm" to come back to the Clinic. It was just Dr. Holm and Dr. Steinberg on staff then, so they worked long hours and even drove the ambulance. Young

Summer Holm

Bill kept asking if his dad was a doctor or the ambulance driver. Soon, Dr. Bill Bevan came to work at the Clinic, and then Dr. Eck. The Clinic was getting very busy, and an ambulance driver was finally hired.

The Red Lion was a great place to eat, and the children loved the Gold Brick Sundaes. We loved the magical surrounding of bright stars at night. The Elementary School (grades 1-6) was held up above the Clinic. After school, Winter would go down and watch her dad in action some days. Dr. Bevan or Dr. Eck always gave her a candy bar or a soda. When young Bill started kindergarten, it was held in the church basement, and Miss Schiavi was the teacher.

One day in early spring during Mud Season, Dr. Steinberg's wife Flo called and invited me to drive to Denver with her. How exciting. The drive over Loveland Pass was a ride that I would never forget. I kept saying that there should be guardrails. Flo just said, "It's not a good drive in the dark." We truly loved Vail. There were always a lot of house parties and family dinners in friends' homes. When the creek was low, we would put tennis shoes on and take inner tubes into town and then go for ice cream.

SUSAN BRISTOL

I grew up in Michigan and lived across the street from Vail's first mayor Ted Kindel. I came to Vail from Boston in 1970, after first job doing PR for The Architects Collaborative and Walter Gropius (Bauhaus Founder). After his death, I lived in the house he designed near Walden Pond, finishing up the exhibit of his life's work with his widow, Ise. I had graduated from Connecticut College for Women in 1968 in German Language and Literature.

I met Roger Staub at a meeting in Boston and liked the look of western skiing. Ise Gropius put me in touch with the Aspen Institute for a job, but I came to Vail first and loved it immediately. I decided to move to Vail after a job offer doing PR for the Vail Resort Association with Dale McCall. My PR work for VRA included "Fam Tours" with media and the first Ski Golf Tournament. I was a member of the first all-girls ski team with Maggie Finch, Doris Bailey, and Brooke Franzgen.

Skiing and my marriage to Wolfgang Herzog plus the wonderful lifestyle are the reasons I stayed. It was a great place to bring up our son, Alexander. I never grow tired of or take for granted the good friends and natural beauty of this place. I purchased a little house on Gore Creek because I couldn't find any other place to live.

I love my friends. It's wonderful to have the depth of camaraderie with so many people who worked to make Vail what it is today. I am perhaps the closest to a group of moms informally called the Mother Tuckers. Although my parents initially thought I'd moved to La-La Land, I found Vail to be more of a community than a resort. I hope to ski till I die. I also love swimming and hiking in the valley. Alex grew up under the French Corner at La Tour with escargots and lobster bisque. He skied with Rumplestiltskin School (with Hatsie Hinmon) before he talked much and had free run of the mountain and hiking into the Gore – a superb way to grow up.

After some wild nights at the Nu Gnu and listening to Jo Jo Lyles at The Clock Tower, I settled into cozy nights in front of the fire, alternating with great enjoyment of wonderful local restaurants. I was fortunate to enjoy an adventurous marriage and a wonderful son. Vail, to me, meant sunshine and great skiing. The on-mountain celebrations were the best. The American West was at our feet; it was such a fantastic opportunity.

SUSAN FRITZ

I came to Vail first in the fall of 1964 on my way to Arizona to see a boyfriend. I had graduated from the University of Wisconsin with a degree in Chemistry. When I got there, I could not find a job in Tucson and was told, "Oh, get out of here, you'll love Aspen." I planned to go to Vail and then Aspen. I came here and found four jobs but no place to live, which is still a level of natural selection. If you want to stay with enough passion, you will find a place to live. The Deli was the place to meet in the morning. I went to the Deli to get coffee, and there were Dickie Pete, Pepper Etters, and Paul Testwuide; they'd all been duck hunting. I just sat there watching the show. Then, I got in my car and went to Arizona until Thanksgiving and returned for the ski season. I met my husband Joel on New Year's Eve on Bridge Street. My daughter, Amy, 35 years later also met her husband on New Year's Eve on Bridge Street.

I came back and started working but still had no housing. On New Year's Eve, I was working at the Casino and had my sleeping bag with me; the next morning, I was sound asleep on a long banquette when New Year's Mass started. The congregation was very amused as I walked out carrying my sleeping bag over my shoulder. I worked at Donovan's Copper Bar and at the Clock Tower, too. My story made the rounds in short order, and people bought me shots. Then I met a gal named Trish who had a place in Matterhorn.

The parking structure had not been built yet, but the Vail Village Inn, Red Lion, and Vail Associates were open. It was an interesting time in some respects; there were really no children except the Kindels, Parks, Burdicks, Seiberts, and Marijke Brofos' boy Erik. The Clinic was in the kitchen of the Red Lion before Steinbergs. Manor Vail had just been built. Gorsuch was tiny. I found things to do here and never made it to Aspen. I found work instantly; people asked me, "Need a job?" It was just a party. I had as many girlfriends as guys – Jebbie Brown, Cheryl Britton, Margo Testwuide – a whole group of girls who were very silly together all the time. We were family to each other. I hope that still exists. We had lots of dinners together. It was ski bumming where there were 10 living in a two-bedroom apartment, and everybody cooked dinner together. We skied all day, played up at the top of Chair 4, and had picnics on a regular basis. Every day that was nice was a picnic lunch and playing all night. I waited tables.

Joel and I got married the next summer. Amy

208

was born in 1968, and Joel skied with her on his back. The winter was harder for me personally because I eventually taught in ski school and waited tables at night. I worked for John Kaemmer until he sold the Clock Tower. I never worked during the summer to play with the kids. We left here one September when Joel took a job with K2 and were back by May. It made our marriage stronger, because we left here and didn't know one person. If we had stayed here with all the shenanigans going on on a regular basis, and even the level of drinking going on, God only knows. It seemed everyone was 21 to 25; it was a college town of drinking. We lived in West Vail in Chamonix Chalets (Byron Brown and Jim Craig built them), and we got one of the first TVs there. The bar business stopped, and everyone came to our house in the afternoon to watch Sesame Street. Chupa, Hatsie and Sandy Hinmon, and Judy Cox were some of the people I played with in those days. A pretty good group of girls skied, went out, and laughed. My family hated that I came here, but they came to visit in the summer. To the day my mother died, she said, "What are you going to do?"

As time went on, Joel and I were pretty absorbed in each other, no one else in our group was. This was clearly home for us. Even when people moved down to Lake Creek, Vail was home. The hardship for me was losing a child. I had a baby on Loveland Pass on the way to Denver. The roads were slippery and closed, and a million hunters clogged the way. Joel finally delivered the baby. When that occurred, I realized that bad things could happen. The baby lived for three days, but there was too much trauma. We were all somewhat blessed in terms of feeling that we could play all night and nothing bad happened, no one died. People went off the road, but no one got hurt. We were sort of invincible. After the baby died, Ski School said, "Go to work; that's the best thing you can do, work!"

Tuck 'Em Inn was an old mattress and a tent up on the hill, a place off to the side of Riva where some people went to smoke dope and sit on the mattress. We just had parties all the time. Somebody would order a lobster, and you'd go to a field for a picnic, like where Potato Patch is now. The boys would be up there shooting their guns, drinking beer, and cooking bratwurst. We would get on the phone and call each other to get together. Dave Garton used to shoot magpies off his deck.

Unquestionably, I had more freedom to be myself with no pressure to conform to somebody's idea of who I should be. I felt equal to the men. It was very democratic. And I'm very content to be by myself; I just never felt any pressure here. I could be outspoken, and I still am. The sense of community and doing things for the community's good was so strong. Yes, you had to make a living, and you had to work hard. I had to tell our kids we couldn't afford to have them do both skiing and hockey; they had to choose.

Barbara Parker was my confidante; she always had common sense and could laugh. But there are too many fine women to name only one. The 10th Mountain pioneers were passionate about being outside. They were in it for a lifestyle but not necessarily making money for their investors. It's not just the weather or the mountains – it's all those things combined. There are days when I miss my privacy and sense of specialness, but that's so overtaken by the convenience of having doctors and grocery stores. There are tradeoffs. Growth is everywhere. I would retire, yes, but I wouldn't pioneer again. I don't see myself working as hard as I do. The best thing about Vail is the lifestyle, and life is pretty good.

SUSAN BROWN MILHOAN

My parents visited Vail in 1959 to decide if they wanted to invest. We stayed in a little yellow house where Red Sandstone School is right now. I was 10 years old. My parents built, if not the first, then the second, home on Mill Creek Circle.

Dad was a partner with Harley Higbie and George Caulkins: their history is well documented. But ours, as children, and eventual full-time residents of Vail, is different. I arrived as a 10-year-old and am still a permanent resident. I've done all kinds of work, from babysitting for the Gorsuch family primarily, working as a waitress at Pepi's, to selling real estate and working in and owning retail stores. Once you've raised a family here and they know this as home, you want to stay and provide that base for them to return to. As a youngster, there really wasn't much for kids to do except steal lunch trays from the International Cafeteria below The Lodge at Vail and go sledding and fool around on the chairlifts. We also did a lot of skitching, or hooking onto the back of cars and sliding around town. We used to hit golf balls onto the 9th hole, which was just outside our door. One time the Knox boys and their dad George were out there playing golf, and they got pretty upset with us. Growing up in Vail was all about being outside whether skiing, sledding, or horseback riding. I had a horse named Colorado Chief that we boarded exactly where Manor Vail is today. The Red Lion had a hitching post outside, and we'd ride bareback into town, hitch up the horse, and have lunch. The Red Lion has another significant memory for me because it was also the location of the first clinic. On April 1, 1964, I broke my leg on the Giant Steps run. It was difficult to convince anyone that I had actually hurt myself, since it was April Fool's day. I was taken to the clinic, then located in the Red Lion kitchen, and put in a full leg plaster cast. It also happened to be the night that "Lost Boy" was lost. All night long, people called our house (there were only four numbers to dial in those days) looking for him, and anyone who could was out searching with torches. I lay awake in pain watching their lights go by all night. I can remember that day and night like it was yesterday. The next day, the boy, who was a Boy Scout, walked out of what is now Game Creek Bowl after having spent the night in a tree well covered in branches. Manfred Schober, a Vail ski instructor, had come within feet of finding him where he lay sound asleep.

My parents, brothers and sisters, and I, spent almost every weekend and all summer in Vail. It took four hours to drive up from Denver. Some of the drives were the most harrowing experiences of my life. Once, we got caught on top of Loveland Pass in a complete white out, like the inside of a milk carton, all of us screaming and hugging each other. That brought us pretty close together. Without TV in the early days, we spent all our time as family, playing games and skiing together. Once I turned 18, Vail became my permanent home and where I married and raised three sons; two of them still live in the valley. Vail is a great place to raise a family, particularly when it was so small and you knew everyone.

Speaking for my parents, Vail was going to be a little ski get-away where we would have a small 'cabin'. never in anyone's imagination could they have dreamed up what it eventually became. As I grew older, my expectations were that it would always remain the same. Those bubbles of illusion were popped one after the other as they floated down the valley, exposing LionsHead then EagleVail, Singletree, Cordillera, then WalMart and Home Depot. Today, nothing surprises us nor do we have any expectations. But to imagine that what is here now happened in one lifetime is incredible.

Vail was a land of opportunity. With so many directions to go to build a community, it was fun and a challenge to get involved in the growth. My perspective changed as I decided to become involved in these important endeavors. My lifetime of involvement with non-profits is fulfilling, knowing that I've been able to make a difference for the good of the valley, my home.

211

SUSAN RODGER

I learned to ski near Mont Tremblant in the Laurentians where my family had a cottage. I grew up in Montreal, Canada, and came to Vail at 19, acquiring my education and job experience here. I had become certified in the Canadian Ski Instructors' Alliance and convinced my parents to allow me to teach skiing in Vermont. With a snowless New England winter, my then-boyfriend and I heard about this new area called Vail and came to teach skiing in January 1965. I actually hitchhiked from Vermont to New York City, boarded a Greyhound bus, and disembarked at the Vail Village Inn bus stop three days later. Of course, my parents knew nothing about it until I called them from Vail. The following autumn, my boyfriend and I married in Canada and returned to settle in Vail. We purchased the first condominium at Red Sandstone.

My first job was teaching skiing. Rod Slifer, the Assistant Director of the ski school, hired me in January 1965. On 200 cm. wood Kastle slalom skis, it took me a long time to learn to ski the deep snow. Rod had nicknames for everyone – especially those Easterners on their stiff skis - and he nicknamed me "Susie Powder." Thankfully, the name didn't stick. I later became the first female ski school supervisor. In the summertime in those days, the choice for women was waiting tables, and men worked construction. I worked for John Kaemmer, a wonderful boss, at the Clock Tower and Pistachio's. I also worked at the Vail Tennis Courts for Bill Wright, another terrific person and role model. At a young age, I became part of a rapidly growing community, established friendships, found interesting and rewarding work, and enjoyed the lifestyle – the things that lead a person toward putting down roots in a community. The wonderful skiing, the small-town atmosphere (everyone knew everyone else in those days), and the sense of adventure kept me here. I divorced and subsequently married Ludwig Kurz.

At age 19, I'm not sure that I had any expectations. It was an adventure to ski "Out West" in Colorado. What started as perhaps a one-season escapade in 1965 has turned out to be home. Although I am occasionally ambivalent about the development in our valley, without that growth, I don't think it would be the vibrant place it is - with opportunities, interesting people, and all the amenities that make it such a great place to live. In those early years, the fun of wonderful skiing and being part of a successful resort company were the main attractions. It is rewarding to be involved in health care and to feel as if I am making a contribution to the community that has been a wonderful place to spend most of my life.

SUSAN POTTS SIMONEAU

I arrived in Vail the fall of 1968 via overnight train from Baltimore to Denver and bus from Denver to Aspen. When the bus stopped in Vail, I was really tired and thought I would overnight and continue on to Aspen the next day. However, the next morning brought a beautiful day and a new perspective. There was a dusting of fresh snow, and the mountain fairly sparkled in the sun. The sky was high-altitude blue, a shade of blue I had never seen anywhere before or since. I spent a busy day talking with many helpful people and by mid-afternoon I had a job waiting tables at the bar underneath the Casino, and a place to live. So hello, Vail and goodbye, Aspen it was. Without a doubt, this was one of the best decisions I have ever made.

Those days, it was fairly common to find a job that included some meals, a ski pass, and sometimes lodging. But to make any money, most people worked several jobs; I know I did. These jobs overlap, but I worked as a waitress, bookkeeper, hotel reservationist, and secretary.

All of us functioned as mountain hospitality and shared our enthusiasm for the area with any visitor who would listen.

Social life then was pretty much bar life. But once in a while, we would organize a big dinner, like Nona Wilke's famous Swiss steak and have a crowd over. Life was centered in the Village with an occasional outing to Jeff's in Minturn, or a great steak place a little further away. There was no television. A special treat was a trip to Denver. Everyone knew everyone else. It was a tight community, and that was both good and bad.

Spring brought mud and usually a giant exodus at least for a couple of weeks. I had some great summer traveling experiences: Europe, Mexico, the Caribbean, and a domestic driving

213

adventure from Chicago to California with Nancy Burnham with lots of side excursions and laughs. "Oldtimers" have said to me, "You wouldn't like Vail now, it is like a city." But for me, it was always about the mountain. I have been back several times, both summer and winter trips. The old haunts are hard to find and the streets are tight, and there is always a bustle of activity. The mountain is as amazing and as accommodating now as it was then. The most recent trip I spent the day skiing the Northwoods area with Nancy Loth. I can get just as excited today standing at the top of Chair 4 and looking down at Mid Vail and the Village or at the bowls, all the while marveling at the color of the sky and the vastness of the mountain.

Suzie Kuehn Shepard

I was a skier and ice skater as a kid in Wisconsin. After attending Colorado University, I knew I wanted to live in the mountains. My husband Ottie Kuehn and I bought property near Aspen, hoping to make a move west. We heard about Vail when Fitzhugh Scott promoted the area in Milwaukee and at our ski club. We came to Colorado the summer of '62 to look at it, went back and had Scott design our building with an apartment above. We decided it was a good opportunity to start out in a new business in a new ski area. We sold our Wisconsin home, finished the Rucksack, and moved in with our three daughters on December 20, 1962. We wanted a life in the mountains, and it was a precious gift to all of us. Dirt streets and muddy parking lots were the status quo. There was no parking for residents except on the north side of Gore Creek. Everything was under construction, including lifts and mountain facilities. We had a hitching post in front of the store, often with a horse

tied there in the summer. Our horses grazed on what is now the Vail golf course in summer and fall, then went to Edwards in the winter.

The town consisted of few buildings: about 30 private residences, The Lodge, the Deli and liquor store, Vail Blanche ski shop, the Night Latch, the Vail Village Inn, the Red Lion, and the Rucksack. Most of them were still being finished on opening day, including the lifts and Mid Vail restaurant. The mountain had very little snow. But the snow soon came with the help of the Ute Indians, and we all had to learn to ski powder. In the early days, the powder lasted a week or two, not an hour or two as it does now. There were few people visiting our new area, and most only stopped for a day on their way to Aspen.

There were six families with children in '62: The Seiberts, Parkers, Shepards, Burdicks, Hilands, and Kuehns. A talented teacher named Allen Brown taught all grades in one room using the Calvert system. School was in the Seibert basement and later moved to the upstairs of the new firehouse. It was a wonderful experience for them, thanks to Allen. I kept busy taking care of my three girls, making their clothes, cooking, and helping run the Rucksack. We never went out for a meal unless it was to someone's home. We were too busy and too broke. I got to ski for an hour a day most days. We swam at the

VVI in the summer. Grocery shopping was in Minturn, where there was a very limited selection of everything. Milk, eggs, and a few items were available at the Deli. An occasional trip to Denver was almost a necessity with a family. There was a doctor in Vail in the winter, but the rest of the time we had to drive to Climax or Leadville in an emergency.

Our third year in Vail, I divorced and reluctantly moved to Aspen where I worked in the ski school program, and two of my girls raced in the Aspen club. I later married Morrie Shepard. When the children went off to college, we moved back to the Valley and the mountains. We are still skiing and consider Vail to be the best snow and mountain in the world.

215

SUZY FITZ PETERSON

I grew up in New England with three brothers and my twin sister. I went to a small women's college in New Hampshire where I got my BS degree in Medical Technology. It was there that I fell in love with skiing. My sister and I ski bummed at Sugarloaf Mt in Maine for the winter of 1963. I then worked at the Hartford Hospital. In

1965, my sister and I and two other girls decided to travel across the country (literally "see the USA in a Chevrolet"). In September, we left in her 1963 Chevy Impala convertible, towing an Apache tent trailer. We traveled 18,000 miles, visiting national and state parks, zigzagging along the East coast, southern coast, inland,

West coast as far as the Columbia River then down through Idaho, Wyoming, and into Colorado. By then it was November and way too cold to camp anymore. Our friends flew home, and my sister and I quickly decided to head to Vail for the winter.

In college, some of the wealthier girls spent their spring break vacations at places like Aspen and Sun Valley. We saw their tans and heard how fabulous the snow was in Colorado, so here was our chance to witness it for ourselves. Vail was a small town with a big mountain, so off we went to look for jobs that would allow us to ski every day. I worked as a waitress at The Lodge at Vail for breakfast and dinner. Partway through the season, Roger Staub asked me to teach in the ski school, which I gladly accepted. I still waited on tables for dinner, so I got to eat meals free. The season pass was only $25.

I spent the winter of '65-'66 in Vail and then the summer back in Massachusetts heading up the Chemistry Department at the Cape Cod Hospital. After Christmas while skiing one day in northern New England, my sister and I decided it was back to Colorado we must go. I got a job in research at the CU Med Center, so I had weekends free and continued to ski and teach in the Jr. Racing Program at Vail. I continued to do that until I married a Winter Park skier. We split time there and at Vail, but he became a powder freak like the rest of us, so we spent most of our weekends at Vail until our

first child was born. After a day on the slopes, my friends and I would go to the Casino (still in our ski clothes and boots) and dance until 2 am (ski boots were left in a pile in the corner). When it was a slow day of teaching, I'd end up skiing with an instructor or ski patroller who was a better skier and improve my technique, especially on the great powder days.

I was crazy about sports. I got into ski racing (for fun) while at Vail and competed in the Standard and Vets races. In 1970, I competed in the Vets Nationals. Though Giant Slalom was what I always raced, I managed to get a 3rd place in the slalom on my Hart Javelins and 13th in the Downhill (on borrowed skis). I ended up 5th overall. I grew up in a family of seven, all good athletes, so we were always playing games of one sort or another. We skied together a few days each winter from the time we were pretty young. I hadn't a clue what to expect when I got to Vail, but knew I'd get to ski on snow we had never experienced back in New England. The friendliness and small-town atmosphere were great. Ski patrollers and fellow instructors were like big brothers, showing me the thrill of skiing deep powder and discovering the best stashes. Skiing all day, waiting on tables at The Lodge and dancing late into the night at the Casino was a terrific lifestyle. They are memories that bring a smile for the great times we had. After experiencing a winter in the Colorado mountains, I knew Denver and the mountains would be my home.

VI BROWN

Back in 1963, my husband Byron asked me a life-changing question, "Vail is brand new, and they need people. So why don't we move there?" We'd lived in Denver and had always wanted to move to the mountains. Some of the talk we were hearing was how exciting this new Vail was. So Byron went into action, got a tent, and camped out in the mountains to decide what would be a good area to move to. Then he happened to talk to Pete Seibert. "Brownie," Pete said. "Why don't you come over and look at Vail? We need ski patrolmen, ski instructors; we need a lot of things up in Vail." So that's how Byron finally decided. He and Pete had met at Loveland when Byron was a ski patrolman and Pete was running the area.

One day, Byron was walking in Littleton and saw Frank Randall with a sign, "Lots for Sale in Vail." Byron said, "Do you need anybody to be an on-site person for the company? I could sell lots up there, because I'd like to move to Vail." Frank replied, "Come on in," and Byron introduced himself. I think a couple hours later Byron walked out and had a job up at Vail and a house for us to live in if he finished building it. We built the first house in West Vail; we were actually the first on South Frontage Road.

It was a corporation house. When we moved in we didn't have windows, and we cooked on a Coleman stove. Todd was a baby, and we put his playpen on cement blocks because there were mice in the house, and we didn't want them to get to the baby. So, we put it up on blocks, and that worked.

When I first saw this place, I was awestruck. We arrived in June and got to go up and see the mountain right away. Vail was beautiful. We liked it immediately. Everyone was friendly and helpful. You could call anyone for help or advice; there weren't social differences. Mike was born in 1962, so he was nearly two; Todd was one; and I was pregnant with Cindy. Byron was a good skier, and I was a beginner.

I'm from Wilmer, Minnesota, and I met Byron skiing at Arapahoe Basin. At the time, I worked in Denver at Sears. He asked me out with this question, "Do you have a sleeping bag?" and I thought, "How rude." So I said that I wasn't interested. I met him again at A Basin my first day on skis. I didn't take a lesson, didn't know what I was doing, and I got off the Poma lift too soon. I rolled down the line and knocked everybody off. I got back on again and he yelled from above, "Don't get off until you get to the top of the hill." That's how I met Byron.

By June of 1964, we had the foundation of the house complete, with the promise that if he finished and used it for an office, too, we could live there. It was a three-bedroom house and office. Byron started out in ski patrol in Vail until he got his real estate license. There were only three companies in town; his business was Byron Brown Real Estate. The main highway was what is now the Frontage Road, Hwy 6. If you went to Minturn to buy groceries or to the corner store in LionsHead to get milk, it was a chance to meet people. You spent a lot of time greeting, because you were very lonesome. No TV. We could mostly just get radio reception at night. I could get recipe shows on KOA in Denver. If the clouds were right, you could get Alaska. One time, I listened to seal hunting on the radio. And then for Christmas my wonderful mother- and father-in-law gave me a record player; I had four records, and I wore them out. Two were Christmas; one was Johnny Mathis, and the other was Bing Crosby.

I met Nancy Reinecke right away. We took our kids outside and played. We met Buddy Werner, and he was so wonderful. He was killed in an avalanche in Austria, and we all mourned. Every ski racer was a hero because we were just getting started. I had learned to ski at A Basin, and I was the fastest snowplower. I left that area being a really good snowplower.

In Vail, we didn't take lessons but learned by watching other people, and we fell a lot. There was always powder snow. You could always stop by skiing into it. I skied three weeks before Cindy was born; you didn't have to worry that someone would run into you. I started a little business where we made (with Diane Pratt) craft items that we sold at Helga Pulis's shop at The Rucksack; our business was Mountain Designs. We put flowers, moss, and stuff on driftwood. Income from the business gave me enough money to buy Christmas presents and clothes. I was an Avon lady, too. You would go to someone's home and they would make you coffee, and you had a chance to talk. In the late '60s, before the Valley Forge, there was Kaleidoscope with Daphne and Anne, Moretti's, and Valley High.

For fun, we invited people over. In the fall, all these single people and couples would move in and leave in the spring. We had hello and goodbye parties. Some didn't stay more than one season; either they didn't like it or needed to make more money. People that stayed were digging in roots and calling this home. We felt this was home right away: the beauty of nature, seasons, skiing. Even in those early years, Vail was very cosmopolitan. People were educated. Vail was a brand new community, unlike Steamboat or Aspen where you already had locals. So everybody felt the enthusiasm and specialness because we were doing it together. Everyone had a sense of humor. A new 'freshman class' came every season, and you'd say, "We're having a potluck. Can you come?" Then they would be your friends for the winter. Anything that happened was cause for celebration. If they were having a baby, we'd have a shower; if they were getting married, we'd have a wedding shower. We did a lot of shopping by catalog. I could get diapers and underwear in Leadville. Wherever we went, we would load our station wagon, you'd spend $100, and the car would be filled to the brim. That's how much cheaper it was. In Denver, we went to the dentist, doctor, got haircuts, and arrived home late at night. The mountain passes were long, and they were bad. You did not go very often, and you had to plan for it and take blankets, flashlights, and shovels.

Sometimes, I was lonesome. If Byron were to come home late, I would practically fall apart. You did not have any neighbors. When the real estate business was slow one time he said to me, "I think we should move to Telluride." And I said, "No, you only have to pioneer one ski area for a lifetime." I had Cindy in Glenwood before we had a clinic. Dr. Gerrick was an intern and practiced in the Red Lion. The waiting room was outside where you sat on wooden benches.

When Goldwater ran for president, we didn't know who the president of the US was until we drove into the village and got the last newspaper. There was one newspaper stand, and the papers came over the passes. We didn't know until about 10 am the next morning who the president was. We found out about Bobby Kennedy by radio. His death made us mad, "Why are they picking on that family?" There were celebrities, but we left them alone. We all gathered at the long tables in the Deli. We talked about world affairs all the time. There was such an intelligent class of people who lived here. We felt everything that happened in the world very deeply up here.

We had local issues that we had to work on, like saving our water. There was a fire by Dowd Junction in a cowboy's house, and the chimney is still there. The biggest tragedy was the electrical fire at the Covered Bridge Store, and it burned to the ground. Byron was in the volunteer fire department, and we had a phone in our house. Whenever that phone rang, we would get the information. They had to get John and Cissy Dobson out of there. The phone melted to the floor.

Women were very vital in the early years; they ran their own shops. We had unbelievably great women ski instructors. To me, they were glamorous. I thought they were really good-looking women and fabulous skiers. They'd walk down the street, and you'd say, "That's a ski instructor." If there was a car accident and the highway was backed up all the way to West Vail and the traffic couldn't get over the pass, people who knew us came and spent the night on the floor. We always had extra blankets and soft pillows.

Our family hiked together. We climbed Holy Cross when Cindy was five years old. She had a pretend backpack on; sometimes we had to carry her to get her to the top. Bob Parker and Pete Seibert started Ski Club Vail right away because we couldn't host a race without it. Byron was very involved. My involvement came later; in fact, I'm still the only lady president of Ski Club Vail. Byron helped start the first Buddy Werner League, and Mike was in it for a very short time; then Ankle Biters Program. Every Saturday Byron and I went to BWL, too; He ran the program, and I was a coach. There weren't many choices of things for kids to do – ice skating lessons, some hockey, skiing, and a few sports in school. Mike went to kindergarten in a trailer in Minturn. We voted to open a public school in Vail. That's when the Rummage Sale started – Barbara Parker, Nancy Kindel – it was to get the wages for the first schoolmaster in town, Allen Brown and Vail Country Day. I did not start the Rummage Sale; I got involved later. Country Day disbanded and started later as Vail Mountain School, above the clinic where Dr. Eck's office used to be. It was a one-room schoolhouse with dividers. Montessori was in the basement of the Rams-Horn Lodge.

We loved the melodramas, and, if anyone criticized them, we got upset, "Of course, it's not professional, it's fun." There was a ski instructor who got involved with somebody's girlfriend, and the next morning the girl's boyfriend chased him down the street naked with a shotgun. Some divorces were funny, and you'd say, "Well I saw that one coming." I didn't think the gossip was mean-spirited. They weren't ostracized; they were accepted for who they were. It was live and let live. I think I was quite spiritual when I was young. I considered my marriage sacred. I think I would have beat up a girl that tried to get Byron. I went to the church services at La Cave because

there was a minister from the Minturn Presbyterian. I went in early to clear away the beer bottles from the night before. Catholics were at the Casino. The first post office was in the Plaza Building, too, where the Mug Shop was. Byron was sitting in his office, two guys had a fight, and one got knocked right through the glass door.

We loved our guests; they were never tourists to us. We were new, and we needed the money. We protected Vail. When anyone criticized Vail, we took it personally. It was such a failure when the gondola went down. We were the families who lived here, helped make the schools better, built the churches, got a library, and helped incorporate a town. Anything that happened we were on the fringes of it, we weren't necessarily the leaders – but everybody that lived here had a pebble to put in the bucket to help make it what it is today.

When a celebrity did come to town we were gracious, because we wanted them to come in and enjoy Vail, so we didn't bother them. Michael Landon came, and I saw him in the Deli. I followed his career after that in Little House on the Prairie, because I had met him. I met Robert Redford when I was working at Gorsuch. When I took his credit card and gave him his receipt, he said, "No, you can have that for a souvenir." Can you believe that? No, I threw it away, because it had his credit card number on there. We were taught in our classes to be very careful with credit cards. I saw OJ Simpson in Gorsuch, how prophetic, with a blonde on each arm. When Jackie Kennedy came into the Deli, we were having coffee. We all looked up and whispered, "Oh, there's Jackie Kennedy." And she went over to the costume jewelry case and bought maybe 10 pieces. People were helpful to her, but nobody went over and bothered her. We would never have thought of asking anybody for an autograph, unless maybe they came to your house. Another thing that was fun in the beginning was getting to be part of everything that was new. For a new lodge, they would have an opening night with hors d'oeuvres and they invited all the locals. Whatever happened in town, you got to be part of it because it was so small. My sister was living in Norway and felt so sorry for me, thinking I was living in the wilderness. I wrote a letter to her and said, "My dear, I have a dishwasher; I didn't have one in Denver. I don't have an outdoor toilet."

My parents sent me a picture postcard from their visit to her in Norway, when we were still receiving mail in Minturn. It was sent back with "Location Unknown."

As we got to know people, there was camaraderie, a sense of adventure, and creativeness. You still have a little bit of the spirit of early Vail. Families come and want to embrace Vail, want to give back; that's not all lost on everyone. It wouldn't be fair for me to say that the only good people were the ones back then. There are still good people now. I read wonderful articles about people who have a really good spirit and care about what happens on the whole earth. Love, love the mountains, the people, the way of life here. It is a good place to raise kids.

VIRGINIA PYKE

I taught school for 10 years in California and moved to Vail in 1967 with my husband, who was the Presbyterian minister for Vail, Minturn, and Red Cliff. I was raised in Southern California and received my degree in Education from Pepperdine University. I taught school, beginning In Minturn then in Vail above the Clinic. We had three teachers in that room: I taught 1st and 2nd, Judy Minger taught 3rd and 4th, and Dwight Lee taught 5th and 6th grades. It was like a one-room schoolhouse. The kindergarten was in the basement of the chapel. I also started to work for Marie-Claire and Walter Moritz at their restaurant the St. Moritz in the Wedel Inn. I followed them to a restaurant in Sandstone and eventually to "La Tour" in Vail.

My husband and I divorced, and I had three children to care for, so I needed to keep teaching and working at the

Granddaughter Olivia

restaurant. I enjoyed skiing and skied with the kids at school and with my family. The restaurant was my social life. I met many celebrities and customers who returned year after year. I also worked for President and Mrs. Ford for three years, supplementing their full-time help. I would go to their house at 7 am, fix their breakfast, and do whatever they wanted me to do. I worked for them when they lived in the Bass house near Golden Peak and continued when they moved to Beaver Creek.

I loved skiing and tennis. I also did a lot of biking. Nightlife centered on the restaurant, and I loved working there. It was as if I had two different lives: one during the day with the children and one at night where I became an adult. I loved both of those lives. I have kept in touch with many of the kids I taught and friends I made at the restaurant. I had three kids of my own who grew up in the valley. My oldest son went into the Air Force and became an Air Traffic Controller. My youngest son Jim still lives in the valley. Unfortunately, my daughter Patti was killed in an automobile accident on Highway 6 in August of 1977, just before her 19th birthday. She is buried in Minturn. Her memories are always a part of me.

I didn't know much about Vail or what to expect before I arrived. It was a brand new ski area, and I wasn't sure what life would be like. I felt like a pioneer going to an uncharted land. My perspective of Vail really hasn't changed. I loved living there and loved my friends and family. It was an important part of my life. As Vail expanded, it didn't remain the quaint little ski town I first grew to love. I always thought of it as a small town but with city attitudes and sophistication. I loved raising my kids up there.

I have many stories I could tell. Most are about my time at the jobs I had. Marie-Claire Moritz and I became like sisters. We did many things together that would probably get us in trouble, but all of it was fun and memorable. My son Jim was an extension of her boys. I couldn't have gotten through some of the hard times without her support. I miss Vail. In many ways, I wish I had never left. But I came back to California where my son Rich and his family live, and I have reconnected with early school friends.

WIDGE FERGUSON

There is a lady, with a rather unusual name, who has been around Vail since the beginning. "Widge" Ferguson has a very unique and useful talent. She knows how to make it snow! When all else fails…Indian

dances, cloud seedings, and even presidential visits…yup, Widge can make it snow. What's her secret? Truly, it's bewitching, and that's why she can do it. When good friends, Pepi and Sheika Gramshammer, first met her

222

with husband, John, they thought her name was Witch...every Austrian pronounced her name that way. Soon, everyone called her the Snow Witch, because of her special talent. Of course, there were many doubters, but the Snow Witch saved the slopes several times in those early years. Word began to get around.

Another close friend and early pioneer was Bob Parker. He had the important job of marketing Vail to the world, and his top selling point was the resort's premier snow. One winter, snowfall was scarce, and the slopes were almost bare. Bob decided to challenge the Snow Witch and put her to the test. The weather forecast called for cloudless skies for several days, but Widge predicted a snowstorm. The next morning, Bob and Widge met by chance in the towline at the bottom of the mountain. Bob pointed to the bright sunshine and blue sky and shook his head. Widge gathered up her courage and promised snowflakes by 2pm that afternoon. By 11am, clouds began to form, and conditions worsened. Skiers left the mountain. By early afternoon, it was a blizzard. The village was snowed in, the roads and passes were closed (in the days before the Eisenhower Tunnel), and Vail became a winter paradise again.

Bob was a believer! He thanked Widge in a very special way. When the trail map for the next season was printed, he called and told her to study it carefully. Guess what she discovered? A previously unmarked, pristine little slope in the Back Bowls now carried the name of "Widge's Ridge." And it happened to be one of her favorite places to ski. Right alongside Seldom, Never, and Forever.

Widge was on the map. Over the years, she continued to work her special magic. Once in a while, she even overdid it. When the 1989 World Championships came to Vail, everyone was concerned about the snow cover. Widge arrived in town the day before the downhill race. It began to snow. Vail received almost 30 inches in the next 24 hours. The downhill was cancelled until officials could uncover the course again. They suggested that Widge leave town for a few days.

And so it goes.... The snow on the mountain isn't always perfect, but Vail is happy to have its own Good Widge Of The West.

223

ZANE HOYT

Memories of those early years in Vail are marvelous. We moved to Vail in April of 1965 - Mitch, me, and five children from three weeks old to age 14. The sun was shining and glorious, a contrast to wet Oregon. We bought a condominium in the "Red and Whites." It was way too small for us, and we made too much noise, I am sure, for Hemmye Westbye, who lived below us. By our move, we doubled the school size in classes held above the Fire House. Jamie was born the following year and completed our large family.

It was a great time to live in Vail. Everyone was working hard but was very friendly and helpful. There were parties, and we made many good friends.

Mitch started a construction company, and from then on, we kept selling houses from under us and moving to the next one.

I loved the mountains, I still love the mountains and the surrounding country. I also loved skiing, but perhaps did not get enough of it because of caring for the children. I remember with great pleasure hikes among the wildflowers in the summer and mushrooming with Barbara Parker in the fall. There were the days skiing and lunches at Camp Robbers. What an adventure those years were. I loved them all.

THOSE WHO HAVE GONE BEFORE US...

Ann Taylor	Judy Nelson
Betsy Robinson	Judy Nicholls
Betty Ford	Julie Kaemmer
Camille Bishop	Karola McMillan
Celine Krueger	Kathy Viele
Cindy Brennan	Kay Wiskerhoff
Cissy Dobson	Lupe Murchison
Daisy Palmer	Marge Burdick
Dana DelBosco	Marty Getz Cogswell
Eileen Scott	Mary Davis
Ella Knox	Mary Ellen Canniff
Flo Steinberg	Nancy Biggs
Fran Moretti	Nancy Kindel
Imogene Doll	Natalie Phillips
Janet Boyd Tyler	Patty Steinle
Janis Lee Ronnestad	Priscilla Hastings
Judy Gagne	

ROSALIE JEFFREY ISOM

I arrived in Vail in 1972 with two babies and no time to write, but I absorbed what I lived, and the kindnesses have formed me. As Vail Town Clerk and assistant to Town Manager Terry Minger, I had the opportunity to meet many residents through my voter registration and business licensing duties, Town Council meetings, and district responsibilities. Perhaps my writing career began with recording meeting minutes. I worked on the Vail Symposium when it was a town project and met Robert Redford, Edward Abbey, and New York's Mayor John Lindsey as a bonus. At the Children's Fountain the Town Council used the Mark Twain quote I chose for the dedication plaque.

I lived for a time in Mayor Dobson's apartment above the Covered Bridge Store then moved to the apartment in Janet and Tim Tyler's home on Beaver Dam Road, thanks to Merv Lapin vouching for me. My first job, André de Lucinges hired me on the telephone in French to work at his café/patisserie in the village. The uniform was a turtleneck, a short suede skirt, and béret - almost France. I met astronaut John Glenn there and remember seeing Paul Anka in a Lodge Promenade shop.

Weaving the fabric of this book has meant transcribing, then writing interviews and editing questionnaire responses from the vibrant and brave women of Vail's first years. As I read their lives, I heard the voices of those I knew back then. Some made me laugh out loud with pleasure, even in second and third read-throughs. I have tried to honor their recollections as I placed punctuation and adjusted a phrase here and there. I want the reader of this book to travel beyond the story on the printed page and share in the lives that each story represents, pausing to revisit Vail's pioneer years.

My single regret is not to have been a Happy Hiker.

MARKA McLAUGHLIN BRENNER

"There is no limit to the good a person can do, if they don't care who gets the credit." Marka jumped in and "did" good things.

My thanks, E.